GW00363980

Treating the
Sexual Offender

Treating the Sexual Offender

Barry M. Maletzky

with **Kevin B. McGovern**

SAGE Publications
International Educational and Professional Publisher
Newbury Park   London   New Delhi

For information address:

SAGE Publications, Inc.
2455 Teller Road
Newbury Park, California 91320

SAGE Publications Ltd.
6 Bonhill Street
London EC2A 4PU
United Kingdom

SAGE Publications India Pvt. Ltd.
M-32 Market
Greater Kailash I
New Delhi 110 048 India

Printed in the United States of America

Library of Congress Cataloging-in-Publication Data

Main entry under title:

Maletzky, M. Barry.
    Treating the sexual offender / by Barry M. Maletzky.
       p.   cm.
    Includes bibliographical references.
    Includes index.
    ISBN 0-8039-3662-1 -- ISBN 0-8039-3663-X (pbk.)
    1. Sex offenders--Mental health. 2. Psychosexual disorders--
Treatment. 3. Behavior therapy. I. Title.
    [DNLM: 1. Behavior Therapy. 2. Paraphilias--therapy. 3. Sex
Offenses.   WM 610 M247t]
    RC560.S47M35 1990
616.85'83--dc20
DNLM/DLC
for Library of Congress   90-8863
                                             CIP

93 94 15 14 13 12 11 10 9 8 7 6 5 4 3 2
Sage Production Editor: Susan McElroy

Contents

Introduction

A decade ago, the behavioral approach in treating maladaptive sexual abuse disorders was fresh and new. Its theoretic underpinnings seemed as solid as science itself, and its technologies were achieving reasonably rapid recoveries in what had been assumed to be hopelessly chronic cases. Unlike many other promising beginnings in medicine and psychology, the behavioral approach to treating the sexual offender has not waned but, instead, has flourished; its accounts in the scientific literature and in anecdotal case studies have continued to be a source of satisfaction to its proponents. Inevitably, however, behavior therapy has not quite gained a monopoly in the therapeutic marketplace. As in other areas, behavior therapy can treat a condition effectively but not fully explain its origin or its course; thus standard individual and group therapies for sexual offenders continue to be practiced both here and abroad. Controversy continues about the merits of these more traditional treatment approaches.

At the same time, most practitioners, psychiatrists, psychologists, social workers, and other counselors alike are being asked to treat increasing numbers of sexual offenders. While part of this increase is attributable to the availability of new treatment techniques, a greater part is due to an explosion of public interest in, and media coverage of, the crimes of sexual approach: heterosexual and homosexual pedophilia, exhibitionism, rape, voyeurism, frotteurism, and the like. Fractured families with unrelated adult males drifting into close contact with the daughters of wives and girlfriends play an additional role in this increase as well. Most sizable communities already have active rape advocate programs, local chapters of Parents United, elementary school curricula teaching students about child molestation, and even television "spots" interspersed with the Saturday morning cartoons, alerting youngsters to possibilities of sexual abuse. These programs have achieved an enhanced public awareness about sexual abuse (especially the pedophilias), have increased patient flow to various sexual abuse programs, and have concomitantly put additional pressure on practitioners to develop effective treatments for the sexual offender.

Literature in this area has grown apace, yet there are still gaps. Most studies of behavioral treatment of sexual offenders are restricted to a small number of subjects and test one treatment manipulation at a time. This approach is, of course, scientifically potent but clinically sterile; in the actual practice of behavior therapy, the clinician must choose, from among the collection of techniques, those particularly suited to each individual. Moreover, he or she must make judgments in an outpatient setting about whether each patient can be treated at large and, if so, what combinations of techniques will prove most effective. Thus the clinician needs sufficient knowledge of proper assessment techniques and of a wide variety of treatment modalities as well to do the job of therapy. The field of behavior therapy for the sexual offender thus lies partly fallow: The theory is well rooted but the application uneven. Here and there throughout the literature, techniques sprout but not regularly and comprehensively enough to yield a lush therapeutic package.

This book is designed to fill these gaps by describing a multitude of techniques for treating the sexual offender in either an outpatient or an inpatient setting. It is not offered as an all-inclusive text for *every* approach in this area but should be regarded as a compendium of behavioral approaches in an overall treatment plan for the offender. Techniques will be described in sufficient detail so that the practitioner reading the account will be able to employ any specific technique in his or her own practice. He or she should also be able to choose, among a smorgasbord of possible techniques, those that particularly suit the patients' appetites and needs. This text will, therefore, be a modest endeavor, clinically based, to bring together a variety of techniques to help the practitioner treat patients face-to-face.

There is, these days, a decided bias against the therapeutic "cookbook." Descriptions of techniques are usually relegated to appendixes, small-print "methods" sections, and archaic references in secondary journals. This book champions the opposite approach: If we banned cookbooks, how well would we enjoy the meal?

1

The Development of Behavioral Treatment for the Sexual Offender

It is not difficult to categorize as a sexual offender a man who molests small children or repeatedly rapes women. The new psychiatric nomenclature codified in the revised edition of the *Diagnostic and Statistical Manual* (American Psychiatric Association, 1987) more clearly than ever before enumerates a variety of paraphilias, each characterized by an essentially repetitive nature, a preference for the use of a nonhuman object for sexual arousal, sexual activity with humans involving real or simulated suffering and humiliation, and/or sexual activity with nonconsenting partners or those unable to consent. Some authors prefer the term *sexual deviation* (Lee-Evans, Graham, Harbison, McAllister, & Quinn, 1975; McGuire, Carlisle, & Young, 1965) to describe the unusual harmful processes and objects we generally associate with sexual offenses. Common to most descriptions are four elements:

(1) a perpetrator—the offender
(2) an unwilling victim

(3) an unusual sexual desire

(4) inferred or actual harmful effects stemming from the offense

The paraphilias, such as pedophilia, exhibitionism, or sadomasochism, must be distinguished from sexual dysfunction in which there is an abnormality in the performance of adult heterosexual activity as, for example, in erectile failures or anorgasmia. In the disorders to be addressed here, there is an inappropriate sexual *approach* that offends society to the extent that the behavior is labeled "criminal." Even this definition, however, may not be all inclusive as, for example, in disorders such as transvestism or bestiality.

It is clear that no single descriptive system can adequately encompass the breadth of human sexual behaviors, usual or unusual:

- A 34-year-old aeronautical engineer was arrested for "public indecency" when apprehended masturbating in his car while watching a girls' high school track team practice. His sexual pleasure (and his erection) was ruined if he became aware that he had been seen. Is he an exhibitionist?

- A retired gardener could achieve orgasm and ejaculation solely when fantasizing he was inserting various objects into the anus of a minor black girl. He had no history of actual molestations. Is this a pedophile?

- A 17-year-old high school student sought consultation with severe anxiety over his sexual orientation. He had always been sexually attracted to boys his own age yet had had no sexual experiences with either sex. Is this "ego-dystonic" homosexuality? Should it be treated; and if so, how?

The variety and intensity of sexual conditioning makes categorization difficult; thus the above questions may be merely rhetorical. The purpose of this work is not to explore the genesis of sexual deviations or to review the copious research findings in this area. Excellent reviews of relevant theoretical and clinical work have been contributed by Adams, Tollison, and Carson (1981), Finklehor (1984), Greer and Stuart (1983), and Marks (1981b). This work will, instead, focus in some detail on the treatment of the sexual offender. By design, this book is a practical, workable guide to treatment techniques explicit enough for the clinician to apply in face-to-face meetings with the patient. Case histories will be presented to demonstrate the methods used and a distinction will be made among different types of offenders to clearly delineate which techniques can best be employed in each particular case.

Data Base

POPULATION

The techniques to be presented here have evolved from the treatment of over 5,000 sexual offenders in a Sexual Abuse Clinic in the northwestern United States between the years of 1971 and 1990 (Maletzky, 1984b). The treatment was carried out almost entirely on an outpatient basis. Tables 1.1 to 1.8 present a demographic definition of the sample; comparisons with other large samples indicate that these patients are fairly typical of the sexual offenders treated on an outpatient basis that have been studied elsewhere (Bonheur & Rosner, 1980; Jason, Williams, Burton, & Rochat, 1982; Jones, 1982; Quinsey, Chaplin, & Carrigan, 1980). In addition, all these offenders were characterized by one outstanding feature shared in almost all other samples: They were exclusively male. Female "offenders" have, until recently, been almost unknown, although this phenomenon has already been discussed in the literature (Eber, 1977; Hollander, Brown, & Roback, 1977). Seventeen female offenders have been treated thus far, but data from their treatment have been deleted from the current sample as it is too early to know whether the

Table 1.1 *Characteristics of a Sexual Offender Population (N = 5,000, all male): Age*

Age Breakdown	Percentage
10–19	7
20–29	27
30–39	26
40–49	15
50–59	16
60–69	7
70–79	2

NOTE: The average age in this sample is 34.7 years, with a range of 13 to 79 years.

Table 1.2 *Characteristics of a Sexual Offender Population (N = 5,000): Educational Level*

Educational Level Breakdown	Percentage
6th to 9th grade	12
10th to 12th grade	44
College started but uncompleted	15
College completed	17
Master's level	6
Doctoral level	6

NOTE: The median educational level in this sample is eleventh grade, with a range from sixth grade to the doctoral level.

assessment and treatment of the female offender will parallel that of the male. The presentations to follow, therefore, deal only with boys and men.

The average age of this sample was 34.7 years with a range of 13 to 79 years (Table 1.1). The majority had completed high school and many had attended college (Table 1.2). These offenders typically were married and employed. Only a minority had never been married or had never lived with a female. Moreover, at the time of the offense, just 21% of these offenders were divorced, a figure below the general population at any one time (Table 1.3). Table 1.4 documents the employment history of this population, and Table 1.5 presents data on social class. It can be seen that most of these men were, in the main, laborers, had stable work records, and belonged to the lower-middle and middle classes. The vast majority of those who had

Table 1.3 *Characteristics of a Sexual Offender Population (N = 5,000): Marital Status at Time of Offense*

Marital Status	Percentage
Married	45
Living with a woman	12
Divorced	21
Never married or lived with a woman and over 21	19
Never married or lived with a woman and younger than 21	2
Widowed	1

Table 1.4 *Characteristics of a Sexual Offender Population*
            (N = 5,000): Employment

Job Analysis	Percentage
Breakdown, duration of all jobs:	
0–11 months	23
1–2 years	26
2–4 years	29
4–7 years	15
Over 7 years	7
Total	100
Type of job	
Unskilled labor	16
Skilled labor	21
Supervisory labor	5
Military	1
Clerical	4
Sales	11
Service	15
White collar	14
Professional	13
Total	100
Ever fired from a job:	27

NOTE: For this sample, 76% were currently employed and the average duration of time employed in previous jobs was 3.6 years.

served in the armed forces had received honorable discharges (Table 1.6). Data regarding past medical histories, presented in Table 1.7, revealed that a minority had a past or present psychiatric diagnosis in addition to their sexual diagnosis; just a few had required prior

Table 1.5 *Characteristics of a Sexual Offender Population*
            (N = 5,000): Socioeconomic Status

Hollingshead-Redlich Group	Percentage
Group I (lower class)	16
Group II (lower-middle class)	38
Group III (middle class)	27
Group IV (upper-middle class)	14
Group V (upper class)	5

Table 1.6 *Characteristics of a Sexual Offender Population (N = 5,000): Military History*

Type of Discharge	Percentage
Honorable	89
General	7
Dishonorable	4

NOTE: In this sample, 37% were previously in the service.

psychiatric consultations or hospitalizations. In addition, very few of these men had required past medical help for any serious illness or were taking prescribed medications at the time of treatment. Finally, approximately one-third of this population had received charges prior to the current episode, and, of these, 76% were of a sexual nature (Table 1.8). Fully 65% of these men had unblemished legal records until the charges for the current episode. (Racial data are not presented in tabular form; 94% of these men were Caucasian.)

In summary, these sexual offenders largely were young, white, and married and employed in labor-related jobs. They did not have

Table 1.7 *Characteristics of a Sexual Offender Population (N = 5,000): Medical History*

Medical History Analysis	Percentage of Entire Sample
Psychiatric history[a]	
other psychiatric diagnoses	29
—sociopathic personality	27
—alcoholism	14
—mixed substance abuse	6
prior psychiatric consultations	9.2
prior psychiatric hospitalizations	0.4
Medical history[a]	
prior hospitalizations	22.7
prior serious illnesses	8.3
prior surgeries	2.9
prior doctor's visits	42.3
taking medications daily	8.2

a. Many offenders carried two or more diagnoses, thus the cumulative percentage of all offenders with psychiatric or medical disgnoses is less than 100%.

Table 1.8 *Characteristics of a Sexual Offender Population*
(N = 5,000): Legal History

Analysis of Charges	Percentage of Entire Sample
Any prior charges	35
Type:	
sexual only	76
nonsexual only	
(non-driving related)	13
sexual and nonsexual	
(non-driving related)	11
alcohol-related only	
(including driving related)	12
Average number of past charges	0.7 (0–22)

NOTE: Breakdown of frequency of past charges: 0 charges, 65%; 1 charge, 29%; 2 charges, 3%; 3 charges, 1%; and more than 3 charges, 2%.

particular histories of psychiatric or medical problems, and the majority had never before broken the law; the overwhelming majority had never been charged with a nonsexual crime.

A small subsample of these offenders were adolescents (*N* = 137). Results of demographic sampling of treatment outcome were not significantly different with this population to warrant isolating it from the mainstream of adult offenders. In retrospect, special considerations in the treatment of the adolescent offender do occur: More time is needed for trust building and sexual education, family therapy assumes a larger portion of the treatment program, and exposure to aversive stimuli is kept to a minimum.

Although the demographic data present an idea of the "average offender," no such concept is viable in clinical practice. There has been no documentation of a typical "offender personality" (Maletzky, 1980a). Rather, these men were characterized by their diversity: An offender could as well have been a professor as a pauper, a minister as an atheist, a teetotaler as an alcoholic, a teenager as a septuagenarian. Moreover, an offender, at least in this series, might as well have had an extensive history of arrests or none at all, and might as well have had associated diagnoses as none; he might have been seen by many therapists or lack any treatment history whatsoever. In retrospect, these patients did not seem to share any definable demographic or personality traits to render them distinctive: One could not have predicted their sexual diagnoses without examining their individual histories. This does not, however, eliminate the possibility of subcategorizations based on future data (Knight, 1989; Knight, Carter, & Prentky, 1989).

The range and frequency of sexual diagnoses for this population are presented in Table 1.9. It is not surprising that heterosexual pedophilia has been the most common condition treated recently. Not shown in the table, however, is the change in these diagnoses over time. During the early years of this work, 1971-1977, exhibitionism was the most prevalent condition, accounting for 47% of all cases, heterosexual pedophilia was the chief diagnosis in 31% of patients, and homosexual pedophilia accounted for 11%. During 1978-1990, however, heterosexual pedophilia was the chief diagnosis in fully 68% of cases while homosexual pedophilia accounted for 17% and exhibitionism just 12% of the sample. A number of factors have combined to produce this dramatic change.

(1) Public exposure to child molesting has increased:
     A 7-year-old girl watched a brief television public service announcement, sandwiched between two Saturday morning cartoons, warning

Table 1.9 *Primary Diagnoses for a Sexual Offender Population*
             (N = 5,000): All Male

Primary Diagnosis[a]	Percentage	N
Heterosexual pedophilia	57.3	2,865
Homosexual pedophilia	17.1	855
Exhibitionism	15.4	770
Rape	2.9	145
Public masturbation	1.5	75
Voyeurism	1.4	70
Frotteurism	1.2	60
Transvestism	1.2	60
Fetishism	0.6	30
Obscene telephone callers	0.5	25
Sadomasochism	0.5	25
Zoophilia	0.4	20
Total	100	5,000

a. In cases of multiple diagnoses, a primary diagnosis was ascertained. For example, 7% of pedophiles were both heterosexual and homosexual in their arousal to minors; these men were always assigned a primary diagnosis of either heterosexual or homosexual pedophilia based upon their histories and arousal patterns.

children to not allow anyone to touch their "private parts." The girl
approached her mother saying, "Daddy did *that* to me!"

(2) Law enforcement personnel, children's services divisions, and district
attorneys' offices have an enhanced awareness of sexual offenses.

(3) Sexual education classes in the early school grades have been initiated
(Nyman, 1989):

An 11-year-old girl came home from school crying. After much
prompting, she told her mother that her 15-year-old brother had been
forcing himself upon her sexually for the past three years: He had
threatened her with physical harm if she divulged this secret. She had
just heard a teacher at school discuss these matters and had read a
booklet she had received as part of a class: "He Told Me Not to Tell"
(Fay, 1979).

(4) There has been an increase in the number of fractured families with a
resulting increase in the frequency with which a stepfather or
boyfriend is living with a young girl who is not his biological relative
(Paveza, 1988; Sugar, 1983).

The diagnoses presented in the table are neither an exhaustive nor
a detailed characterization of this population. Many offenders, for
example, combined two or more paraphilias (Freund, Scher, & Hucker, 1983), while others practiced deviant behavior for a limited time,
then either changed to a different aberrant sexual object or dropped
the deviation entirely:

• A 9-year-old girl accused her grandfather of forcibly undressing her in
a treehouse he had built for this purpose. He denied her accusations
until her 13-year-old brother, learning of the charges, exclaimed "I
know you did it because you did the same thing to me!"

It is clear that an offender with one paraphilia may possess several
others. Mixtures of heterosexual and homosexual pedophilia have
been commonly reported (Bonheur & Rosner, 1980; Jason, Williams,
Burton, & Rochat, 1982). Less frequent, but not rare, are combinations
of exhibitionism with heterosexual pedophilia or with voyeurism.

Of equal importance is the frequent coexistence of a paraphilia
with age-appropriate heterosexual attractions and practices. Indeed,
the majority of heterosexual pedophiles in this series were married or
cohabiting with a female and enjoyed a healthy sexual life with these
partners. Speculation that deficiencies in a man's sexual gratification
result in sexual offenses has not been borne out by scientific investi-

gation (Bonheur & Rosner, 1980; Hayes, Brownell, & Barlow, 1978; Marks, 1981a, pp. 249-287). Apparently, the puzzles of deviant sexual arousal cannot be solved so simply. Thus 71% of these men believed that their nondeviant sexual relationships were gratifying; among heterosexual pedophiles, this figure was 79%. Nonetheless, many men attempted to partially apportion blame for offending on a quantitative or qualitative deficit in sexual activities with their partners. Large multifactorial studies will be necessary to illuminate our as yet dim comprehension of the etiology of these disorders. Nonetheless, as is often true in behavior therapy, important progress has been made in their treatment.

In addition, some care must be taken in affixing diagnostic labels in borderline cases:

- A 50-year-old disabled former logger was reported by his 16-year-old stepdaughter for a six-month history of sexual molestation. This offender became attracted to this girl after she was sexually fully developed. Penile plethysmograph recordings showed no arousal to girls who lacked secondary sexual characteristics.

There is no agreement on when deviant arousal ends and normal arousal begins. Thus some men might become attracted to a teenage girl who is not a biological relative, particularly if they have joined her family recently. Still, only a minority would actually molest her. Many men would experience no sexual arousal for a child they had lived with since that child was an infant, a taboo possibly inbred to maximize genetic success. In some cases, an offender will molest a teenager with whom he has been living for a number of years, a pattern clearly "abnormal." In other cases, an offender will molest a girl "on the borderline," perhaps 12 or 13 years of age. In both cases, however, behavior therapy can usually be employed with sufficient precision so that attraction to a particular age group or to a specific person can be deconditioned without adversely affecting arousal to women of an appropriate age.

REFERRAL SOURCES AND LEGAL STATUS

Table 1.10 lists the sources of referral for this large population of sexual offenders. Although there were a multitude of sources, one

Table 1.10 *Sources of Referral and Legal Status on Referral for a Population of Sexual Offenders (N = 5,000)*

Sources of Initial Referral	Percentage
"Voluntary"	26
professional therapists	8
pastoral counselors	5
self-referred	9
spouses	2
other relatives	1
friends	1
"Involuntary"	74
attorneys	41
—before charges	10
—after charges	31
probation/parole officers	27
children's services divisions	3
police	2
district attorneys' offices	1

characteristic of interest was the distinction between voluntary and involuntary offenders. This dichotomy was not always clear:

- A building contractor often exposed himself from the windows of homes just nearing completion. As he did so on one occasion, friends drove by on the street facing the window. They confronted the patient and informed his wife, who then insisted he enter therapy. He did so "voluntarily" but under clear duress from friends and family.

- A boy in high school often secretly slipped out of his house late at night to visit groups of condominiums nearby. He would peer in lighted windows, hoping to catch a glimpse of naked women or sexual activity. Charges were brought against him in juvenile court and then dropped on a legal technicality. Nonetheless, he followed through with the suggested treatment on his own, at the same time admitting this activity to his parents. He explained that this legal near miss frightened him to such an extent that he became eager for help to eliminate this condition.

To some extent, many sexual offenders voluntarily entering treatment without coercion from the judicial system are still responding to pressures from family, friends, attorneys, or even their own consciences. Nonetheless, the literature occasionally makes these distinctions (Bonheur & Rosner, 1980; Smith, 1980; Smith & Meyer, 1980). The only data at hand indicate that, with behavioral methods of treatment, voluntary and involuntary, patients do equally well. The sole difference in one study was attendance: It is perhaps not surprising that involuntary patients had a better record in this regard (Maletzky, 1980b).

Sexual offenders were most likely to be referred through the legal system, chiefly during the period between arrest or arraignment and pleading or sentencing. The major referral sources for such offenders were attorneys; this group accounted for exactly half of all involuntary referrals. Other sources, however, included children's services divisions, corrections divisions (probation and parole officers), district attorneys, and police officers. Of the voluntary patients, most were referred by other therapists and family members, chiefly wives or girlfriends. These women generally stood solidly behind their partners, even though often the patients had to leave the family setting. They encouraged the offender to seek treatment but persisted in the relationship and even looked ahead with anticipation to the reunification of their families. While the pertinent literature reflects the firmly held belief that, within these families, the men were dominant and the wives or girlfriends weak and dependent, in clinical practice, a wide variety of intrafamilial dynamics were seen (Adams, Tollison, & Carson, 1981).

Although these men were, in the main, first- or second-time offenders, they had typically committed a number of offenses before being charged. Table 1.11 lists offending characteristics for pedophiles and exhibitionists. Of chief interest are the comparisons between these diagnostic categories for duration of symptoms and number of victims. Heterosexual pedophiles had significantly shorter durations of deviant behavior ($p < .01$) and significantly fewer victims when compared with exhibitionists ($p < .01$). However, homosexual pedophiles had the longest duration of symptoms ($p < .01$) and a significantly greater number of victims than heterosexual pedophiles ($p < .01$). It is surprising that none of these offenders spent much time incarcerated or on probation or parole. All categories averaged less than one year in custody and less than three years under supervision. The commission of a sexual offense appeared to result in less severe penalties than those handed down for burglary, forgery, or other forms of assault. In addition, these data are

Table 1.11 *Offender Characteristics for Pedophiles (N = 3,720)*
and Exhibitionists (N = 770)

Characteristics	Pedophiles		Exhibitionists
	Heterosexual (N = 2,865)	Homosexual (N = 855)	(N = 770)
Average duration, in years, of symptoms	7.5	12.7	9.3
Percentage with prior sexual charges	30.4	36.5	35.2
Percentage with prior sexual convictions	22.5	29.7	42.5
Average number of years in custody	0.8	0.9	0.6
Average number of years on probation or parole	2.1	2.3	1.9
Average age, in years, of victims	10.8	11.4	N/A
Average number of victims	1.4	3.6	14.3[a]

NOTE: N/A = not available.
a. Estimated.

provided mostly for offenders who were apprehended. A significant number may elude the justice system and never enter treatment (MacMurray, 1988, 1989).

A distinction has often been made between the situational or circumstantial offender and the predatory, opportunistic, or preferential offender (Finklehor, 1984).

- A 42-year-old, unemployed mechanic molested his 6-year-old biological daughter on five occasions. His wife was away at conferences or on vacation during these episodes. He denied a general sexual attraction to girls, and his penile plethysmograph evaluation showed excellent arousal to adult, consenting activities, yet an absence of deviant sexual arousal.

- A 27-year-old elementary school teacher commonly "helped" young girls off with their coats and wet clothing after a rain. He fondled these children quickly as he did so. He spent a good amount of time watching girls in a nearby park and would invite them to his apartment where sexually oriented materials awaited. His plethysmograph tracing documented 100% arousal to sexual stimuli associated with young girls and just 17% arousal to stimuli associated with adult females.

Although it cannot be assumed in every case, it does appear that many offenders, especially those coming to an outpatient clinic, will have molested because the situation presented itself. This by itself cannot be a sufficient cause, as it is clear that many men live with attractive young girls or even teenagers who are not their own progeny and demonstrate no arousal or, if experiencing it, do not act upon it. There are other offenders, though perhaps a slight minority, who prefer youngsters as sexual objects and may seek them out. As detailed further in Chapter 10, this latter group is somewhat more difficult to treat, and some among its members may be dangerous remaining at large and may require institutionally based treatment programs.

Table 1.12 places these distinctions in clearer perspective by examining four characteristics believed typical of situational versus predatory patterns of pedophiliac behavior. Histories of each of the 2,865 heterosexual pedophiles and 855 homosexual pedophiles were examined to determine whether there were single or multiple victims, whether the offender was well known or a relative stranger to the victim, whether most or all of the molesting occurred in the victim's or offender's home as opposed to sites in the community (such as rest rooms or parks), and whether or not the offender enjoyed heterosexual, adult, consenting relationships. It was relatively easy to group these men into one or the other category within each parameter. Doing so demonstrated that the majority of both types of pedophiles were situational offenders, as might be expected in an outpatient population. However, significant differences did emerge when heterosexual and homosexual pedophiles were compared. Within each parameter, there was a significantly greater frequency of predatory behaviors in the homosexual pedophiles. Some of the increased difficulty in treatment with this group might be due to their lower level of arousal to appropriate stimuli and the consequent necessity to positively condition increasing arousal to those stimuli in addition to deconditioning inappropriate sexual arousal to boys. Indeed, the problems in treating this group lay in the extra time needed to successfully complete treatment rather than a marked reduction in ultimate treatment efficacy. There is, however, an increased danger for homosexual pedophiles to remain at large, especially during the early phases of treatment.

Thus a basic difference often alluded to in the literature may exist between a man responding for the first time to a provocative situa-

Table 1.12   *Percentage of Heterosexual and Homosexual Pedophiles Showing Situational Versus Predatory Patterns of Offending (N = 3,720)*

Parameter	Heterosexual Pedophiles (N = 2,865)	Homosexual Pedophiles (N = 855)	P
More than one victim	34.8	51.1	<.01
Offender not well known to victim	29.8	57.4	<.01
In-community molestation	19.0	37.5	<.001
Unsatisfactory adult heterosexual relationships	17.7	43.7	<.001

tion and living with a minor female (though recognizing that most men would not be attracted to that stimulus) and a man actively and perhaps preferentially seeking out sexual opportunities with children. Chapter 10 will more completely analyze these differences in a beginning attempt to ferret out the factors rendering an offender amenable to a treatment program and safe to remain in the community.

CONDITIONS OF TREATMENT

The majority of sexual offenders upon whom this work is based were treated as outpatients. This only partly limited the seriousness of their disorders.

- A 22-year-old, unemployed truck driver was referred for outpatient treatment after committing his fourth violent rape in one and a half years. At sentencing, treatment personnel testified that he was highly dangerous. The presiding judge believed that his prospect of a job in the near future would help mold him to be a responsible citizen and sentenced him to five years of probation (his second such sentence), with required treatment at a sexual abuse clinic.

In the main, however, these men manifested only a small to moderate amount of violence and were judged safe to be at large. The techniques of treatment to be described here are applicable to both an in- and an outpatient setting, but an inpatient setting was employed with these offenders in only a few isolated cases, chiefly due to environmental, rather than safety, factors. For example, an offender who lived a great distance from the clinic was admitted to a psychiatric hospital for two weeks of intensive behavior therapy; following discharge, he needed to travel to the clinic only twice per month, thus obviating expensive weekly trips.

The techniques of behavior therapy have been demonstrated to constitute part of an effective treatment program regardless of the seriousness of the offense, whether judged in terms of presence or absence of violations, the duration of deviant sexual arousal, or the frequency of offenses (Kelly, 1982; Maletzky, 1980a, 1980b; Quinsey, Chaplin, Maguire, & Upfold, 1988). Obviously, with greater environmental control in an inpatient or other secure setting, an enhanced use of a variety of modalities can occur: Contingency programs can be constructed, assignments can be monitored, and group therapy can be more effectively employed. In addition, the treatment course can be intensified and perhaps shortened as well. Longo (1983) has reviewed the application of some of these techniques to an inpatient setting.

Regardless of setting, the treatment program to be described here is derived from the premises and practices of behavior therapy. Whether one ascribes to the conditioning theory of the genesis of paraphilias (Little & Curran, 1978; McGuire, Carlisle, & Young, 1965; Vanceventer & Laws, 1978) or to an analytic (Allen, 1974, 1980) or physiological (Berlin & Coyle, 1981; Rieber & Sigusch, 1979; Schmidt & Schorsch, 1981) etiology, a number of studies have demonstrated the comparative efficacy of behavioral techniques when contrasted to more traditional methods of treatment. This literature has been expertly summarized by Adams, Tollison, and Carson (1981), Little and Curran (1978), and Marks (1981a, pp. 249-287, 1981c) and will not be extensively reviewed here. It is likely, however, that a strictly behavioral program applied in a rigid and stereotyped fashion will not be effective unless allowance can be made for human idiosyncrasy.

- The techniques of aversive conditioning were chosen for a 32-year-old laborer with two prior arrests for molesting his two stepdaughters, 1 and 6 years old. Following four months of active outpatient treatment, he was again charged with molesting; this time, the victim was his young stepson, aged 11. He had been deconditioned to arousal for young girls and boys but later explained that it was the children's smooth skin, not their genital areas, that was most arousing. A more careful sexual assessment might have prevented his reoffense.

- A 21-year-old college student was repeatedly arrested for stealing women's undergarments. He would occasionally cross-dress in them, but more often he would masturbate while staring at them. An initial penile plethysmograph evaluation revealed sexual arousal at the sight of undergarments he had stolen but not to others bought for the purpose of treatment. Further scrutiny revealed that the patient's thought of successfully stealing these items from stores or homes of relatives was a crucial ingredient producing sexual excitement. A treatment program encompassing cognitive as well as behavioral elements was ultimately successful.

Techniques of behavior therapy have often been combined with other treatment elements to tailor a program suited to the individual patient's needs. Most often, principles and practices derived from group therapy, cognitive therapy, existential therapy, and family approaches must be combined with methods of behavior therapy to produce an effective treatment package. Occasionally, although not often, even the addition of chemotherapy must be considered.

In addition, treatment with just one type of behavior therapy, aversive conditioning, can often be incomplete.

- At 23, a graduate school student was arrested on campus for following an Asian girl to her car, then suddenly grabbing her breasts and genital areas. His history revealed that, at the age of 13, his parents had taken him to Japan on a business trip. As he took a solitary walk near his hotel, he was approached by a prostitute. He recalled being both terrified and sexually fascinated and had entertained repeated sexual fantasies involving Asian females since that time. Frightfully shy, he had dated just three times before this sexual approach. Aversive conditioning was only moderately effective, but the addition of a social skills training program produced a marked increase in heterosocial approach behavior and, at nine-year follow-up, there was no evidence of repeat offenses.

All treatment to be described here was delivered in a sexual abuse clinic composed of a psychiatrist-director, a group of psychologists with special training and experience in evaluating and treating deviant sexual arousal, and a number of mental health technicians with similar specialized training and experience. Chapter 10 details the operation of the clinic and presents results of all treatment offered.

Therapy with sexual offenders is rarely facile or pleasant. Most offenders, at least partially if not totally, deny their sexual problems and/or their need for treatment. Many blame the victim for the offense or attribute responsibility to the police or another adult for concocting the offense or for coaching the victim into fabricating a story of abuse. (Clinicians recognize that it is important to use the victim's story of what occurred, combined with police reports, presentence investigations and the like. While victims *do* sometimes make up stories, experience dictates that, if they do, they do so at a comparatively low rate—Faller, 1984; Goodman, 1984; MacMurray, 1989; Riggs, Murphy, & O'Leary, 1989. In the current sample, 87% of offenders, on first visit, denied all or part of their offenses. Minimization and denial, frequently combined with the coercive nature of treatment, make this population more difficult to work with, and often therapists may need "vacations" from treating only sexual offenders. They may appreciate working with a variety of clients from time to time as well as being given assignments in administrative and research areas.

The major goal of treatment for each offender has been the *elimination* of deviant sexual arousal; the goal of decreasing the probability of a repeated offense by strengthening resistance to deviant impulses has not been considered sufficient. The distinction between these two goals was usually, though not always, clear. The methods of assessment discussed in Chapter 2 were devised to maximize this distinction.

The techniques to be described did not always correspond to a behavioral interpretation of their mechanisms. Several of these could, with varying degrees of facility, be explained using a variety of theoretic paradigms. The treatment plans were, therefore, an amalgam of techniques forged through experience: They were empiric and eclectic; most important, by and large, they were effective and their benefits were measurable.

Most of these techniques were deployed in a typical physician's suite of offices with specialized equipment such as slide and movie projectors, electric shock and odor presentation equipment, and penile plethysmographs, all of which are readily available in the United States and Canada (see Appendix D).

The timing of treatment varied with individual patient requirements, but, in general, the following phases were delineated:

(1) the active treatment phase—four months of weekly sessions
(2) the intermediate treatment phase—four to six months of
     bimonthly/monthly sessions
(3) the booster treatment phase—six months of sessions every three
     months

To provide an overview of treatment techniques, Table 1.13 presents a compendium of the chief methods found useful within a
typical time course. The division of categories is arbitrary but possibly useful. In the chapters to follow, detailed descriptions of all
techniques will be given.

Table 1.13   *Chief Treatment Techniques Employed in a Sexual Abuse Clinic with
             Average Durations of Treatment*

 I. The Active Treatment Phase (four months of weekly sessions)
     A. Aversive conditioning techniques
         1. assisted covert sensitization
         2. electric shock aversion
         3. aversive behavior rehearsal
     B. Positive conditioning techniques
         1. desensitization
         2. amyl nitrate conditioning
         3. plethysmographic biofeedback
     C. Homework assignments
         1. reconditioning techniques
             a. masturbatory fantasy switching
             b. masturbation satiation training
         2. foul taste aversion
         3. assisted covert sensitization via tape recordings
         4. covert sensitization
II. The Intermediate Treatment Phase (four to six months of bimonthly/monthly
     sessions)
     A. Aversive conditioning techniques, as in I A
     B. Positive conditioning techniques
         1. desensitization
         2. success imagery
         3. fading techniques
     C. Cognitive techniques
         1. thought stopping and changing methods
         2. deviant cycle awarenes
         3. relapse prevention techniques

Table 1.13 *Continued.*

D. Ancillary techniques
   1. social skills training
   2. assertive training
   3. impulse control training
   4. plethysmographic biofeedback
   5. anxiety management training
   6. empathy training
   7. marital and/or family therapy
E. Group therapy
   1. sexual education
   2. confrontation of minimization and denial
   3. empathy training
F. Homework assignments as in I C

III. The Booster Treatment Phase (six months of sessions every three months)
   A. Aversive conditioning techniques
      1. assisted covert sensitization
      2. electric shock aversion
   B. Ancillary techniques
      1. empathy training
      2. marital and/or family therapy
   C. Homework
      1. assisted covert sensitization tapes and foul odor once per week
      2. covert sensitization two to five times per week
      3. foul taste aversion as needed

Methods of Assessment

Although Chapter 2 will present, in detail, the common assessment tools used by those providing care or engaged in research in these areas, Table 1.14 presents an abbreviated compendium of these methods of assessment. Results discussed in several chapters will be expressed in terms of these assessment techniques. In general, such methods can be divided into those that are subjective and those that are objective. The penile plethysmograph would seem to be an objective test, though, even here, this instrument can provide confusing as well as helpful information.

Table 1.14 *Methods of Assessment for a Population of Sexual Offenders*

I. Self-report
    A. Covert deviant sexual behaviors
        1. deviant sexual urges
        2. deviant sexual fantasies
        3. deviant sexual dreams
    B. Overt deviant sexual behaviors
        1. actual sexual behavior with a victim
        2. masturbation using deviant sexual fantasies and/or material
II. Therapist and significant other reports
    A. "How much has this patient progressed?" (0–4 scale)
    B. "How well is this patient following through with treatment?" (0–4 scale)
III. Legal records: search of computerized police files for charges, arrests, and convictions for any sexual crime
IV. The penile plethysmograph: results generally expressed in percentage of full erection
V. The polygraph ("lie detector")

- A plant foreman for a large lumber company was suspected by his family of molesting several young boys in his neighborhood. He had a complicated medical history, which included arteriosclerosis and diabetes mellitus. Penile plethysmograph testing indicated low arousal to homosexual pedophiliac materials, but arousal to all stimuli seemed diminished. After confrontation by his family, he admitted to erectile failure of many years' duration due to his medical conditions, a fact that he had not divulged on admission to the clinic. Accepting his plethysmograph results alone might have led to erroneous diagnoses and treatment approaches.

- An elderly drifter was seen frequenting school yards and parks where children played. He was apprehended by witnesses after trying to feel a young girl's genital area while lifting her skirt. He denied any sexual intent, and a distant relative who had known him for his entire lifetime denied any knowledge of prior offenses. Penile plethysmograph testing revealed very high erectile responses to stimuli associated with young girls. The patient, when confronted with these results, admitted a long history of deviant sexual arousal.

A variety of subjective (Maletzky, 1973b, 1974b, Marks, 1981a, pp. 259-287), semiobjective (Maletzky, 1974b), and objective (Adams, Tollison, & Carson, 1981; Adams, Webster, & Carson, 1980; Freund, 1975; Josiason, Fantuzzo, & Rosen, 1980; Nolan & Sandman, 1978) assessment techniques have been used and reported in an extensive and at times divergent literature. The earliest and simplest methods consisted of patient reports. These were severely criticized due to the obvious advantage a reporting offender would have in minimizing his deviant arousal. However, evidence casts such self-reports in a slightly more favorable light (Maletzky, 1980a).

Observer ("significant other") reports are also subject to bias, even when gathered from those living with the patient. A somewhat more objective measure, however, comes from scrutiny of police records obtainable via computer, reflecting arrests, charges, and convictions during treatment or follow-up periods (Maletzky, 1973b, 1974b, 1980a).

Psychological monitoring has been employed for a number of years in attempts to render sexual assessment more valid and reliable (Rosen & Kopen, 1978). Although polygraph evaluation (including combinations of electrodermal, pulse, blood pressure, and respiratory responses) has not been as helpful as originally anticipated (Smith & Meyer, 1980), erectile responses via the penile plethysmograph have assumed the leading if not definitive role in present-day assessment of deviant sexual arousal. Such arousal in males does not occur on a random basis (Abel, 1976; Abel, Barlow, Blanchard, & Guild, 1973; Henson & Robin, 1971). The plethysmograph response appears highly specific: A male without deviant arousal, for example, will generally not respond to depictions of heterosexual pedophilia; a rapist will often respond to aggressive sexual scenes but not to descriptions of sexual activity with young boys (Abel, Blanchard, Barlow, & Maviscakalian, 1975; Malamuth & Clark, 1983). Moreover, the plethysmograph is relatively consistent within the same individual and within a cohort of offenders with similar behaviors (Abel, Blanchard, & Barlow, 1980). In addition, it can often graphically demonstrate progress during a course of treatment.

While the plethysmograph cannot be used to prove that an event did or did not occur, it can frequently point to deviant arousal patterns not previously suspected, monitor the progress of therapy, and assist, via its biofeedback capacities, in the treatment itself (Marquis, Day, Nelson, & Miner, 1989). It must be remembered, however, that this instrument has not been as extensively validated across a large number of nondeviant subjects as have many psychological tests. Ongoing studies are currently attempting to correct that deficiency.[1]

In the evaluation of the sexual offender with the penile plethysmograph, the therapist must choose among a wide variety of stimuli, including slides, stories, movies, and videotapes. Although slides depicting explicit sexual activity have been most often used, some authors believe that sexual arousal to such static visual stimuli is relatively low (Abel, Blanchard, & Barlow, 1980; Earls & Marshall, 1981). Nonetheless, slides will probably continue to be employed because of their low cost and ease of transport as well as the wide latitude they afford in timing of presentation. In addition, separate slides can be handpicked for each patient, according to their desirability and ability to produce measured arousal. Each patient may then have his own collection of scenes, specifically designed for him.

Some clinics have recently experimented with videotape; its production of very high arousal levels has been noted as a distinct advantage. While movies and videotaped sequences do produce generally higher arousals in offenders (Malamuth & Donnerstein, 1982; Quinsey, Chaplin, & Varney, 1986), it is sometimes difficult to know which elements of the stimulus are especially attractive. It is also difficult, though not impossible, to return to exact sequences to produce more specific conditioning using videotaped presentations.

Spoken scenes—by the therapist at the time of treatment, by the offender, or by the therapist via a tape recording—have also produced surprisingly high levels of arousal (Abel, Blanchard, Murphy, Becker, & Djenderedjian, 1981).

- In a retrospective review of 100 randomly selected charts of sexual offenders within the current sample, 66 manifested their highest arousals to audiotaped scenes, while 21 experienced their highest arousal with movies, and just 13 with slides alone.

It may be that verbal presentations of sexual material allow an individual to visualize (and perhaps idealize) his own picture of sexual activity, unencumbered by others' ideas of what should be arousing to him. Studies are now ongoing using drawings made by an artist based upon feedback given by the offender in order to tailor the stimulus to a more precise fit.

There has been much comment in the literature about the ability to suppress the penile plethysmograph, producing false negatives (Rosen & Kopen, 1978). In general, offenders with "straight lines" on the machine are not rare: They constituted 29% of all offenders in the present sample. It appears, based on multiple assessment techniques, that these individuals can be successfully treated with the usual behavioral methods, but success cannot be verified as objectively as for offenders showing deviant arousal on this instrument. Often, however, these individuals would do one of the following:

(1) Begin to manifest low arousal (10%-20%) to deviant stimuli and very low arousal (0%-10%) to normal stimuli: The differential responses usually defined a limited but valid range within which to work.

(2) Fail to suppress a full erection when deviant material was presented after normal consenting sexual activity: It appears to be much more difficult for men to reduce their erections once fully aroused than it is for them to prevent an increase from a baseline state (Malcolm, Davidson, & Marshall, 1981).

(3) Demonstrate a series of initial arousals to deviant stimuli, interrupted by reductions in tumescence once the same level of arousal was reached with each stimulus presentation: Arousal to normal stimuli was prompt and complete. This pattern was suspected to indicate attempts at suppression of erectile responses of deviant stimuli.

Research exploring the use of a variety of physiological monitors, including pupillography, penile temperature changes, measurement of penile *length* changes (in addition to circumference changes), computerized electroencephalographic responses, and even positron-emission tomography of the central nervous system is brisk and, combined with plethysmograph data, promises more comprehensive and hopefully valid barometers of sexual response in the future (Adams, Tollison, & Carson, 1981).

No mention will be made here of treatment for the victims of sexual abuse. Recent and excellent reviews of this subject are part of a rapidly expanding literature in this once-neglected area (Adams-Tucker, 1982; Berliner & Wheeler, 1987; Cox & Maletzky, 1980; Wheeler, 1987). It is important to note again that it is best to use the victim's story of what occurred, combined with police reports, presentence investigations, and similar material. Experience mirrors the suggestions in the literature that offenders often shade their stories in their own favor in attempts to camouflage their own complicity (Adams-Tucker, 1982; Cox & Maletzky, 1980; Nadelson, Nothan, Zackson, & Gornick, 1982).

Specific techniques may apply to just one form of sexual offender. The method of aversive behavior rehearsal, for example, has been almost exclusively applied to exhibitionists. However, the use of such techniques has often been encouraged for other disorders as well.

- A middle-aged businessman with two counts of molesting his 6-year-old stepdaughter was asked to reenact the molestation employing a life-size doll-replica while being observed by male and female treatment staff. Several such sessions reduced his plethysmograph readings to zero in association with images of the real event.

The following material presumes some familiarity with behavior theory and a rudimentary knowledge of basic conditioning techniques. While literature references documenting the effectiveness of these techniques will be given, an exhaustive review will not be undertaken so that we will be better able to concentrate on the actual descriptions of techniques. The references will assist those who wish to pursue relevant subjects further.

Note

1. Personal communications with Steven Mussack (Ph.D., Eugene, Oregon) and Robert Irwin (Ph.D., Albuquerque, New Mexico).

2

The Assessment of
Sexual Offenders

KEVIN B. MCGOVERN

This guest chapter is contributed by a psychologist with extraordinary experience and expertise in the assessment and treatment of sexual offenders. Dr. Kevin McGovern brings to this work many years of experience not only in the treatment of the maladaptive sexual approach disorders but also in teaching the crucial assessment and treatment skills necessary for such therapy as well. Dr. McGovern is the founder of two organizations associated with sexual abuse: Alternatives to Sexual Abuse, an educational organization involved in workshops and seminars, and Sexual Abuse Free Environment, through which educational materials concerning victims of sexual abuse are distributed to community agencies and the general public. Although this chapter is limited to behavioral and psychological assessment, Dr. McGovern's breadth of experience in treating these disorders contributes an added dimension to his effort in the present work.

— BARRY MALETZKY

For decades, mental health care providers have been asked to make predictions about future disruptive behaviors. Although some clinicians claim a high level of accuracy, others question the overall validity and reliability of clinical assessment procedures. During the last several years, abusive sexual behavior has become a recognized national tragedy. Society wants reassurance that identified sexual offenders will not engage in other deviant or aberrant activities. Clinicians are often asked to predict whether identified sexual offenders will assault, coerce, or seduce others into abusive sexual acts. The clinicians providing these assessments utilize an array of clinical procedures. The clinician carefully assesses subconscious thoughts, preoccupations, fantasies, sexual arousal patterns, and behavioral acts. By examining these and other pertinent factors, clinicians become more familiar with the psychological deficits and assets of each sexual offender.

Brief clinical staffings and peripheral evaluations will not provide adequate information. To make reasonable decisions about the psychological status of the sexually impaired offender, clinicians should carefully review as much pertinent information as is available at the time of assessment. While completing an assessment, clinicians should strive to provide a comprehensive evaluation that will identify the psychological assets, deficits, and excesses of the sexually impaired.

The Clinical Interview

In many cases, a carefully taken social history will provide a clear historical picture of an individual's developmental background, including his or her ability to control behavior. When an individual's past social history is contrasted with his or her current psychological status, cognitive abilities, responses to an array of psychological tests, and sexual arousal patterns, a psychological profile will emerge. This profile may be used to make realistic forecasts regarding future behavior. There is a major difference between making realistic forecasts and infallible or ironclad predictions about future events. Realistic forecasts are based on the collection of sound information about an individual's psychological characteristics. On the other hand, "infallible" predictions are often based on subjective opinions, skewed data, and unreliable biases.

While providing a clinical evaluation, a comprehensive multidimensional assessment is also highly recommended. An individual's past social history, sexual development, psychological characteristics, and sexual arousal patterns should be carefully examined.

When numerous clinical symptoms are apparent, a thorough evaluation may reveal a long history of aberrant activities. In cases where a character disorder is apparent, the individual's verbal self-report is often unreliable, especially when specific inquiries are made about an individual's sexual history. Individuals with serious character disorders often minimize their psychological problems during an evaluation. They clearly recognize that their current deviant acts may lead to institutionalization or incarceration. In these instances, the offender will often minimize his level of sexual deviance. Instead of revealing his actual sexual fantasies and preoccupations, he may describe a long history of innocence and naïveté. In a number of instances, an offender will have seriously distorted what has really occurred between the victim and himself. Minimization, denial, rationalization, and claims of seduction are often observed during these interviews. The above variables represent a number of factors that should be carefully examined during the clinical evaluation.

The evaluator must always remember that there are false positives and false negatives. Some individuals are extremely adept at disguising their sexual pathology, while others may exaggerate their symptoms in a histrionic fashion. In many cases, the sexual offender will simply not provide accurate information.

Sexual offenders represent a broad population of individuals. Although the majority of arrested offenders are men, there is an increasing number of cases of sexual abuse by women (Finklehor, 1988). These abusive sexual behaviors can range from exhibitionism to homicidal rape. The types and frequencies of aberrant sexual behaviors and their range of victims also vary. Some offenders search for youthful victims each day, while others engage in aberrant sexual activities on a very limited basis. In some circumstances, the sexual addict may enjoy engaging in forms of multiple deviations including exposing, voyeurism, fondling, and public masturbation.

Various evaluation procedures have been used to clinically assess the sexual offender's psychological deficits and assets (Groth, 1979a; Laws, 1988). Through the use of a systematic assessment approach to obtaining historical information, the clinician will be able to make more sensible decisions about future treatment and placement (Abel, Blanchard, Becker, & Djenderedjian, 1978; Barlow, 1977; Herman, 1976; Hindman, 1987; Laws & Osborn, 1983). When evaluating the historical characteristics of a sexual offender, clinicians are continuously faced with an array of pertinent diagnostic challenges. In many cases, mental health care providers, social agencies, and court officials are interested in determining (a) the extent or magnitude of the sexual deviance; (b) whether or not there is an immediate or long-term threat to society; (c) if the aberrant thoughts, attitudes, emotional reactions, and behaviors can be changed; and (d) what treatment programs or residential care facilities would be most appropriate.

These clinical evaluations will often have significant and long-lasting effects upon the sexually impaired. In many cases, these reports will be circulated among mental health care administrators, counselors, probation officers, and courts. For example, in some communities, these evaluations are utilized by the corrections division during presentence investigations. Probation officers often incorporate these clinical assessments into their final reports. These documents will be reviewed by the court before final recommendations are made regarding incarceration, hospitalization, outpatient treatment, and probation.

Because these evaluations can provide an array of valuable information, each clinical assessment should include a thorough and comprehensive analysis of the sexual offender's strengths and weaknesses. During these evaluations, the clinician is often asked to determine whether or not the sexually impaired (a) is an adequate candidate for an appropriate treatment program, (b) is hampered by aberrant sexual arousal patterns, (c) has seriously distorted his perceptions of these aberrant sexual events, and (d) is motivated and willing to change his behavior patterns.

The clinical interview involves not only the gathering of data but an ability to establish a bond with the offender, a difficult goal in cases that are mandated for treatment by the judicial system. Thus it is often not wise to attempt to gain all information in just one or two sessions, even if pressures are exerted to send information to third parties. Crucial information may only seep out slowly, and indeed the process of obtaining historical data continues throughout treatment. Nonetheless, it is important to obtain critical information as soon as feasible in several areas:

(1) a history of the present offense
(2) a history of sexual arousal patterns
(3) a history of prior legal problems
(4) any history of drug- and alcohol-related problems
(5) any history of current medical problems and medications

During the course of several subsequent sessions, the therapist can delve deeper into these areas while also obtaining other information regarding

(1) developmental history
(2) educational history
(3) military history, if any
(4) vocational history
(5) a history of social interactions and significant relationships
(6) genetic history

In addition, every attempt should be made to interview a significant other (also see below), such as a wife, girlfriend, or parent, as few individuals are skilled in observing their own behaviors. As detailed in a later section, interviews with the victim(s), if feasible, should also occur to gain as much material as possible.

Supplemental Reports

Sexual offenders usually minimize their aberrant behavior patterns. These distortions are influenced by a number of factors, including (a) social embarrassment, (b) the threat of divorce, (c) serious economic sanctions, and (d) the fear of long-term incarceration. As the offender prepares for his day in court, his perceptions of what actually occurred between himself and his victim(s) may become quite distorted. Because these distorted perceptions occur frequently, police reports, victim statements, past criminal records, collaborating evidence, presentence investigation reports, medical records, prior psychological evaluations, and any other related documents that have already been accumulated by the police, mental health care providers, or the defendant's attorney should be carefully reviewed.

While reviewing this information, the evaluator should search for any indicators of previous assault, disruptive developmental patterns, antisocial acts, or past incidents that substantiate erratic and impulsive behavior patterns. In addition, the police reports should be carefully examined to determine the degree of violence, force, and abuse employed by the offender. Specific attention should be given to the duration and frequency of these impulsive acts. While examining these critical characteristics, the clinicians should also carefully study the type of relationship that existed between the victims and the sexual offender, the number and ages of victims, the type of intimidation used, the various forms of sexual behaviors (i.e., exposing, public masturbation, fondling, oral stimulation, assaultive rape), and any paraphernalia utilized by the offender (McGovern & Peters, 1988).

The Assessment of Aberrant Sexual Arousal

Some sexual abusers develop long-term aberrant arousal patterns. Although these individuals often minimize their sexual disorders, many have cultivated aberrant sexual fantasies and deviant masturbatory behaviors for years. During a clinical assessment, these aberrant sexual arousal patterns and deviant sexual fantasies may not be adequately evaluated. In addition, therapists may not always adequately confront the sexual offender about distorted fantasies or aberrant masturbatory habits, perhaps from a desire not to unduly confront or embarrass him. During the course of therapy, the offender may continue to conceal his aberrant fantasies or may minimize his aberrant sexual arousal patterns, discount his collection of erotic materials (i.e., child pornography), or disclaim masturbation to any deviant sexual arousal materials. A number of sexual offenders, once involved in treatment, have confided that their therapist did not ask them about aberrant arousal patterns and masturbatory practices during the course of the evaluation. Because many offenders are required by court to obtain treatment, they often minimize their problems to successfully complete a treatment program in a brief period of time. During their therapeutic contacts, they proclaim high levels of self-control.

To obtain more reliable information regarding an individual's sexual arousal pattern, the implementation of physiological assessment procedures is highly recommended. By having each sexual offender participate in a penile plethysmograph evaluation, the clinician can obtain objective data. There may be a significant difference between an individual's verbal estimation of his arousal and the actual level of arousal as measured by these physiological changes (Greer & Stuart, 1983; Laws, 1988).

Some offenders have a distorted perception of their own sexual arousal patterns. During an assessment, for example, they may verbalize that they are not sexually attracted to scenes describing assaultive sexual behavior with children. However, their actual arousal patterns may indicate that they are highly aroused by these sexual materials. Because their verbal self-report is at times so much at variance with other data, physiological evaluations are needed to determine whether or not the sexually impaired are accurately perceiving their environments.

Physiological Assessment

Five basic physiological responses have been examined regarding male sexuality (Tollison & Adams, 1979). These indices include (a) electrodermal responses, (b) cardiovascular responses, (c) respiratory responses, (d) pupillary responses, and (e) penile arousal. This section will focus on the plethysmograph measurement of arousal as the first four assessment modalities either are still in the developmental stage (pupillary responses) or have been largely abandoned (electrodermal, cardiovascular, and respiratory responses).

Numerous clinicians endorse the use of the penile plethysmograph as the optimal measure of normal and aberrant sexual arousal patterns. In a seminal report, Laws and Osborn (1983) have described how their assessment procedures are used to evaluate and treat sexual deviance. These physiological data provide clinicians with quantifiable recordings of male sexual arousal patterns. With this information, therapists are able to continuously study the sexual offender's patterns.

As an additional approach, Abel, Blanchard, Becker, and Djenderedjian (1978) are now completing studies comparing pupillary responses with penile circumference changes. These research results may identify which physiological methods provide the most reliable way to assess deviant and normal arousal patterns. The combination of sensory receptor movement in the eyes and penile circumference changes may in the future provide more consistent and accurate information about deviant arousal and subsequent behavior.

As these and other physiological approaches are being more thoroughly researched, many clinicians have routinely incorporated penile plethysmograph evaluations into their armamentarium of physiological assessment techniques. During a physiological assessment, the clinician attempts to obtain an objective measure of arousal. Although a chart recorder is one standardized way of obtaining this information, other evaluators have used analog or digital recording machines. Various penile transducers are also available for purchase. The more popular transducers include the Barlow strain gauge (1977) or the Parks gauge (Laws & Osborn, 1983).

However, the plethysmograph and its gauges can be used indiscriminately. State licensing boards have not yet established reasonable certification guidelines; neither are there any standards yet established for performing a plethysmograph evaluation. In some cases, the sexual offender is not provided with privacy while completing a physiological assessment. In addition, clinicians differ in the attachment of the gauge. Occasionally, some evaluators have implied that the plethysmograph is a phallic lie detector or an instrument to measure whether an offender committed a crime. None of these practices is warranted given the current state of the scientific literature.

These potential abuses need to be addressed by recognized certification boards. Recently, an international nonprofit organization, the Association for the Treatment of Sexual Abusers,[1] has set about formulating a series of guidelines (see Appendix D) and training courses for plethysmograph technicians and therapists. It is hoped that these guidelines will eventually be endorsed by local, state, and national professional organizations.

Although these limitations are painful realities, the plethysmograph has a number of positive advantages. By using this assessment tool, the clinician can gain valuable information regarding an individual's arousal patterns. Although some sexual offenders will not become aroused during this evaluation, the majority of individuals will be able to generate some patterns during this assessment. When the therapist reviews the actual arousal patterns with an offender, he is often more willing to engage in a behavioral treatment program designed to modify his current aberrant thoughts, tendencies, and related masturbatory activities.

Operation of the Penile Plethysmograph

During plethysmograph evaluations, it is crucial that the clinician use relevant materials that will provoke accurate responses. Various types of sexual materials can have differential effects on the obtained patterns. In some situations, an offender may become more aroused to visual than to auditory cues. In other circumstances, an offender will not become aroused to audiotapes or slides but will generate arousal while viewing videotapes. A more thorough and detailed explanation of arousal patterns, laboratory procedures, and other clinical approaches can be found elsewhere (Laws & Osborn, 1983).

Before a sexual offender participates in the physiological evaluation, he will have provided a sexual history and an explanation of his inappropriate sexual activities. The offender then signs a consent form and is given a brief overview of what will occur during the assessment. The individual is then invited into a comfortable room and is instructed to sit in a relaxation chair, commonly a reclining lounger. He then places a strain gauge on his penis and is asked to become as relaxed and as comfortable as possible. The client then views a variety of slides that portray a wide range of sexual scenes varying from nudity to hard-core explicit sexual behavior. After each slide is presented, the offender is asked to rate his level of sexual arousal on a scale of 0 to 100. His verbal report of arousal and the score obtained on a chart recorder are then placed on a summary form. Following the slide presentation, the individual listens to a number of audiotapes describing an array of deviant sexual behaviors. He may also be exposed to sexual stories pertaining to his own deviant actions as well as to videotapes and movies.

Again, the offender is asked to rate his arousal. After the materials have been displayed, the offender is asked to bring himself to full erection through fantasy or self-stimulation. Comparisons are then made between his arousal responses to normal and aberrant materials.

After the offender has removed the gauge, his arousal responses are reviewed with him. In many cases, this is the first time that anyone has provided this individual with objective data regarding his normal and deviant arousal patterns. Often, but certainly not always, the offender is surprised by these data. By reviewing these chart recordings, the offender can see which materials actually caused the highest levels of arousal. Because many sexual offenders often underestimate their aberrant arousal, these recordings provide them with more realistic and accurate information. In numerous cases, sexual offenders have rated their deviant arousal responses as extremely low or nonexistent. By reviewing their arousal responses, distorted perceptions are often replaced by realistic and accurate descriptions of arousal patterns. Although it may be extremely difficult to convince an offender that he should obtain treatment because of his responses to a true-or-false questionnaire or an inkblot test, he can better understand the need for treatment if he has become highly aroused by themes describing sexual behavior with children and adolescents or aggressive, sadistic behavior with adults. In many cases, the sexual offender's aberrant arousal patterns have not been previously assessed or modified, as shown in the following example.

* * *

L.R., a 38-year-old male, had sexually abused his biological daughter, Becky. A review of his past history revealed that he had not been previously arrested and there were no other indications of deviant sexual behaviors. During an evaluation, L.R. reiterated that his inappropriate sexual behaviors occurred only between himself and his daughter. L.R. reported that he had fondled her genitals weekly for at least seven years. While attending a recent school retreat, Becky had reported these inappropriate sexual behaviors to a school counselor.

At an omnibus pretrial meeting, L.R. agreed to move out of the family residence. His wife eventually divorced him. At the time of his final court hearing, several mental health counselors testified that L.R. was no longer a threat to the community because he would not be living with Becky.

Although this man had been removed from his family, he was still preoccupied with his deviant sexual fantasies. A careful review of his history revealed that L.R. (a) had been sexually abused as a child by several baby-sitters; (b) had been verbally, psychologically, and physically abused by his parents; (c) had cultivated aberrant sexual fantasies for years; and (d) had engaged in inappropriate sexual behaviors for seven years.

During one interview, L.R. calculated that he had inappropriately touched his daughter's genitals on over 500 occasions. After touching her, he would usually vividly fantasize about what had just occurred and stimulate himself to orgasm. In addition, he would imagine having intercourse with his daughter while sexually stimulating his wife. Although his behaviors had been confined to one victim, he had spent many hours engaging in aberrant behaviors. After his divorce, L.R. still reminisced about his sexual behaviors with his daughter. He eventually married a woman who believed his contrived story about his seductive and promiscuous daughter.

The probation officer concluded that L.R. no longer had a significant psychological problem. In addition, the psychological evaluation indicated that L.R. could control his behavior. Unfortunately, L.R.'s sexual arousal patterns had not been evaluated. Without this information, an accurate decision could not be made about his aberrant arousal patterns.

At a later hearing, the court ordered L.R. to complete a physiological assessment. The results, displayed in Figure 2.1, clearly demonstrated that he was highly aroused by both visual material and audiotaped scenes depicting fellatio, cunnilingus, and intercourse between adults and minor females. In addition, he was minimally aroused by materials describing or visually depicting sexual behaviors occurring between consenting adults. A correct physiological assessment resulted in an appropriate referral for treatment.

* * *

As illustrated in this example, sexual offenders can provide authorities and therapists with erroneous information regarding their aberrant sexual activities, either by design or by unconscious lapse.

Because most sexual offenders have cultivated aberrant sexual fantasies, a thorough physiological evaluation at some point during assessment is highly recommended. The timing of a plethysmograph evaluation can be flexible in most cases, to ensure that adequate historical information has been collected and some rapport built. Intermittent physiological monitoring is also recommended. In some cases, an individual's aberrant arousal pattern will recycle at another point in his life. With this in mind, sexual offenders need to learn how to both monitor and modify their aberrant arousal patterns throughout a lifetime.

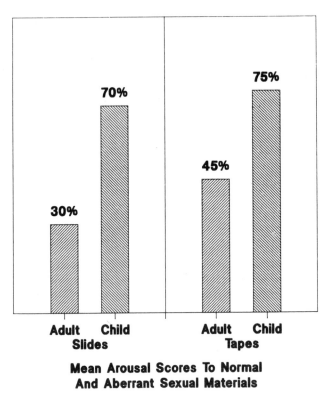

**Mean Arousal Scores To Normal
And Aberrant Sexual Materials**

Figure 2.1 Penile Plethysmograph Assessment for L.R.

Psychological Assessment Techniques

It has proven advantageous to conduct a psychological assessment utilizing a male and female team, if at all feasible, to make observations of any differential responses and to obtain as much data as possible. During the first phase of this evaluation, the interviewers study the police reports, presentence investigations, victims' statements, and other pertinent historical information including past medical records, previous hospital discharge summaries, and other psychological reports. The clinical interview, and frequently the physiological assessment, is completed during this period. Thereafter, testing is begun.

Clinicians have designed a constellation of physiological assessment procedures. These assessment procedures have been used to identify intelligence, personality characteristics, emotional deficits, learning disorders, brain damage, and a host of the other psychological traits, characteristics, and behavioral patterns (Newmark, 1985).

For the psychological assessment of the offender, each client is placed in a separate testing room and is given an explanation of a number of paper-and-pencil tests. These instruments include the Cornell Medical Index, the Minnesota Multiphasic Personality Inventory, the Rotter Incomplete Sentence Blank, and the Sone Sexual History Background Form (Sone, 1984; see Appendix A). After the individual has completed these materials, he then participates in a second interview with a male evaluator. At this time, his social history is reviewed. The sexual offender is again asked to discuss his perception of what occurred between himself and his victim(s). In addition, he is asked to respond to a number of psychological tests.

In the majority of cases, sexual offenders are *not* administered an intelligence test. Clinical experience indicates that approximately 80% of these individuals have either graduated from high school or completed additional college courses. In addition, 95% of these men are generally literate and not impaired by an organic impairment, a developmental disability, or a learning disorder. In some cases in which intellectual functioning is suspect, however, a Wechsler Adult Intelligence Scale, Revised, is administered. In a few selected cases, the sexual offender can be referred for other neuropsychological testing, as indicated.

In addition to the standardized assessment procedures mentioned above, a number of informal, supplementary evaluation techniques have been utilized either during the evaluation or throughout the initial phases of an outpatient treatment program. These approaches have included (a) a card sort technique, (b) a detailed autobiography, (c) a written statement of specific deviant sexual interactions, (d) the construction of an audiotape describing deviant arousal patterns, and (e) supplementary questionnaires.

Infrequently, blood tests are obtained to determine whether certain medications, alcohol, or drugs were being used to suppress arousal patterns. In rare instances, a urological evaluation is performed to determine whether an individual has been impaired by organic impotence (LoPiccolo, 1985).

Although it is beyond the scope of this chapter to delineate, in detail, major psychological tests, a general description of most of these clinical assessment procedures, along with additional references, will be provided.

THE CORNELL MEDICAL INDEX

The Cornell Medical Index consists of 195 items that describe a number of major medical problems. This paper-and-pencil questionnaire is divided into 17 sections. Although the first 144 items pertain to major medical concerns, the remaining 51 questions relate to psychological problems. By carefully examining the "yes" and "no" responses, the clinician can acquire pertinent health care information during the evaluation.

After reviewing the responses on this questionnaire, the clinician may decide to obtain past medical records. Information obtained from state hospitals, private clinics, or other medical facilities may provide the clinician with valuable reports regarding the psychological assets and deficits of the sexual offender.

- A sexual offender, diagnosed as schizophrenic for years, was administered a standardized battery of tests. These led to the suspicion of brain damage. Neurological examinations confirmed the existence of brain damage and a seizure disorder. Following the institution of appropriate medications, bizarre behavior and aggressive tendencies were markedly reduced.

- A sexual offender, previously doing well in treatment, began to complain about chronic headaches and to act inappropriately during group therapy meetings. His behavior became increasingly immature. During a neurological examination, an inoperable brain tumor was found.

While reviewing an individual's medical history, questions may arise regarding the efficiency of pharmaceutical agents, such as depo-Provera. This synthetic hormone (Walker & Meyer, 1981) has been utilized to extinguish obsessional sexual thoughts and deviant behaviors. Although some oppose this pharmacological therapy, others profess that the combination of depo-Provera and a multifaceted treatment program can be used to successfully reduce the frequency and intensity of aberrant sexual fantasies, impulses, and behaviors. Before this medication can be used, the clinician must thoroughly review an individual's medical history and carefully evaluate the short- and long-term side effects of this approach. The use of chemotherapy as an occasional aid in the treatment of the sexual behavior will be more completely discussed in Chapter 8.

THE MINNESOTA MULTIPHASIC PERSONALITY INVENTORY

This multi-item, true-and-false questionnaire was developed to identify an array of psychological assets and deficits. Since its initial use, over 5,000 research studies have been conducted on this instrument. After the sexual offender has completed this self-report questionnaire, his responses can be scored either by hand or with a computerized scoring system. The computerized scoring system usually provides a profile analysis that discusses the individual's psychological strengths and deficits.

This valuable test provides information regarding the sexual offender's test-taking response set. These scores indicate whether an offender is purposely portraying himself in an overly positive or overly negative fashion. These test results also demonstrate whether or not the offender has endorsed an overabundance of unusual or bizarre items. Then a series of scores are provided for 10 basic clinical scales. Additional information can be obtained for an array of other subtests of this instrument (Greene, 1980).

These scores provide valuable information regarding the presence of a characterological disorder, depression, anxiety, cognitive distortions, manic disorders, antisocial personality disorders, chronic impulsivity, sexual identity conflicts, and a host of other psychological characteristics.

THE RORSCHACH AND THEMATIC APPERCEPTION TESTS

Two projective tests, the Rorschach and the Thematic Apperception tests, provide additional information regarding the offender's psychological abilities. Although objective data are not viable to document their use in all cases, these tests have been of use in identifying distorted thinking, psychotic thought processes, levels of intellectual functioning, depression, anxiety, impulsivity, somatic concerns, and a preoccupation with sexual themes. In some cases, a sexual offender may be able to camouflage his current psychological deficits during the clinical interview and while responding to the standardized psychological tests. However, during the administration of these projective tests, he may reveal a number of aberrant psychological characteristics. As he reacts to these materials, the sexual offender may become less confident and begin to reveal a number of deficits and disturbances:

- A pedophile arrested for multiple accounts of sexual abuse portrayed himself as a healthy individual during clinical interviews and while completing the Minnesota Multiphasic Personality Inventory. However, while responding to the Thematic Apperception Test, he described a number of unusual themes. In addition, his responses to the Rorschach Test portrayed him as an impulsive individual who was extremely preoccupied with sexual objects and anatomical parts. It is interesting that, after responding to the projective tests, this man revealed that he had not openly discussed many of his previous responses. During the second administration of the Rorschach, he provided an even higher incidence of unique responses, including an array of child, prepubescent, postpubescent, and adult female genitalia.

THE ROTTER INCOMPLETE SENTENCE BLANK

This questionnaire consists of 49 open-ended items. The respondent is instructed to fill in each incomplete sentence with whatever words appear to be appropriate. In reviewing a sexual offender's responses, the clinician may delineate a number of clinically significant patterns. In some cases, the sexual offender is extremely defensive and cannot respond to these ambiguous materials. In others, the offender will openly portray his concerns, anxieties, and fears. By examining these 49 items, the evaluator in many cases can gain valuable information about the offender's inner concerns, thoughts, and emotions. Frequently, responses to the projective instruments provide revealing information that might otherwise be buried.

In summary, after completing the initial data collection, the sexual offender is asked to complete a number of standardized psychological tests and questionnaires. During a subsequent interview, based on these test results, the individual may be requested to respond to the projective testing. In a few cases, the offender may be referred for other forms of psychological or neurological testing. In occasional cases, offenders have been found to be illiterate; in these situations, the questions are read to them aloud.

Although the aforementioned tests are extremely helpful in clarifying cognitive deficiencies, affective disorders, personality deficits, and other psychological problems, these assessment procedures do not always provide specific information about an individual's sexual behavior. Thus those protocols will not always identify a prevailing sexual dysfunction, disorder, or dissatisfaction. To obtain specific information regarding an individual's sexual behavior, additional protocols, as described below, are recommended.

Other Assessment Techniques

Since the completion of Masters and Johnson's (1970) initial research in St. Louis, a series of questionnaires have been developed by clinicians to identify specific sexual dysfunctions and concerns. For example, the Survey of Sexual Interactions (SSI) and the Background Information Questionnaire (BIQ; LoPiccolo & Steger, 1978) provide information regarding an individual's current level of sexual satisfactions and disappointments. In addition, the Sone Sexual History Background Form (Sone, 1984), a 15-page questionnaire designed specifically for sexual offenders, often provides valuable information; it is presented in Appendix A. This form poses questions regarding the individual's sexual development and history, sexual arousal patterns, fantasies, masturbatory behaviors, heterosexual and homosexual experiences, and a host of other pertinent topics.

In responding to the Sone questionnaire, the sexual offender answers 54 questions pertaining to his sexual history. The initial questions refer to early childhood development; for example, "Where did you obtain your sexual information as a child?" or "To what degree of comfort was sex discussed at your home?" The questionnaire then focuses on adolescent sexual activities, including self-stimulation, sexual fantasies, and initial sexual encounters. The offender is then asked to respond to questions pertaining to his interactions with sexual partners and how he would rate his own sexuality.

Additional questions focus on specific sexual dysfunctions, such as erectile difficulty, retarded ejaculation, penis size, and orgasmic deficiencies. After completing questions pertaining to his sexual activities with partners, the sexual offender then responds to 10 specific questions regarding the nature of his sexual crimes. This information supplements police reports, children's protective services documents, and the verbal sexual history provided by the offender. Information obtained on this protocol is then compared with the physiological results generated through the penile plethysmograph evaluation.

Some clinicians have also advocated the use of a card sort technique (Brownell & Barlow, 1977). In this procedure, each offender is asked to read through a variety of aberrant and normal sexual scenes that are written on 3×5 index cards. These cards are then sorted into six separate stacks. The offender is instructed to use a rating scale from –3 to +3: –3 indicates no arousal while +3 indicates high arousal. In reviewing responses to this card sort technique, a general profile of sexual interest, arousal patterns, and preferences can be obtained for each offender. Responses to these cards can then be contrasted to arousal patterns obtained during the penile plethysmograph evaluation.

During a clinical assessment, each offender can also be asked to write a descriptive explanation of his aberrant sexual behaviors. While not a standardized "test" in the usual sense, responses can be instructive. One offender wrote:

> I love young boys' bodies. The size and shape makes a big difference to me. I have spent hours at public swimming pools watching them dress and undress. When the urges become really strong, I either go to my car and masturbate or hide in a bathroom stall and play with myself. These rituals have gone on for years. They first started at a public pool when I was a lifeguard.
>
> When I sit in a bathroom stall, I watch these young boys through the cracks between the door and the wall. I imagine that my lips are caressing their tiny balls—I hate pubic hair—my mother always complained about it. So I focus on the little ones—their tender, small, yet hard cocks in my mouth.
>
> On some days, I help these young boys dress or undress. Some of the real young ones have a hard time closing their zippers or untying the knot in the cord that keeps up their swimming trunks. On some days, I'll play with them in the pool or have them swim through my legs under water. They see these actions as a game or just a helpful hand while they are changing clothes.

Many of these voyeuristic actions and actual fondling activities strengthen my fantasies and encourage my deviant sexual behavior.

In order to gather more data, a sexual offender might be asked to masturbate to his favorite deviant fantasy at home while verbalizing this fantasy on a tape recorder. This request can be made when the offender cannot become aroused during the customary physiological assessment or is unable to write about his inappropriate sexual activities.

During this assessment procedure, the individual is first instructed to (a) relax in a peaceful and private setting at home, (b) cultivate a fantasy that portrays his inappropriate sexual behavior, and (c) tape-record this scene while masturbating to climax. While listening to this tape, a clinician can learn which elements of the offender's fantasies are most arousing and can gain greater insight into the extent and depth of the individual's sexual thoughts. This clinical assessment technique encourages frank and candid discussions between the offender and the clinician. As the sexual offender becomes more comfortable with this assessment technique, he will more openly discuss his sexual fantasies.

In other situations, the sexual offender is asked to verbalize his most vivid deviant sexual fantasies while his arousal responses are being monitored on the penile plethysmograph. In other cases, the sexual offender's arousal responses are measured on the chart recorder while he then listens to a description of a vivid sexual scene that he has written. Through these assessment procedures, the clinician can determine whether or not the individual is still highly aroused by specific aberrant materials. As can be seen, assessment continues throughout treatment and often merges imperceptibly with treatment itself.

The P and M Rating Scale (presented in Appendix B) is another valuable tool that can be utilized during the assessment of sexual offenders (McGovern & Peters, 1988). This 13-page rating form is divided into a number of major categories, including past criminal history, evidence of prior mental illness and/or deficits, alcohol and drug dependency, asocial activities, and past aberrant sexual activities. The offender is assigned a separate score on each of the 45 items. A high score implies multiple psychological deficits and problems, whereas a low score indicates that the individual is not hampered by a known array of serious psychological or sexual problems. Sexual offenders obtaining lower scores on this scale are normally adequate candidates for outpatient therapy. High scores can imply the need for residential placements, in-hospital treatment, or intensive custodial care. The scores obtained on this protocol must be correlated with psychological test results, a physiological assessment, other objective rating scores, peer observations, and victim statements (Groth, 1979a).

As this forensic field continues to grow, clinicians will continue to both create and utilize an array of additional assessment tools that appear to have merit. These assessment techniques, to name a few, include Self-Efficacy Rating Scales (Hall, 1988), the Multi-Phasic Sex Inventory (Nichols & Molinder, 1984), the Millon Clinical Multiaxial Inventory (Millon, 1977), and the Clarke Sexual History Questionnaire (Langevin, 1983). In addition, residential treatment programs for sexual offenders use an array of other diversified assessment techniques (Prithers, Martin, & Cummings, 1988).

Victim Interview

In some situations, the clinician will be able to interview the victims. Because sexual offenders often minimize their sexual involvement, a candid discussion with the victim will often provide valuable information, as in the following examples.

- L.S., a 35-year-old male, would frequently digitally penetrate his 8-year-old stepdaughter's vagina. As his stepdaughter described these sexual assaults, she became visibly upset and cried throughout the interview. She explained that her father was an abusive man who also frequently struck her mother and little sister. On a number of occasions, he threatened to burn down the house. During one fit of anger, he strangled her dog.

  She reported that her father would pull her by the hair and throw her on the bed. After telling her to stop crying, L.S. would pull down her pants and painfully push his finger into her vagina. When she complained about the pain, he would laugh and tell her to "shut up." On several occasions, he tried to force his erect penis into her mouth. This distraught child was relieved that her father had been arrested and removed from the house; she perceived him as a belligerent, hostile individual who frequently behaved in a sadistic manner.

• The 14-year-old daughter of offender J.B. described her father as a benevolent, loving, and caring individual, despite the fact that he had been encouraging her to masturbate him frequently and perform fellatio on him as well, occasionally ejaculating on her. In fact, she was quite confused about his aberrant sexual behavior. She recognized that her father would only behave inappropriately after consuming alcohol. Although she felt anxious and awkward during these sexual acts, she had not yet developed resentment toward her father. At the time of the interview, she indicated that she wanted her father to stop drinking, obtain professional assistance for his emotional problems, and eventually be reunited with the family.

J.B. had minimized his sexual involvement with his daughter. Although he was willing to discuss the forced manual stimulation of his penis, he would not admit to fellatio and ejaculation. However, during the physiological evaluation, J.B. became highly aroused while listening to a tape describing a vivid scene of fellatio between an adult male and a pubescent adolescent female. As these results were discussed, J.B. began to vaguely recall the oral stimulation that occurred between the two of them. As he continued to discuss this episode of fellatio, J.B. explained that "that damn booze must have screwed up my memory. I used to remember everything."

Although both men sexually abused their children, the actual behaviors differed with regard to the types of sexual behavior employed, the frequency of physical force and violence, and the subsequent patterns that followed each inappropriate act. Both L.S. and J.B. had developed a distorted perception of what had actually occurred between themselves and their victims; the victim interview was significant in assisting with the evaluation and treatment of both offenders.

However, in many situations, the victim's parents are apprehensive about an interview. From the parents' point of view, the child has already participated in enough potentially traumatic events involving the abuse. In addition, some parents may be concerned that a clinician may verbally abuse the child. In these circumstances, both the parents and the victim must be reassured that he or she will not be aggravated or humiliated through this experience.

During these interviews, victims have an opportunity to share their perceptions of what occurred. Their initial statements can be compared with the information that has been provided in the police reports, agency documents, and other pertinent interview materials.

In many cases, the perpetrator has provided the clinician with erroneous information regarding the physical stature, secondary sexual characteristics, and cognitive abilities of the alleged victim. For example, in some cases, perpetrators describe victims as promiscuous and seductive individuals. During these interviews, the clinician has an opportunity to assess the victim's cognitive abilities, social skills, and other relevant behavioral characteristics and compare these observations with the sexual offender's perceptions, thereby broadening the data base and enhancing treatment.

Interview with a Significant Other Observer

During early sessions, and following trust building, the offender should be asked for permission to interview a significant other, an observer who knows the offender intimately, such as a wife, girlfriend, or parent. This person can often provide the clinician with pertinent information about the offender's overall demeanor, his reactions to the accusations, his prior sexual and criminal history, and his level of employment and relationship stability. These perceptions can be correlated with the information obtained through the other assessment techniques already mentioned. Major discrepancies can be reviewed and discussed with this observer and the offender, at times in joint sessions. Through these interviews, the clinician will gain other insightful information about the overall psychological assets and deficits of the sexual offender. In addition, repeated contacts with such an observer can keep the therapist aware of ongoing progress.

It is only through a combination of assessment methods that a thorough and reliable picture of the sexual offender can emerge. The following case illustrates the application of these methods in the evaluation and treatment of a typical offender.

* * *

While talking to an adolescent friend, a 16-year-old girl confided that she was engaging in nonconsenting sexual activities with her stepfather, W.B. Because the friend had experienced a similar relationship with a distant relative, she decided to discuss this matter with a high school counselor. State law obligated the counselor to report these assaultive incidents. Children's protective services was thus notified. After a thorough investigation was completed by this agency and the local city police department, W.B. was arrested. Initially, he denied any sexual involvement with his stepdaughter; after discussing these allegations with his attorney, he agreed to undergo a clinical evaluation.

During the first phase of this evaluation, the interviewer reviewed the police reports and victim statements that had been provided by the attorney. Because W.B. had not been previously arrested and was not medically impaired, there were no other major documents available. In reviewing these reports, attention was paid to the degree of correspondence existing between the victim's and perpetrator's perceptions of these offenses, the degree of coercion or force used during these sexual activities, the number and types of sexual behaviors, and the victim's psychological and behavioral reactions to these aberrant behaviors.

During the initial clinical interview, W.B. was asked to provide an extensive social history. He was questioned about perceptions of the current criminal allegations and asked whether he had participated in any other recent psychological, psychiatric, or polygraph evaluations. In this case, W.B. had failed two independent polygraph examinations administered by two separate polygraphers hired by his attorney. He had also completed a psychiatric evaluation. Although these documents were not yet available for review, W.B. explained that their clinical conclusions were "highly favorable yet inconclusive." W.B. also implied that his attorney had told him not to discuss these previous evaluations with anyone. However, W.B. was certain that his attorney would eventually send these documents in the mail. These reports were never received.

During the first meeting, W.B. continued to reiterate his innocence. He believed that his stepdaughter had made several false accusations in order to emancipate herself from the family. After concluding this clinical interview, W.B. was then placed in a separate testing room and asked to complete an array of paper-and-pencil tests, including (a) the Cornell Medical Index, (b) the Minnesota Multiphasic Personality Inventory, (c) the Rotter Incomplete Sentence Blank, and (d) the Sone Sexual History Background Form. He readily agreed to cooperate with the clinical assessment, stating, "I want to prove my innocence."

During the next clinical interview, which occurred two weeks later, W.B. again reiterated his innocence. As in the initial interview, the police reports were again reviewed with him. W.B. explained that his stepdaughter's accusations were "absolute lies and that the truth would finally come out in the end."

After again reviewing his past social history and his current perceptions of these allegations, W.B. was given an opportunity to react to the Rorschach and the Thematic Apperception tests.

W.B.'s stepdaughter and wife were then contacted for separate interviews. During this component of the assessment, the stepdaughter gave vivid verbal descriptions of a variety of inappropriate sexual behaviors that had occurred with her stepfather. She stated that these interactions began approximately four years ago when her stepfather would intermittently come into her room after she had fallen asleep, ostensibly to adjust her covers. While he was doing so, W.B. would begin to fondle her breasts. Uncertain of how to respond, she pretended to be asleep. As the years passed, this became a regular ritual. Approximately once a week, W.B. would spend inordinate amounts of time in the room adjusting her bed covers, touching her breasts, and eventually placing his hands on her genitalia.

About one year before referral, this young girl finally voiced her objections to her stepfather. At that time, he became defensive and indicated that she had misunderstood his intentions. However, one afternoon after drinking beer for several hours, W.B. demanded that she engage in intercourse. During this interaction, he became physically abusive, telling his stepdaughter that, if she were old enough to have sex with her boyfriend, she could certainly share "some of those goodies" with him. After this episode, she decided to tell her girlfriend about what had happened.

After her stepfather's arrest, this victim felt fearful, depressed, and ambivalent about these inappropriate sexual activities. She recognized that W.B. had a serious psychological problem but was also aware that her mother had become seriously depressed about these allegations. She had threatened to kill herself if W.B. were sent to jail.

During the clinical interview with W.B's wife, she described her husband as a loving and benevolent man who had not engaged in other forms of abusive behaviors. When she first learned about those inappropriate sexual interactions, she could not believe that her husband would sexually stimulate her daughter. She felt that her daughter had lied about these incidents. However, after attending a self-help group for mothers of sexually abused children, she gained some insight into her husband's problems. She began to realize that her husband had spent large amounts of time up and walking around the house at night. She had wondered why W.B. would spend an additional 15 to 20 minutes in the bathroom thereafter. When she questioned him about these activities, W.B. would inform her that he was simply constipated.

W.B.'s wife indicated that they had had a dissatisfying sexual relationship for many years. Although they engaged in coital activities approximately twice a month, there was very little romantic touching and concomitant sexual activities. She felt that their disappointing sexual relationship may have contributed to their current disharmony and her husband's abusive sexual behaviors.

During the next clinical interview, W.B. was again asked to describe his perceptions of these sexual activities. As the police reports were again reviewed, W.B.'s verbal statements became more inconsistent. At this point in the assessment, W.B. became frustrated and confused. He was then referred for a physiological evaluation.

During the plethysmograph assessment, W.B. viewed 14 slides covering an array of sexual materials and listened to six erotic tapes. The slides portrayed both inappropriate sexual interactions with minors and appropriate heterosexual behaviors with adults. In addition, the audiotapes explicitly described sexual interactions between consenting adults and inappropriate sexual interactions between children and adults.

W.B.'s responses to these materials were automatically recorded on a chart recorder. After each presentation, he was asked to verbally rate his arousal to each visual and audiotaped presentation. The differences between his verbal self-report and the actual circumference changes as measured by the penile strain gauge and chart recorder were then analyzed and compared. Figure 2.2 portrays W.B's arousal patterns to these sexual materials. It is interesting that W.B. did not become aroused by any of the slides. However, while listening to the erotic tapes, W.B. showed significant responses to a story describing inappropriate sexual fondling and stimulation of a young girl and a female adolescent. His overall arousal responses to appropriate adult sexual behaviors were extremely low.

When these results were reviewed with W.B., he became agitated. He appeared to recognize that he was unable to fully suppress sexual responses while listening to tapes describing inappropriate sexual

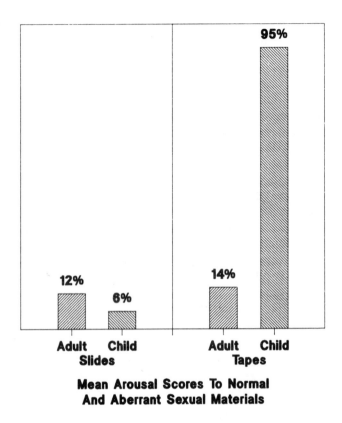

Figure 2.2   Penile Plethysmograph Assessment for W.B.

behavior between adults and children. Although he had managed to close his eyes periodically throughout the slide presentations, he could not screen out taped descriptions of sexual activity with female minors.

W.B. then provided the following history: Several years ago, he became preoccupied with adolescent sexual fantasies. While on a trip to a large city, he purchased a number of magazines describing sexual behaviors between men and female teenagers. He would read these erotic materials in his hotel room and stimulate himself to orgasm.

As these fantasies became a regular component of his life, he thought about actual sexual interactions with his stepdaughter. At night, he would enter her room and check her bedding. While being aroused by his sexual fantasies, he would begin to touch her breasts and, eventually, her genitals. After obtaining a full erection while stimulating his stepdaughter, he would go into the bathroom and masturbate to orgasm.

When questioned about his marital relationship, W.B. disclosed that he was able to have intercourse with his wife. However, to obtain an erection, he would need to fantasize about sexual experiences with teenagers or preteens. During coitus, he would continue to think about aberrant fantasies. He explained that he had become dissatisfied with his marital relationship. In his eyes, his wife had aged and become overweight and less attractive. On occasion, he felt suffocated when his wife would sit on top of him during intercourse.

At the end of this interview, W.B. admitted that he had lied about his inappropriate behavior; however, he wanted to discuss these latest revelations with his attorney. A conference call was arranged. During a subsequent pretrial conference with an assistant district attorney, W.B. and his attorney accepted a plea-bargaining agreement. After spending a month in a work-release program at a county jail, W.B. was required by the court to participate in a behavior therapy program. This multifaceted treatment approach included (a) a group behavior treatment program and (b) individual behavior therapy sessions (McGovern & Jensen, 1985).

* * *

This case is typical in some ways, as it demonstrates not only some advantages in employing these assessment techniques but some pitfalls in doing so as well. Psychological problems in offenders can at times revolve around their inept sexuality, low self-esteem, subassertiveness, and poor decision making. These negative traits are accompanied by their inappropriate fantasies, cognitive distortions, unhealthy masturbatory behaviors, and aberrant arousal patterns. In probing these weaknesses with such assessment methods, brittle egos may shatter. The application of these techniques must occur within a framework of trust building, no matter how alienated the offender may be. In many cases, a traditional psychological evaluation may not uncover these inadequacies. Therefore, while a comprehensive, multifaceted assessment is highly recommended, it must be approached from a position of rapport and within a spirit, if at all possible, of mutual exploration.

Clinical Perspectives

In the evaluation of over 2,000 sexual offenders, these assessment procedures continue to be revised. Although the majority of these evaluations have followed routine assessment guidelines, individual differences have also been taken into account. Thus this systematic approach provides both flexibility and the opportunity to add additional assessment procedures. For example, one evaluation candidate had experienced several myocardial infarctions during the past three years. During the clinical interviews, he readily admitted that he had engaged in inappropriate sexual behavior with several minors. Because this man was experiencing serious health care problems, a physiological evaluation was deemed unwarranted because of his unstable medical condition.

In other situations, additional psychological tests or second opinions have been encouraged. In a recent case, a client appeared to be preoccupied and delusional. He was referred for an assessment by an independent clinical psychologist to determine whether or not these deficits were contrived. This second opinion confirmed that he was indeed hampered by several serious psychological deficiencies, and appropriate referral was initiated prior to treatment for his sexual problems. Thus, while this assessment approach uses a number of standard components, there is always room for modifications and improvement.

This evaluation approach also allows an opportunity to contrast various modes of information. By examining police reports, relevant medical documents, military discharge summaries, past criminal history forms, and presentence investigation reports, information can be contrasted with the offender's perception of his own social history. By carefully reviewing these materials and the clinical notes, the clinician can search for major inconsistencies.

Because each assessment candidate is usually interviewed by at least two interviewers, his degree of consistency can be evaluated. In some situations, the accused will make significant changes or will provide different information during these meetings. In addition, although the sexual offender may be extremely defensive and guarded in the first interview, during the second interview, he may provide a more detailed explanation of his inappropriate sexual behavior. Thus multiple assessment techniques provide an opportunity to repeatedly check the offender's own history and perceptions.

As with any assessment approach, there are also a number of limitations. Some offenders falsify or distort relevant information. These individuals may exclude pertinent bits of information or distort past sexual history. Obviously, most sexual offenders recognize that these clinical evaluations will have a major impact on their future freedom and financial stability. In some cases, they understate their psychopathology to deliberately mislead the clinician. During the course of these evaluations, a number of procedural problems can thus arise. Offenders may not answer specific questions or may refuse to complete certain tests. They may claim to be unable to experience sexual arousal during the physiological assessment. On at least one occasion, an assessment candidate confessed that a friend taught him how to cheat. This man explained that he masturbated several times the day before the assessment, stayed awake the night before, and took a number of sedatives the morning of the assessment. Because these individuals are often facing severe legal and social consequences, some of them will use a number of such ploys to prove their innocence and psychological stability.

Other problems, procedural in nature, may arise. Because a multidimensional evaluation requires a number of interviews and sufficient amounts of time, some evaluees complain that they cannot afford an extensive evaluation. Some offenders may state that their employers will not allow them to be absent from work; some argue that they must complete other family or vocational tasks that are more important than the clinical evaluation.

Scheduling may also present its own challenges. In some cases, attorneys will want their client evaluated within several days. Because the assessment consists of multiple evaluation components, the entire evaluation may take a period of four to six weeks. Examiners should try to be as flexible as possible in meeting these conflicting demands in order to build better rapport. Nonetheless, the importance of checking validity and utilizing multiple assessment techniques will generally outweigh questions of expediency. A rushed

and careless assessment can be more misleading than no assessment
at all.

Implications for Treatment

A variety of therapeutic programs are now being provided by an
array of therapists, some more qualified than others. A sexual offender can technically be treated by anyone professing some expertise in this area, although standardization is being attempted.[2] Sexual
offenders have previously obtained professional assistance from pastoral counselors, psychology interns, psychiatry residents, police officers, volunteer counselors, prostitutes, health educators, and mental health care providers. In addition, a wide variety of modalities
have been employed, including self-help groups, bibliotherapy, hypnosis, behavior modification, homone treatment, and Gestalt therapy.

In some cases, therapists view aberrant sexual behavior as a symptom or behavioral manifestation of a personality disturbance or characterological disorder, and the sexual problem itself may not be
directly treated.

- E.L., 49 years old, was arrested for fondling his 14-year-old
  stepdaughter's breasts and vagina. During his first marriage, he had
  engaged in similar behaviors with another daughter. E.L. had not
  reoffended for six years, but, during his second marriage, he began to
  notice arousal for his stepdaughter as she reached pubescence, and he
  eventually began molesting her.

  During the clinical interview, a number of interesting factors
  emerged. Although E.L. had already participated in 32 sessions of
  psychotherapy, the majority of these meetings consisted of discussing
  his early childhood, his interactions with peers, and his occupational
  stress. E.L. had faithfully attended these sessions, but only a few comments were made by his therapist regarding his inappropriate sexual
  behavior.

  Although E.L. had successfully completed his therapy program, he
  had not modified his inappropriate arousal patterns, masturbatory
  behaviors, or unhealthy sexual fantasies. On numerous occasions, he
  would vividly fantasize about his sexual encounters with his first
  daughter while having intercourse with his wife.

The situation in this example is not uncommon, and it underscores the premise that continuous ongoing evaluations must occur during the course of therapy. To effectively assess the efficiency of treatment, the sexual offender's assets and deficits must be continuously monitored and evaluated throughout his treatment program. In one such program (McGovern & Jensen, 1985), the offender's arousal patterns are reevaluated by the penile plethysmograph every 60 to 90 days. In addition, intermittent polygraph examinations are also required. During the polygraph evaluation, the offender is asked whether or not he has engaged in any other deviant sexual acts with victims since the inception of his treatment program. While controversy exists about the subjectivity, reliability, and validity of this instrument, this test has often been useful in promoting fuller disclosure during treatment. When these two assessment procedures are used, the offender understands that his sexuality, arousal patterns, and propensity to engage in aberrant sexual activities will be more closely monitored during the course of treatment.

Conclusions

Sexual abuse has become a recognized national tragedy. In many states, the courts are now requiring a more thorough and comprehensive clinical evaluation. Because many sexual offenders deny or minimize their participation in criminal sexual activities, the clinician is often asked to provide an undistorted perception of reality. Many of these offenders are reluctant to discuss their aberrant sexual activities because of serious social sanctions, potential financial losses, and possible civil lawsuits. At the same time, the therapist/evaluator must attempt to build trust under adverse clinical conditions.

To provide comprehensive evaluations within such a framework, the clinical assessment team must utilize a multidimensional evaluation approach, including historical, psychological, and physiological components. Throughout this comprehensive and systematic process, the clinician will be able to more carefully study the offender's psychopathology and behavioral abnormalities. With this strategic information, the evaluator will be able to make reasonable and accurate clinical recommendations regarding outpatient therapy, inpatient care, community correctional programs, or long-term residential placements. In doing so, a delicate balance must be achieved between the desire to help the patient while protecting the rights of his community. As most clinicians realize, such a balance is not easily gained, but, if achieved, it can benefit all concerned.

Notes

1. The Association for the Behavioral Treatment of Sexual Abusers: P.O. Box 66028, Portland, Oregon 97266.

2. Standardization is being attempted by the Association for the Behavioral Treatment of Sexual Abusers.

3

Aversive Respondent
Conditioning Techniques

The animal conditioning literature demonstrates that aversive conditioning is a powerful way to alter behavior (Kazdin, 1978), yet the literature on human conditioning techniques is parochial: Almost all studies and case reports involve attempts to decondition inappropriate approach disorders such as overeating (Kennedy & Foregt, 1968), drug and alcohol abuse (Maletzky, 1973a), and the paraphilias (Becker & Abel, 1981). Although a modest amount of literature has accumulated in the treatment of addictive disorders, it is in the maladaptive sexual approach disorders that aversive conditioning has emerged as a major weapon in the therapeutic armamentarium.

A variety of aversive stimuli have been used to reduce inappropriate sexual arousal, although two modalities, electric shock and foul odor, predominate. These aversive stimuli can vary across several dimensions:

(1) intensity
(2) duration
(3) aversiveness to the individual patient

(4) economy

(5) ease of use

(6) acceptability

For example, foul taste could be administered with bitter substances but might be difficult to vary in its timing, duration, and intensity (Quinsey & Marshall, 1983). Electric shock is often frightening to the patient and his family, even when demonstrated to be harmless; hence its acceptability can be poor (Cautela, 1967; Sajwaj, Libet, & Agras, 1974). Moreover, shock often requires sophisticated equipment to coordinate presentation of sexual stimuli in association with the electric stimulus. In addition, its brief duration of effect does not allow its use in association with many stimuli that may require time in which to build an adequate sexual response, such as movies or slide presentations. Similarly, more exotic aversive techniques, such as the administration of drugs to temporarily paralyze the respiratory muscles in a conscious patient (D. R. Laws, personal communication), or the use of apomorphine to induce spasmodic vomiting (Morganstern, Pearce, & Linford-Ness, 1965), are viewed as *too* aversive and even inhumane. In these circumstances, many writers, clinicians, and patient advocate groups have voiced the belief that the therapeutic ends do not justify these means.

In the 1960s, researchers and clinicians believed that they had discovered an ideal alternative to the use of physically aversive stimuli in a technique called either covert sensitization or aversive imagery (Cautela, 1967; Gold & Neufeld, 1965; Maletzky, 1974a). In this technique, inappropriate sexual stimuli, such as slides or stories, were paired not with actual negative stimuli but with *imagined* aversive consequences. Imagination was thus substituted for electricity or odor:

- A 38-year-old school superintendent admitted to homosexual pedophiliac urges and activities occasionally involving children in his own school district. His treatment program emphasized the association of pedophiliac scenes spoken to him or by him with imagined aversive consequences such as discovering sores on the boys' genitalia, maggots in their hair, being vomited upon, or being discovered by angry parents and police. Eleven conditioning sessions accompanied by homework tapes and assignments removed any homosexual pedophiliac arousal as tested by the penile plethysmograph; a seven-year follow-up demonstrated continued freedom from deviant arousal.

However, some reports have been equivocal regarding the success of these strictly covert techniques (Brownell & Barlow, 1976; Kolvin, 1967; Maletzky, 1974a). Some patients suffered relapses when re-exposed to pretreatment conditions. Others complained that such sessions "were not strong enough" (Maletzky, 1973a, 1974a).

- Covert sensitization seemed helpful, at first, to a 39-year-old married apartment manager with heterosexual pedophilia. He and his wife reported favorable progress through early conditioning scenes, but, five weeks after treatment began, he molested his 11-year-old step-niece once again. He admitted that the aversive scenes were not very powerful compared with noxious stimuli. The therapist thereafter added a foul odor (rotting placental tissue) to the aversive cognitive elements in his scenes with excellent remission of deviant arousal.

- When a 21-year-old exhibitionist was apprehended while exposing himself to teenage girls near a high school, he was placed on probation with mandated treatment in a sexual abuse program. He experienced no difficulty imagining sexual components of covert sensitization scenes but said that he could (or would) not visualize the aversive elements such scenes contained. The addition of a nauseating odor(rotting placenta combined with human urine and cat feces) strengthened such elements and led to a more rapid improvement.

- A 19-year-old youth complained of homosexual urges that both troubled and bewildered him. He had heterosexual urges as well and could not understand or accept his homosexuality. He requested elimination of his homosexual arousal. He was given 10 sessions of covert sensitization in which he was asked to imagine a hierarchy of homosexually explicit scenes, each with an adverse ending. For example, one scene depicted a homosexual encounter unexpectedly interrupted by his girlfriend abruptly entering the room, a severely negative outcome for him. However, aversive images without any accompanying physically aversive stimuli were not effective in diminishing his homosexual urges, fantasies, or dreams. A modification of his treatment program was inserted: A foul odor was combined with the aversive imagery; that led to elimination of his ego-dystonic homosexual urges.

- A 54-year-old lumberjack had been convicted for molesting two step-daughters, 6 and 8 years old. He consented to a treatment program employing slides, movies, and descriptions of sexual activities with young girls, related by both the therapist and himself. Each scene ended with a negative consequence, such as being arrested or coming into contact with urine, feces, or vomitus. Little progress had been made by the twelfth session. Thereafter, with the patient's consent, the therapist introduced an electric aversive stimulus in association with sexual scenes involving young girls. The therapist, at the beginning of each session, self-administered the electric stimulus to demonstrate its irritating but safe properties. Approximately seven months of weekly to bimonthly sessions markedly reduced (but did not eliminate) this patient's deviant sexual arousal.

Foul odor has been used to good effect in such combinations, but shock and foul taste can be employed as well. Odor, however, offers the advantage of flexible duration in its presentation. It can be administered during a variable time scale from one to two seconds up to several minutes and can be discontinued with precision. Thus it can be combined with aversive elements in slides, pictures, movies, and stories. Its administration can be relatively simple, such as holding an open bottle under the patient's nose, although more sophisticated equipment is available; an odor delivery system has been marketed that can deliver foul and pleasing odors directly.[1] Such equipment is described in more detail in Appendix D (Hayes, Brownell, & Barlow, 1978). Noxious odors that use compounds such as hydrogen sulfide (Maletzky, 1980a), ammonia (technically not a foul odor but a physically irritating substance; Colson, 1972; Wolpe, 1969), valeric and butyric acids (Levin, Barry, Gambero, Wolfinsohn, & Smith, 1977; Maletzky, 1973b, 1974b), and rotting animal and human tissues (Maletzky, 1980b) have been used with some success in the treatment of maladaptive sexual approach disorders.

The use of any aversive technique, even one involving only imagery, raises questions of ethical concern. This is particularly so because many sexual offenders are treated under court mandate and cannot be considered to be voluntary patients. In addition, some writers in this field have questioned whether strongly aversive techniques, such as those that elicit nausea and pain, should be used in cases in which harm to the victim is uncertain, such as exhibitionism, public masturbation, or transvestism (Rachman & Teasdale, 1969b; Rosenthal, Rosenthal, & Chang, 1977).

However, evidence does exist to indicate that these "victimless" crimes cause harm; victims often suffer prolonged trauma (Abel, Blanchard, & Barlow, 1980; Adams, Tollison, & Carson, 1981), and the perpetrator is also a victim himself. In addition, in a small and probably as yet uncertain minority, these crimes, while apparently of lesser degree, can predispose the offender toward more aggressive inappropriate sexual approaches, such as pedophilia and frotteurism (Maletzky & Price, 1984). Many investigators and clinicians have accepted and tolerated the use of these aversive techniques as a necessary evil while expressing the hope that positive conditioning techniques will replace these negative methods in the future (Becker & Abel, 1981). A review of the literature in this area, however, indicates that this promise is as yet unfulfilled, although it appears to be a valid and obtainable goal.

A further ethical issue concerns the manner in which an offender enters treatment. Can the sexual offender ever be considered a truly voluntarily patient? Most offenders enter treatment under pressure from the courts, their attorneys, children's protective services divisions, their families, and even from themselves. Recent data indicate that even the putative "voluntary" patient can identify a number of external forces propelling him to treatment. Yet a comparison of treatment results in voluntary and involuntary patients showed that both received similarly beneficial results (Maletzky, 1984b). In another study, the sole significant difference between these two groups occurred in compliance: The involuntary patients missed fewer appointments (Maletzky, 1980b). It is possible that the patient's desire and energy to change sexual orientation are not as crucial an ingredient to treatment success as had previously been believed.

Nonetheless, it is essential that treatment consent be obtained. Indeed, major portions of the first several sessions with the sexual offender generally involve explaining and clarifying concepts of treatment. It has been helpful to use case examples and videotaped or audiotaped vignettes in the course of the initial sessions to ease entry into therapy at a time when a new patient is understandably cautious and, quite often, suspicious of treatment. Formal conditioning sessions should always be preceded by trust building. It is not uncommon to include a spouse, parents or other significant individual not only to gain his or her observations of the patient but to garner his or her support and understanding of the treatment as well. Chapter 10 will detail the typical time course of various stages of treatment for a variety of offenders.

In the remainder of this chapter, the major aversive treatment modalities will be described. In a summary at the conclusion of the chapter, recommendations regarding their integration will also be presented.

Aversive Conditioning Techniques

COVERT TECHNIQUES

These procedures, variably known as *aversive imagery* or, more popularly, *covert sensitization*, avoid an overt, physically aversive stimulus and rely instead on spoken stories, usually combining inappropriate sexual stimulation with adverse consequences (Brownell & Barlow, 1976; Cautela, 1967; Hayes, Brownell, & Barlow, 1978).

- A 47-year-old laundry owner had a nine-year history of exposing himself to high school girls in the area near his shop. Among other scenes, he was asked to imagine exposing himself to a young girl but then getting his penis stuck in his fly zipper with subsequent bleeding and pain; only when he zipped himself up did the pain disappear.

  The same exhibitionist was also asked to imagine exposing to a young girl as seen only from the rear. As she turned to face him, he realized it was his own daughter who screamed, "Daddy, how could you?"   .

There are typically three components to each such scene:

(1) a build-up of sexual arousal associated with the deviant stimulus
(2) a negative affect connected with the act:
   (a) disgust (sores, contact with feces, vomitus, and so on)
   (b) pain (zipper caught on penis, apprehended by father of victim and assaulted, and so on)
   (c) causing physical pain to others (attempting intercourse with a young girl and ripping her vaginal vault, chasing a victim who falls and sustains a head injury)
   (d) causing emotional pain to others (victim screaming hysterically, requiring medical and psychiatric attention)
   (e) being discovered committing the act (by police, relatives, friends)
   (f) natural adverse consequences (being apprehended by police, facing a judge, being imprisoned)

(3) relief or escape from adverse consequences with reversal of the act

Here are some examples of complete scenes used in the treatment of several offenders:

"You're on the prowl again, looking for boys at night. You pull up by a video game store where the kids hang out. There is a boy, maybe 13 or 14, just standing around outside. You offer to take him home and he accepts. He is so pretty, blond, blue eyed, just reaching puberty. He is thin and angular, like you like the boys. You park by his house and reach over to put your arm around his shoulder. He does not resist—he likes your touch! You start to caress his shoulders and neck. He wants it. You reach down to feel his crotch. He's got a hard-on! You slowly unzip his fly and pull it out, stroking it back and forth. You can hear his heavy breathing as you go down on him. You can feel the shaft of his penis with your mouth and tongue, wet, sliding it back and forth . . . but suddenly there is a foul odor; it is disgusting, like rotting flesh, putrid and nauseating. You glance down and there is a sore on the underside of his penis. It's red and full of pus and it's broken and some of the blood and pus have gotten into your mouth and down your throat. It's nauseating—you can feel the pus in the back of your throat and you gag. Food comes up in your throat and your mouth. You're going to vomit. You upchuck all over him and your clothes. The smell is driving you mad as big chucks of vomit dribble down your chin. His prick is full of vomit too. It's disgusting. You've got to get out of there. You leave the car and get a rag to clean yourself off. As you get away from the boy, that smell goes away and you can breathe the fresh night air. Getting away from sex with boys, you can breathe deeply, getting away from that putrid odor. Now, you can relax again."

"You're out again on the prowl, looking for an inviting window. You sneak behind some apartments and you see a light come on in a ground-floor apartment—in the bathroom. You carefully go over and peek in. It's a girl, maybe 18 or 20, and she's undressing! Very quietly, you get some old crates to stand on to see better. She's taking off her blouse now and then her bra. You can see her breasts really clearly now. She's bending over. You're really getting hard now. You take it out and start to jack off, really getting excited, but suddenly there's a noise behind you. It's the police—it was a trap! They caught you doing it! They slap handcuffs on and push you into the squad car. There's no escape now. You know you're headed for jail."

There are a number of factors inherent in such scenes that need to be taken into account in their construction:

(1) These scenes work best when the initially sexually attractive part is composed of real elements. However, it is not always practical to use actual occurrences. Therefore, a certain percentage of scenes can be totally imaginary and, indeed, perhaps they should be to capture and try to decondition the important sexual fantasies of each patient.

(2) Scenes should be constructed using the patient's own words and phrases, even if these are offensive to the therapist.

(3) Scenes work best when they are not overly detailed but are sufficiently explicit to facilitate imagery.

(4) Scenes should be constructed with the aid of the patient; they can be idiosyncratic and may not need to contain all the elements mentioned above. For example, the scenes for the voyeur described above lacked an escape but worked quite well nonetheless.

(5) The offender should always be asked to participate in arranging the use of negative images. He should be questioned on the stimuli that are most unpleasant for him, such as pain, contact with feces, and the like. Often the plethysmograph can be employed to check the aversive nature of such images by noting how rapidly they elicit declines in arousal following exposure to sexually exciting material.

(6) Adverse consequences do not always need to be a logical outgrowth from the scene (but compare with Diamet & Wilson, 1975): An exhibitionist was asked to imagine exposing, being discovered by his wife, and developing severe nausea and vomiting as a result of discovery.

(7) The timing and detail of each scene needs to be adjusted for each offender. In general, highly detailed scenes can take from one to three minutes to present and be followed by another 30 seconds to enable the patient to continue focusing on the scene and its natural outcome. For some patients, however, a 30-second presentation will suffice.

(8) The scenes should be read or presented realistically using appropriate inflections.

(9) Each session, typically consisting of three scene presentations, should be preceded by relaxation (or hypnotic) induction techniques. A variety of methods are used, through the most common technique is that of a modification of Jacobson's relaxation exercises, demon-

strated first, then practiced by the patient using a prerecorded tape (Wolpe, 1969). Usually an idiosyncratic pleasant scene (gently rocking in a boat on a lake, watching waves on an ocean beach, revisiting a vacation spot) is presented from one to two minutes after general relaxation to enhance the depth of relaxation and help the patient practice imagery skills.

(10) The aversive elements in such scenes can be introduced earlier and earlier in the scene to decondition the initial steps in the chain leading to sexual abuse.

(11) If the offender insists he did not commit a crime, scenes are taken from police records and then similar scenes are constructed with the offender. There will occasionally be a refusal to make up such scenes. In this case, the therapist should construct his or her own scenes in front of the offender, asking him at different points to signal yes or no, depending upon how appropriate he believes the scene to be. The plethysmograph can help in determining any arousal during this process.

It is important to note that the timing and duration of scene presentations and the entire treatment course differ with each patient. Flexibility must be maintained to mold a given program to the framework of each individual patient.

It is sometimes advisable to build a hierarchy of scenes, somewhat similar to the procedure of desensitization for a phobic patient (Wolpe, 1969). Table 3.1 details an actual hierarchy for an exhibitionist patient with scenes presented in abbreviated form for the sake of clarity. The scenes are arranged from the least to the most sexually exciting for the offender, rated by him on a "sexual pleasure rating" scale of 0 (no pleasure) to 10 (maximum pleasure). In the progression of treatment, less attractive scenes are presented first, increasing in arousal until some of the most exciting deviant scenes are reached. Hierarchies are helpful if the patient is not making progress or if there is initial difficulty in reducing sexual arousal because the early scenes were found to be too exciting.

Some patients experience difficulty imagining scenes, whether sexual or nonsexual in nature. It may be helpful to have such patients practice imagery not only with pleasant scenes but by focusing on an object close at hand, then imagining it with eyes closed immediately thereafter. After some progress, the patient can be asked to practice imagining familiar scenes (such as at work or home) and faces,

Table 3.1 *Hierarchy of Scenes (abbreviated) Presented to an Exhibitionist Patient for Covert Sensitization*

Scene	Abbreviated Content	Sexual Pleasure Rating
1	Seeing young girls walking home from school while sitting in car, masturbating, being discovered, getting sick to stomach, vomiting.	10
2	Standing behind tree in park, masturbating while watching young girls go by, being apprehended by policeman.	30
3	Inviting young girl behind tree in park, exposing self, girl laughing, inviting friends to see.	45
4	Driving past high school, exposing to group of girls, feeling apprehensive, getting sick and having uncontrollable diarrhea.	60
5	Driving through shopping center at night, approaching pretty girl, no one nearby, unzipping pants, getting penis stuck in zipper, much pain, bleeding.	75
6	Driving to laundry, seeing young blond on street alone, trying to expose, bad smell from factory nearby, nausea, vomiting.	85
7	Driving to laundry at night, approaching pretty young blond to expose, seeing witnesses taking down license number and police approaching.	100

progressing on to less familiar ones, in an effort to enhance the entire visualization process.

Although patients differ, in general, it is possible to collect data, build trust, introduce the offender to the equipment and procedures, and teach relaxation skills during the early visits. Treatment then usually progresses to a phase combining relaxation with pleasant scenes and then, finally, pairing sexual scenes with aversive images, thereby accomplishing a central goal of conditioning therapy—the association of previously pleasurable but deviant sexual arousal with aversive images.

However, although certain patients improve with covert sensitization, many show only moderate reductions in deviant sexual arousal as measured by self-reports, observer reports, or the penile plethysmograph. Others demonstrate excellent early progress but relapse soon after treatment ends (Maletzky, 1980a). Newer, apparently stronger techniques have been developed that can deepen the therapeutic reservoir and enhance treatment results (Maletzky, 1973b, 1974b).

OVERT TECHNIQUES

The initial attraction of covert techniques lay in their avoidance of physically punishing stimuli; in addition, the purchase and setup of costly equipment was not necessary. An ideal technique would not merely be effective but be acceptable to the patient and to the general community as well. Such a technique has yet to be developed, although work on combinations of covert methods, positive conditioning, and cognitive approaches may one day replace the use of actual aversive stimuli (Abel & Becker, 1984). However, to date, the overt techniques have proven to be one of the mainstays of most successful treatment programs for the sexual offender (Maletzky, 1973b, 1974b, 1980a; Rachman & Teasdale, 1969b).

Fortunately, these techniques are not *terribly* noxious and are certainly not dangerous, although the therapist must be certain that the offender understands that these methods produce sensations that are uncomfortable, although generally only briefly so. The message should be clear: Treatment will often be unpleasant not only in the need to reveal embarrassing sexual histories, endure restrictions on one's personal liberty, and bear an expense in time and money but in tolerating unpleasant stimuli as well.

This discomfort is rendered only slightly more bearable when the therapist administers a noxious stimulus to him- or herself within view of the patient. Each time electric shock is to be used and, at least before the first application of foul odor or foul taste, the therapist should self-administer the stimulus in the same dose the offender is expected to endure. It is vital, especially with the use of electricity, that the offender and the community at large understand the level at which aversive stimuli are to be employed.

ELECTRIC STIMULATION

Electric shock has never been popular as a behavioral treatment device, despite the fact that is has proven effective in a number of studies (Abel, Lewis, & Clancy, 1970; Evans, 1980; Maletzky, 1980a). It is frightening to many patients, some of whom may confuse it with electroconvulsive therapy, which is usually reserved for major depressive disorders. Its use can provoke an outcry against shock as an inhumane procedure associated with torture, electric fences, and science gone awry. Popular literature expresses the fear that mind control is the hidden goal of this therapy and that it could, therefore, be employed for unscrupulous political purposes.

It is for these reasons that therapists who use electric shock aversion must be compulsive in explaining and demonstrating its theory and practice to prospective patients, taking extra time to review all options, side effects, and risks and keeping clear notes about patient consent. Patients should be asked to paraphrase this information and sign a consent form. It might be judicious to ask a relative to sign as well, even if the patient is not a minor, to reflect the fact that the patient himself was not coerced into accepting electric shock.

Paradoxically—and in spite of its frightening image—until recently, electric shock aversion has been the most frequently employed overt aversive technique in the treatment of the sexual offender. This is partly because it was the first such method applied in this field but also because it worked relatively well with patients who were chronic treatment failures with more traditional methods (Marshall, 1973). For such a patently odious technique to be so widely employed, it probably has been of some help for many sexual offenders.

Historically, there are a multitude of techniques employing aversive electric stimulation, but they can be divided into two general categories:

(1) Associative conditioning: In these techniques, the electric stimulus is presented in association with deviant stimuli (Maletzky, 1980a; McGonaghy, 1972).
(2) Anticipatory avoidance: In this technique, the patient receives an electric shock within a few seconds after the presentation of the deviant stimulus; however, he has the opportunity to avoid the shock by switching off the stimulus quickly before those few seconds have elapsed (MacCulloch, Waddington, & Sanbrook, 1978; Sanbrook, MacCulloch, & Waddington, 1978).

Numerous modifications of these techniques have been presented in the literature. Interesting variations on these themes can be created for the individual patient:

- A patient with homosexual pedophilia was asked to sort cards containing words and phrases associated with deviant sexual arousal, such as *teenager*, *pubic hair*, and *prick*, rank ordering them from least to most sexually arousing. He did the same with pictures displaying graphic homosexual pedophiliac scenes. A brief electric shock was then administered when these stimuli were projected onto a screen. Following successful inhibition of arousal, the patient was asked to voluntarily remove from the screen any homosexual words/images within three seconds. If he failed to do so, a red light would flash to indicate that he must self-administer the electric shock. Any escape from shock coincided with the presentation of appropriate heterosexual stimuli.

- A frotteur was asked to imagine sexually exciting scenes in which he rubbed up against a woman as, for example, in an elevator. He was simultaneously monitored on the penile plethysmograph. With an increase in penile circumference above a predetermined level (greater than 25% of full tumescence in this case), a red light flashed and a brief electric shock was administered. Employing the plethysmograph in this fashion as a biofeedback device was highly effective in reducing deviant sexual arousal.

Certain parallels are evident in comparing electric shock aversion techniques with those of purely covert approaches. A deviant sexual stimulus is presented in both, followed by an aversive stimulus (image or electricity), with termination of the aversion contingent on escape or refusal to enter the deviant situation.

- An exhibitionist was asked to imagine a scene in which he had the urge to expose, experienced the beginnings of an aversive stimulus (covert or overt), turned away from the setting and did not expose, thus resulting in immediate removal of the aversive stimulus: in a sense, a temptation successfully resisted.

Differences with covert methods should also be apparent. Aside from the covert/overt dichotomy, the purely imaginary procedure can present an aversive *idea* for a variable length of time within the scene. In contrast, electric shock cannot humanely be administered continuously over the period of time required for presentation of scenes, usually one to two minutes. Although frequent, brief, individual pulses could be administered, these have usually proven so distressing as to inhibit cooperation with treatment. Clearly, electric shock procedures are more compatible with physical stimuli such as slides, videotapes, and movies, while covert techniques are better applied to sexual stories, whether spoken by the therapist, on tape or in person, or spoken by the offender himself. (Please see Appendix D for a technical description of electric shock equipment, equipment to present stimulus materials such as slides, videotapes, and movies, and methods of obtaining pornographic stimulus materials.)

Despite the historic significance of electric shock aversion and the many reports of its efficacy, there has been a trend away from the use of electricity toward the use of either purely covert techniques (Cautela, 1967) or the use of foul odors (Maletzky, 1980a). This is due in part to studies directly comparing one form of aversion with the other (Maletzky, 1980a); in part to the popular distaste for, and mistrust of, electric shock; in part to the practical difficulties inherent in the more sophisticated applications of shock; and in part to the occasional increase in anxiety and aggression noted with this procedure (Evans, 1980). Perhaps contributing to this decline is the expense of equipment needed to coordinate slides, audiotapes, and live story presentations. This combination of drawbacks has resulted in the increasing use of foul odors as noxious stimuli in an attempt to decondition inappropriate sexual arousal. In actual practice, however, a combination of these aversive techniques has yielded results exceeding those of any method alone (Evans, 1980). The techniques for this coordination are presented later in this chapter.

ODOR AVERSION

Results of covert sensitization alone have occasionally proven to be excellent for some sexual offenders, but more often covert sensitization has proven marginally effective. It has been possible to improve the success rate by "assisting" the covert procedure by combining a foul odor (or, occasionally, electric shock) with deviant stimuli.

The earliest work in this area employed chemically noxious odors such as smoke (Leichtenstein & Kretzer, 1969; Sanbrook, MacCulloch, & Waddington, 1978), ammonia (Colson, 1972; Wolpe, 1969), or butyric (Foregt & Kennedy, 1971) or valeric (Levin, Barry, Gambero, Wolfinsohn, & Smith, 1977; Maletzky, 1973b, 1974b) acids. More recent efforts have employed the odor of putrifying tissue (usually human placenta inoculated with bacteria; Maletzky, 1980a, 1980b; see

Appendix D for details of preparation). There are several advantages to the use of odors:

(1) The aversive stimulus can be precisely timed to be presented during the duration of the deviant slide, during the deviant part of a videotape or movie, or, more commonly, during the deviant part of a story line.

(2) Very little technical equipment is necessary.

(3) The odor is long lasting and stable and can be "doped" from time to time with additions of meat, fish, cheese, urine, or feces.

(4) Patient acceptance is relatively high.

The 11 factors listed earlier for covert sensitization also apply to the construction of scenes using foul odors.

Physically aversive stimuli such as lemon juice on the tongue, ammonia in the nasal mucosa, or electric shock to the fingers have been chosen because they seem to be aversive to everyone. However, there may be something about a putrid odor that directly deconditions the appetitive responses. Single-trial learning in animals and man can occur with such an association (Kazdin, 1978).

- A heterosexual pedophile also had a history of intercourse with several species of farm animals. He related a history of attempted coitus with a sheep without realizing that a pregnant sheep was giving birth nearby. The new birth was actually a stillbirth and, along with it, came a horrifying odor of decaying flesh, just as he penetrated the sheep. He became nauseous and regurgitated; from that date, he lost any urge to copulate with animals.

It is of theoretic interest that this patient did not become nauseated when he looked at or even touched sheep following this experience; he simply lost any sexual attraction to them. This phenomenon of eliminating deviant arousal without conditioning actual nausea seems to be true in the majority of patients receiving aversive olfactory conditioning.

Work with exhibitionists has demonstrated that a nauseating odor is more effective than a chemically noxious one (Maletzky, 1980a). With the direct neural connections between the olfactory epithelium, the first—or olfactory—cranial nerve, the olfactory bulbs, and the limbic system in the brain, there is possibly a direct unlinking of sexual arousal previously bonded to a deviant (or theoretically non-deviant) stimulus.

In contrast, a physical irritant, such as ammonia, produces a burning sensation transmitted from submucosal elements via the fifth, or trigeminal, cranial nerve to the thalamus. This may be a factor limiting its efficacy in deconditioning work. Moreover, its irritating effect on the nasal mucosa can produce inflammation and eventually lead to ulceration.

Covert sensitization, thus "assisted" with putrid odors, can be applied across the broad spectrum of maladaptive sexual approach disorders.

- A male transvestite was asked, under relaxation, to imagine the following scene: "Imagine you are beginning to pull a beautiful slip on over your naked body. You can feel its satiny-smooth surface glide over your legs and press tightly against your penis. You're beginning to get hard, just feeling it on you, when (odor introduced) that horrible smell comes back. The odor of rotting flesh makes your stomach turn; just having the slip and touching it makes you sick to your stomach. You begin to puke and chunks of vomit dribble down onto the slip. It's disgusting to be there with that slip on. You quickly pull the slip off (odor removed) and wash yourself off. Now, you can breathe again. That horrible odor is gone and you can relax, feeling glad you finally got that slip off."

- A heterosexual pedophile was asked to imagine, under relaxation, undressing, caressing, and performing cunnilingus on his 11-year-old stepdaughter when he suddenly noticed a vile odor coming from her vaginal area (odor introduced). He saw white maggots crawling in and out of her vagina and he had swallowed some. Leaving the area (odor removed) was associated with relief.

As demonstrated in the first example, a nauseating odor need not always be presented as a logical consequence of the deviant sexual act. Thus scenes of pain, embarrassment, or apprehension by the police can also be paired with the actual odor, even though a foul stench would not necessarily follow. It has been the impression of some investigators, however, that, if negative imagery flows more naturally from a scene, enhanced treatment effects can occur (Diamet & Wilson, 1975).

In practice, the foul odor used, usually bacteria-inoculated placental tissue "doped" with rotting fish, meat, cheese, or urine or feces, can be introduced by holding an open bottle of the tissue in front of the patient's nose. However, several clinics have used odor reservoir and pump mechanisms that, at the touch of a button, deliver any of a number of odors to the patient through a nasal cannula.[2] This setup greatly facilitates odor presentation while reducing laboratory background smell. Appendix D contains a more complete description of such equipment.

Although this technique has been called "assisted" covert sensitization (Maletzky, 1973a), there is clearly nothing covert about it. It is simply associative or respondent aversive conditioning and hence similar in several respects to covert sensitization and electric shock aversion. The scenes, again, are tripartite, with increasing sexual arousal to the deviant stimulus first, then associating this arousal with negative consequences and stimuli, and, finally, portraying an escape situation in which actively leaving the deviant stimulus configuration results in removal of the aversive stimulus and subsequent relief. In addition, these scenes contain unabashed examples of suggestion. Although it is doubtful that suggestion alone can decondition a maladaptive sexual approach disorder, it is probably advisable to include this element, especially under deep relaxation or hypnosis.

In addition, such olfactory conditioning can be carried out with a hierarchy of presentations, beginning with milder scenes and progressing to those of utmost sexual pleasure. Truly noxious elements must be used; frequently, the patient will grimace in disgust. He must be encouraged to allow nausea to occur, as the best possible results will be obtained in this fashion. Occasionally, scenes can be constructed in such a manner that escape from aversion is associated with turning *toward* a normal sexual stimulus:

- A young exhibitionist was presented with the following scene: "Imagine, now, that you're hiding in the bushes of a park. Several young girls go by on their way to the swings. You can clearly see their faces, their hair, what they are wearing, their young bodies. You start to unzip your pants and pull your penis out. It's getting hard as you rub it back and forth. The girls can see you now. They're staring right at it, shocked as you pump it back and forth. But suddenly, as you're showing it to them, there's a terrible odor. You stepped in some brown, slimy, dog crap; it smeared onto your shoe and some has gotten onto your socks and pants. The odor is nauseating. You're going soft. The whole thing is making your stomach turn, making you sick. You zip yourself up and clear yourself off as quickly as you can and start

running to your girlfriend's house closeby. You can breathe again as
she suddenly welcomes you with open arms."

Moreover, as with covert sensitization, the noxious elements
(image plus odor) can be introduced earlier and earlier in the scene to
decondition the patient's first approaches in the behavioral chain
leading to offending (Abel & Becker, 1984).

The combination of covert and overt elements in the presentation
of stimuli, particularly stories or stories combined with slides, videotapes, or movies may be especially advantageous in these disorders
because of the importance imagery plays in sexual behavior. Deviant
sexual fantasies, whether during intercourse, masturbation, or even
during idle daydreaming, may well sustain maladaptive urges (Lovibond, 1963). Self-directed imagery techniques, particularly those
using masturbation fantasies, which will be further described in
Chapter 4, have also proven to be a valuable addition to the treatment repertoire of the sexual therapist (Conrad & Wincze, 1976;
Kremsdorf, Holman, & Laws, 1980; Marquis, 1970; Vanceventer &
Laws, 1978).

TASTE AVERSION

There are but a handful of references in the behavioral literature
that acknowledge taste aversion as a potential technique in the treatment of sexual arousal (Maletzky, 1980a; Sajwaj, Libet, & Agras,
1974). This is curious, given the usual association of taste and odor
receptors and their anatomical proximity. However, in considering
the criteria previously listed in the choice of an aversive stimulus,
taste aversion does possess some drawbacks. The available bitter
substances are not readily obtainable except by physicians, yet the
majority of therapists treating sexual offenders are not M.D.s. Moreover, the stimulus itself, whether in the form of pill, powder, or
liquid, can be difficult or impossible to deliver to a patient. Outside of
extraordinary circumstances, it must be self-administered. In addition, the timing variables are difficult to gauge. The onset of the
aversive taste can be pinpointed with some accuracy, but, once in the
mouth, a substance can be swallowed variably, leading to uncertainty about the concordance between an inappropriate sexual stimulus and the bitter taste itself. In addition, tastes are more variable
than smells; what is bitter to some may be judged sweet by others.

These drawbacks have limited the use of taste aversion in most clinics. One area, however, that seems promising is the use of foul taste in homework assignments given to sexual offenders:

- A 22-year-old college student, convicted of two rapes, was given a supply of propantheline (Probanthine) tablets with instructions to thoroughly chew and taste a half tablet if he experienced any urges to attack women sexually. He was instructed to chew and taste the bitter substance while focusing on aggressive sexuality for one minute; then he was asked to spit the substance out. As he expelled this foul taste, he was asked to concentrate on fleeing the potential rape scene and finding his girlfriend happily accepting him back into their relationship.

Many potentially useful tastes are too toxic to be ingested or even swished about the mouth, such as corrosive liquids or household chemicals. A number of bitter medications in liquid, capsule, or tablet form have potentially harmful effects that limit their even occasional use. The quinine and quinidine fall into this category: Exquisitely bitter to most people, even their infrequent use could jeopardize cardiac contractility.

One substance, however, has proven to be safe and consistently foul tasting: propantheline. This antimotility drug, used in the treatment of peptic and gastric ulcers, is manufactured to be swallowed whole. When chewed, the tablets produce a noxious taste that most patients agree is not only bitter but nauseating as well. Of equal importance is its safety. Any adult chewing or even swallowing it in its entirety would, at worst, experience mild drying of the mouth and temporary constipation. In practice, while the patient is instructed to spit the residue of half of a tablet out after one minute, those patients swallowing it have not experienced even these side effects. Each patient is told not to chew more than two pills in any 24-hour period. Offenders could be given three to five tablets to have in their possession at all times; even were the patient to ingest all five at once, however, no medical harm would ensue.

As cited in the case example above, taste aversion is particularly suited to homework assignments. Although it is theoretically possible to devise equipment that would deliver doses of bitter substances into a patient's mouth during office settings, this technique would seem unduly awkward when electric shock and odor aversion are simpler to administer.

Instructions to the patient in the administration of taste aversion are critical to ensure appropriate deconditioning of maladaptive sexual approach behaviors. The following instructions are given to the offender on a card before using propantheline:

(1) This medication is called Probanthine. It is used in the treatment of peptic and gastric ulcers.
(2) This medication should be used at the first sign that you are becoming sexually aroused to an inappropriate stimulus.
(3) Take one-half tablet and chew it thoroughly for one minute while contemplating the inappropriate sexual behavior.
(4) After one minute, spit out the residue. You should try not to swallow the residue, but, if you do, no adverse effects will occur except, rarely, dry mouth and constipation.
(5) Do not chew any more than two tablets in any 24-hour period.
(6) Call the clinic if you experience any problems with these pills.

Despite such drawbacks with taste aversion as loss of therapist control and possible side effects, one striking advantage to this form of therapy is its application in the in vivo sexual situation. It would be awkward, to say the least, to pull out a bottle of foul-smelling tissue and sniff it while viewing an inappropriate sexual scene in real life. This is equally true with the self-administration of an electric shock, at least with present-day equipment, although it is conceivable that miniaturized equipment may soon be available. However, one can place a tablet in the mouth and chew it relatively inconspicuously. In public situations, the pill is often swallowed, as spitting it out is usually awkward. Often the most convenient and least embarrassing techniques for the patient will be those most frequently used.

AVERSIVE BEHAVIOR REHEARSAL

Known also as "Shame Aversion Therapy" (Server, 1970), this technique has enjoyed both fame and notoriety as much for its novel simplicity as for its effectiveness. It has been almost exclusively employed in the treatment of exhibitionism:

- A 23-year-old law student could not stop his compulsive exposing on campus to attractive co-eds. Arrested twice by security police, he was threatened with expulsion unless he obtained therapy. He gave consent to an unusual procedure in which he exposed in a hospital psychiatric setting to male and female staff for a period of three minutes on each of three occasions. Staff were instructed to make no response but merely to watch silently. Following the first session, he reported that he lost all urges to expose.

- A 62-year-old retired grocer and grandfather frequently exposed from his truck to young girls in his neighborhood. He agreed to expose from his truck for three minutes to male and female hospital staff who offered no response. He achieved no erection. The procedure was debriefed immediately thereafter. He had not reexposed on six-year follow-up.

Aversive behavior rehearsal has been remarkably effective in certain cases of exhibitionism (Jones & Frei, 1977; McGonaghy, 1972; Wickramaserka, 1976), but by no means is it so for every exhibitionist (Maletzky, 1980a; Wickramaserka, 1980). To repeat a dominant theme, it usually should be combined with other procedures for full therapeutic advantage. Nonetheless, the technique offers several advantages:

(1) It requires no equipment.
(2) It is inexpensive.
(3) It can work astonishingly quickly and well.

As expected, there are some drawbacks:

(1) It is so aversive that it is only with great difficulty that consent can be obtained in many cases, even with court-mandated offenders.
(2) It is sometimes difficult to obtain staff to observe.
(3) It is sometimes difficult to guarantee that staff will not respond, for example, with smiles or scorn.
(4) The procedure causes intense anxiety for the patient and usually for the observing staff members as well.

It appears that the very advantages of this technique contribute to some of its drawbacks. It is likely that the intense anxiety associated with exposing in such situations contributes, at least in part, to its therapeutic effect.

In practice, aversive behavior rehearsal is used with a minority of exhibitionist offenders, despite the fact that it appears to be a powerful technique that could contribute to shortening treatment and thereby curtailing the increasing costs of therapy. For certain offenders who are making slow progress or in whom it is difficult to measure progress, the therapist can legitimately encourage the patient to follow through with this technique.

As aversive behavior rehearsal is usually practiced, three to five male and female staff personnel are invited to be present in a suitable room. If at all possible, a natural exposing situation, however, should be re-created, as in the second example above, in which the offender was asked to expose from his truck. Only rarely will any sexual excitement or an erection occur under these conditions, but staff should be coached to make no discernible responses such as grimacing, smiling, or disapproving. It may be that this neutral nonresponse heightens the intended anxiety.

It is because of the adverse and possibly demeaning effects of this technique that great care must be taken to obtain truly informed written consent not only from the patient but from the participating staff as well. Based on the current literature and on experience with aversive behavior rehearsal, the therapist should suggest this technique only after trust has been established and after there is either slow progress or none at all with other treatment techniques. The majority of sexual offenders can be treated without this technique, although, if favorable reports of speedy recoveries continue, the economics of treatment may dictate its increasing use.

Can the use of this innovative technique be extended to other maladaptive sexual approach behaviors? Perhaps so:

- A patient with a history of heterosexual pedophilia was placed in a room with three female and two male staff members who observed, without response, while for three minutes he "molested" a life-size pediatric mannequin that hospitals use to teach cardiopulmonary resuscitation. He was instructed to act out on the mannequin what he had actually practiced in real life. Three such sessions were believed to have contributed to the elimination of deviant sexual arousal, reflected in normalization of his plethysmograph tracings.

- A grocery store checker, in his late twenties, had been arrested for molesting two daughters of his live-in girlfriend, aged 6 and 7. He was asked to demonstrate, on videotape, how he molested them, using anatomically correct dolls. His parents were then asked to view the tape with him, twice.

The plethysmograph can also be employed to advantage in aversive behavior rehearsal. While he demonstrates with dolls what he has actually done to children, the offender's arousal can be measured simultaneously on the plethysmograph. Aversive stimuli can be introduced in the presence of deviant arousal. With this procedure, an offender can be assessed for deviant arousal and treated at the same time. Experience with this technique reveals, however, that the majority of patients show no arousal and consider the procedure itself a negative experience.

Although this potentially powerful technique may not be limited to the treatment of exhibitionism alone, it will be cumbersome, at times, to reproduce some of the conditions that pertained at the time of deviant sexual acts. Nonetheless, it may be worthwhile, particularly for those patients who do not seem to be progressing in therapy. Whenever used, however, aversive behavior rehearsal requires a sensitive approach to the patient.

NEGATIVE PRACTICE

The principles inherent in aversive behavior rehearsal, combined with its efficacy, give rise to several modifications that may make it more acceptable to certain patients (see Yates, 1958):

- A middle-aged businessman with heterosexual pedophilia was a previous treatment failure and returned to treatment after a second conviction. He was asked to tape-record detailed accounts of his pedophiliac exploits and listen to them daily. Three different tapes with nine different scenes were produced. The experience was "devastating," in his words. However, he has experienced no arousal to heterosexual pedophiliac material since that time.
- A 33-year-old electrical contractor gained maximal sexual pleasure while masturbating dressed in women's nylons and panties. He declined an offer to duplicate this behavior before observers but did consent to do so in front of an unmanned videotape camera. Thereafter, he agreed to view the tape with his wife. He credited this proce-

dure with eliminating his transvestism; however, the condition recurred one year later and more conventional aversive conditioning was required to eliminate it.

- A patient with a 22-year history of sexually assaulting young boys agreed to use an anatomically explicit boy mannequin to duplicate his behavior privately but in front of a full-length mirror. Such sessions, five times per week, were thought to be helpful in eliminating his deviant arousal pattern.

These techniques all seem to share a common denominator with aversive behavior rehearsal: the production of extreme anxiety and shame with a total or partial re-creation of the offense and hence the "unhooking" of the operant response from its sexual gratification. Moreover, a similarity exists between these techniques and the "orgasmic reconditioning" techniques to be described in Chapter 4. Simpler explanations of aversive conditioning alone, however, should not be overlooked in explaining the efficacy of these techniques.

As these techniques are more imaginatively and industriously applied, further knowledge about their mechanisms of action may be gained. Extensions to sexually inappropriate behaviors in addition to exhibitionism should become increasingly feasible as well.

Summary

The aversive conditioning techniques have provided what appeared at first to be a strong arsenal in the battle against sexual abuse. These techniques not only were highly effective but also provided a framework upon which to develop theories about the origin of the maladaptive sexual approach disorders. If conditioning methods could eliminate inappropriate sexual arousal, it would appear that sexual behavior might have been initially caused by learning errors acquired through faulty experiences, perhaps at especially critical stages early in sexual development (Berlin & Coyle, 1981). Even if critical stages were invoked, the basic role of errant conditioning was assumed because deconditioning techniques were largely successful in eliminating deviant arousal.

There is, however, reason to question this simple assumption. A number of patients treated with apparent success using aversive techniques *alone* did not believe that their overall improvement was as satisfying as the plethysmograph demonstrated.

- A middle-aged salesman with heterosexual pedophilia recalled early sexual experimentation with neighborhood children. From the ages of 8 to 12, he regularly participated in a neighborhood "sex club" with frequent games of "doctor" and "show me" with same-age female peers. A later fixation on girls of this same young age was assumed to have been conditioned by these early sexual experiences. Aversive conditioning removed any sexual attraction to young girls, but the patient continued to complain of little sexual interest in his wife, a deteriorating family situation, and increasing tension at work.

- A 17-year-old homosexual pedophile recalled sexual experiences with boys from the age of 7 onward. He wished this attraction removed, and aversive conditioning did so convincingly. Following treatment, he experienced satisfaction at being free of sexual urges toward young boys but continued to be shy and introspective. He could not ask girls for dates, was subassertive in most social situations, and reported difficulty reaching orgasm when masturbating to heterosexual fantasies.

If the goal of therapy for the sexual offender is the elimination of deviant sexual arousal, then aversive conditioning offers the most convincing array of techniques to gain this end. But, as the above cases illustrate, aversion therapy of the sexual offender, by itself, can accomplish technical triumphs that may be sterile. The elimination of troublesome sexual behaviors may be thought to be sufficient, and, indeed, the proponents of the aversive therapies have generally never laid claim to any greater gains. Here, however, while the careful goals of the research lab may be justified in simplifying and purifying data collection, the clinician often cannot afford the luxuries of the double-blind or the isolated single-treatment approach. Fortunately, during the past decade, research and clinical findings have merged to demonstrate how aversive conditioning, reconditioning, positive conditioning, and adjunctive techniques can blend into a usually satisfying total treatment approach.

There are additional reasons to question whether aversive techniques by themselves can constitute a total treatment approach to the sexual offender. Many such patients do not have a clearly identifiable history of sexual conditioning that can explain their inappropriate arousal. For example, although some exhibitionists recall early experiences in which their exposure was associated with sexual pleasure, most do not (Allen, 1980; Rader, 1977). A lack of unambiguous deviant conditioning also occurs in many if not most pedophiles, voyeurs, and frotteurs (Bonheur & Rosner, 1980; Gebhard, Gagnon, Pomeroy, & Christiansen, 1965).

- A 24-year-old unemployed mill worker with an extensive history of voyeurism could not recall any early sexual experiences of surreptitiously observing sexual scenes. He vividly recalled his first voyeuristic experience as an impulse to peek into a window conspicuously lit at night. He saw nothing sexual but felt the experience was exciting nonetheless. His first four such attempts were fruitless, but the fifth and ninth produced sexually satisfying scenes. This variable ratio of positive reinforcement was sufficient to induce continuing voyeurism.

Even if aversive conditioning methods were universally successful at eliminating deviant sexual arousal, the conditioning theories themselves that spawn these aversive techniques could not be automatically invoked to explain their etiology. Lithium carbonate is helpful in treating manic-depressive illness, but its benefit does not imply that the illness is secondary to a lithium deficiency. Galactosemia, an inherited inability to metabolize galactose, a sugar found in milk, is treated by eliminating milk products from the diet; this treatment does not help us understand, however, the basic genetic and metabolic etiologies. Recent reviews have noted benefit in cognitive therapeutic approaches to major depressive disorders (Beck & Rush, 1976; Carson & Adams, 1981), yet several lines of evidence point to genetic and biochemical deficits as causes of this condition (Schatzberg et al., 1983). Such evidence, however, does not invalidate the cognitive approaches. Often, identical treatments can help two separate conditions, but this also does not imply shared causes. Aspirin, for example, helps prevent cerebrovascular thrombosis and reduces pain, but those two conditions cannot thereby be automatically assumed to spring from the same source. Behavior therapy, in particular, has been very helpful in the treatment of psychophysiological illnesses such as hypertension (Blanchard, 1979) and migraine (Rallman & Gilmore, 1980), but its mechanisms of therapeutic action may not automatically indicate that faulty conditioning caused these disorders.

Although the development of inappropriate sexual arousal may be conditioned, it might be so only at certain critical stages of sexual development (Berlin & Coyle, 1981; Freund, 1980). It would appear that the brain continues to evolve even after birth, and some neuroscientists believe that, in this evolution and maturation, there are *critical stages of learning* (MacLean, 1965). Thus children from 2 to 6 years of age may be most adept at acquiring language skills, or children at 8 to 15 years of age may be at a maximum of potential for sharpening coordination in sports.

- A 39-year-old schoolteacher with homosexual pedophilia could recall no early sexual experiences with young boys. His wife, however, reminded him of a time when he was 4 to 7 and an older male baby-sitter showed him some nudist magazines. The baby-sitter focused on the young naked boys in the pictures and, through his pants, this youngster could see he was getting an erection. He remained fascinated by this for several years, but then almost forgot about the experience.

Another difficulty in employing aversive conditioning techniques alone is the frequent need to treat more than the deviant arousal. If the heterosexual pedophile or exhibitionist loses his inappropriate sexual attractions, wlll he thus automatically increase his appropriate nondeviant sexual arousal? Some evidence indicates this is not necessarily so (Vanceventer & Laws, 1978). Although some heterosexual or homosexual pedophiles do show an increase in appropriate sexual arousal with aversive techniques alone, many do not, especially those who have never developed strong sexual responses to adult females. Many pedophiles and most exhibitionists are attracted to the adult female but sometimes just marginally so. Those offenders who are mostly or completely attracted just to the inappropriate stimulus and undergo aversive conditioning alone may never increase their arousal to appropriate female stimuli. In addition, as demonstrated in the case examples above, aversive conditioning does little to improve the social problems that often accompany the offender's deviant arousal. Problems such as social awkwardness, subassertion, and marital instability can be as devastating as the deviant sexual arousal to the offender and, not infrequently, even more so.

Yet another problem in restricting treatment to aversive conditioning techniques is the specter of symptom substitution. In the traditional literature on the subject of the sexual offender, symptoms such as pedophilia, transvestism, and exhibitionism are considered superficial facades that camouflage more profound difficulties (Allen, 1980; Remberg, 1975). If so, merely eliminating the symptoms should result in the reappearance of problems somewhere else as, for example, in another sexual deviation, a phobia, or a physical symptom such as chronic headaches.

- A 65-year-old retired office worker, arrested for molesting his 7-year-old granddaughter, was treated exclusively with aversion therapy. Following six months of therapy, he lost any urge to fondle young girls but his neighbors began to complain about his parading nude in front of open windows in his home.
- A 14-year-old boy who had repeatedly sexually attacked young boys in his school and had several episodes of bestiality was treated with odor aversion and electric shock techniques. Following one year of treatment, plethysmographs indicated no sexual arousal to these stimuli, but his grades had dropped in school and his behavior had become increasingly noncompliant at home.

It is surprising that there is no convincing and objective body of evidence to support or refute the phenomenon of symptom substitution. While the above case examples can be interpreted as symptom substitution, it is only one of a number of alternative explanations for these same data. Designing an objective study of symptom substitution is difficult given the current methods of investigation.

The aversive conditioning techniques, whether covert or overt, boast the most extensive documentation of all the behavior therapies in the treatment of the sexual offender. An earlier hope that overt techniques could be replaced solely by covert ones has not yet been realized. In addition, as will be discussed in Chapter 5, the use of positive rather than negative stimuli to condition appropriate sexual responses has been demonstrated to be helpful but not definitive. A combination of positive and negative techniques still appears to be necessary in the comprehensive care of the maladaptive sexual approach disorders.

Innovative techniques have sprung from the behavioral literature in this field. It is certain that the ingenuity already shown to be characteristic of behavior therapists will continue to flourish, adding richness and variation to the texture of treatment approaches for the sexual offender.

Notes

1. For information, contact MECTA Corporation, 7015 McEwan Road, Lake Oswego, Oregon 97035.

2. Contact MECTA Corporation (address in note 1, above).

4

Reconditioning Techniques

The behavioral methods of aversion therapy have yielded impressive but narrow victories in the battle against deviant arousal. These methods have successfully eliminated such arousal but have not clearly explained the genesis of such behavior or provided a comprehensive treatment approach in themselves. They have not laid to rest the troublesome specter of symptom substitution and have been unable to use the sexual act itself—or its close representative, masturbation—in the deconditioning process.

Reconditioning techniques employ the arousal already present in sexual fantasies and masturbation and, by slightly shifting the timing and sequence of images, weaken deviant arousal while strengthening appropriate arousal. In this and the following three chapters, a variety of techniques that can be combined with aversive conditioning will be described, hopefully contributing to a more satisfying, meaningful, and comprehensive therapeutic approach to the sexual offender.

Fading

If sexual pleasure can occur in response to one set of stimuli, these in turn can be used to increase sexual responses to another set of stimuli presented in proximity with the first set. The "fading" in and out of such discriminative stimuli has been described in terms of nonsexual conditioning for some time (Barlow & Agras, 1973). For example, a patient with fear of flying might be briefly shown slides of flying scenes, just after scenes of favorite vacation spots or favorite foods. Gradually, the flying scenes are "faded in" by increasing the duration of the stimulus presentation or its fearsome properties. For example, scenes of boarding the airplane or taxiing to the runway can be followed by scenes of the airplane taking off and then actually being in the air. These scenes are combined with pleasant slides, but eventually the pleasant scenes are "faded out" until positive responses remain to the flight scenes alone.

Obviously, the timing of stimulus presentations is crucial in this process, and the patient must play an important role in planning treatment by describing his responses with accuracy. One hopes for the lingering effect of the positive stimulus to condition desired behaviors. The same result can be obtained when attempting to decondition inappropriate sexual disorders (Braun, 1976)

- A young heterosexual pedophile had little sexual response to adult women. As part of his treatment program, he was shown slides of sexual situations with inappropriately young girls, very rapidly followed by slides of sexual situations involving adult women. The adult slides were shown for increasing durations as treatment progressed, while the inappropriate pedophiliac slides were gradually faded out. Use of the plethysmograph assisted in determining when to substitute the adult slides: A rapid increase in tumescence to an inappropriate slide was quickly followed by an appropriate adult presentation. Gradually, sexual pleasure began to build to the adult slides.

- A transvestite achieved maximum sexual arousal when cross-dressed; he had a normal sexual response to adult women as well. The stories he had constructed about cross-dressing were read to him but, at points of increasing sexual arousal, brief aversive videotapes were shown, generally of contact with feces or vomitus. Gradually, the cross-dressing scenes were intensified and, as sexual pleasure was reduced in response to these, the aversive videotapes were reduced in duration and intensity. This fading in of increasingly provocative but deviant stimuli in association with fading out of aversive imagery markedly diminished his sexual arousal to transvestite stimuli.

- A heterosexual pedophile attracted neighborhood girls to his home with video games and ice cream. He would fondle their genital areas and rub his erect penis against them when they sat on his lap to play the games. He was asked to imagine scenes with his victims, but, gradually, images of his beloved granddaughter were substituted and supplemented with family slides, causing an adverse response with subsequent reduction of arousal.

- Similarly, a teenage exhibitionist was asked to gradually change the image of an actual victim until it resembled his mother.

Thus fading can be used as an aversive technique to reduce deviant sexual arousal, or as a positive technique to enhance normal arousal, or as both. Used either way, it relies upon two principles:

(1) the overlap of negative or positive responses to stimuli so that a previously conditioned response is extended to cover a new stimulus
(2) the gradual introduction of new stimuli so that the patient is not required to make large and difficult leaps of associative conditioning

In addition, it should be clear that fading can be carried out in a covert (but not surreptitious) or overt manner. Thus a patient can be directed to imagine deviant sexual activity that is then faded out gradually as nondeviant imagery is faded in, using some of the sexually pleasurable feelings associated with the deviant activity but that are now conditioned to the appropriate sexual act. Alternately, slides, videotapes, or movies can be employed in association with foul odor or electric shock, while the deviant responses are gradually shifted so that they occur in association with the aversive stimuli.

The timing of such shifts is, of necessity, an individual matter; however, Table 4.1 displays sample programs and indicates average stimulus durations in two separate cases. In these endeavors, the plethysmograph has proven doubly valuable as it not only can provide immediate feedback to the therapist on when to fade stimuli in or out but can also serve as a biofeedback instrument providing data to the patient so that he can participate in his own treatment plan. The therapist will want to know, in constructing protocols, how long and at what strength an arousal response was. By examining the

Table 4.1 *Two Examples of Fading in Sexual Offenders*

A homosexual pedophile:

    Deviant stimuli = slides of sexual scenes with young boys

    Appropriate stimuli = movie clips of adult consenting heterosexual activity

    Session 4: 60 seconds of a deviant stimulus→plethysmograph arousal
       (criterion = over 40% of full erection)→10 seconds of an appropriate stimulus

    Session 8: 30 seconds of a deviant stimulus→plethysmograph arousal
       (criterion = over 30% of full erection)→20 seconds of an appropriate stimulus

    Session 11: 10 seconds of a deviant stimulus→plethysmograph arousal
       (criterion = over 20% of full erection)→40 seconds of an appropriate stimulus

A fetishist:

    Deviant stimuli = actual contact with women's undergarments

    Appropriate stimuli = scenes describing adult consenting heterosexual activity

    Session 7: 120 seconds of fondling a variety of deviant stimuli→plethysmograph
       arousal (criterion = over 50% of full erection)→10 seconds of an appropriate
       stimulus

    Session 12: 60 seconds of fondling a variety of deviant stimuli→plethysmograph
       arousal (criterion = over 30% of full erection)→30 seconds of an appropriate
       stimulus

    Session 15: 10 seconds of fondling a variety of deviant stimuli→plethysmograph
       arousal (criterion = over 10% of full erection)→60 seconds of an appropriate
       stimulus

plethysmograph data, the patient and therapist can arrive at appropriate stimulus configurations and durations in designing a treatment program.

    Such programs can begin with subliminal stimuli if specialized equipment is available and if the offender is informed ahead of time that such a procedure will be employed:

- As part of his reconditioning program, a successful attorney was told that initially some stimuli might be presented so briefly as to preclude his awareness of the homosexual part of his bisexuality. Triplets of stimuli were then presented during each half-hour session for 15 sessions, consisting of (a) homosexually arousing scenes of 30 seconds each sandwiched around a one-tenth of a second presentation of a heterosexual scene and (b) homosexually arousing scenes of 30 seconds each sandwiched around a nauseating scene of 30 seconds. The heterosexual scene was increased from one-tenth second (outside the patient's awareness) to 30 seconds, while the nauseating scene was reduced from 30 seconds to one-tenth second. This had the effect of gradually conditioning sexual arousal to the heterosexual scene while deconditioning it to the homosexual scene.

How does one know, however, that an opposite effect will not occur? Is it as likely that deviant arousal will be increased because it is paired with pleasant sexual responses? Here, the plethysmograph is of value in demonstrating, in a timely fashion, whether such "backward conditioning" is occurring. With experience, it is possible to use this instrument to time the stimulus durations so that positive overlaps occur:

- A 40-year-old mechanic had been convicted of four rapes during a six-month period of time and had already served the majority of his 20-year sentence when, in an effort to reduce the prison population, he was placed on parole. A fading technique was devised in which a combination of slides and stories of rape activities were presented for progressively shorter periods of time while slides and stories of adult, consenting heterosexuals were immediately substituted once the plethysmograph showed arousal. However, one of the clinic's plethysmographs was inoperative for sessions 6 through 10. Once repaired and placed back in service, this instrument registered *increasing* levels of arousal to rape scenes. It appeared that the high levels of arousal to nondeviant scenes carried over to the presentation of deviant stimuli, thus reinforcing rape fantasies. This patient was then treated only with assisted covert sensitization and had adequate remission.

Fading is a promising technique little explored in the sexual conditioning literature thus far. It can be employed as one link in the chain of therapy and can be conveniently individualized to fit many response patterns. Moreover, it can be employed with real or imagined stimuli, and its progress can be monitored with the plethysmograph. Further studies are needed to explore this technique further.

Plethysmograph Biofeedback

Although the initial enthusiasm for a technology employing bio-feedback to cure high blood pressure, ulcers, and migraine head-aches has not been sustained by clinically meaningful changes, it has nonetheless altered perceptions about volitional control over mind and matter. One very worthwhile use of this technique included the plethysmograph in the treatment of the sexual offender (Goodman, 1984).

In a typical session of plethysmographic biofeedback, the patient reclines in a lounge chair, with plethysmograph gauge attached, and views explicit slides, videotapes, and movies or listens to sexual stories or experiences both combined. The plethysmograph is connected in series to a vertical array of 20 lights, which are connected to the plethysmograph's output and are positioned to the side of the viewing screen. Every 5% of increasing plethysmograph arousal triggers a light above the next to flash on; signs by the lights tell the offender the level of arousal, spaced every four lights apart ("20%, 40%, 60%, 80%, 100%"). Alternately, red, green, and yellow lights can be used, keyed to varying levels of arousal at the discretion of the therapist. The offender can thus see his arousal increasing or decreasing and, combined with instructions from the therapist, can engage in attempts at self-control:

- A 41-year-old heterosexual pedophile, while being treated on the ple-thysmograph, was asked to keep the green biofeedback light on as much as possible. Thereafter, a series of slides of explicit sexual activity between a man and two young girls were shown. The plethysmograph was connected to the light array so that any value above 20% activated the red light, a 15%-20% value activated the yellow light, and any value below 15% kept the green light on. By the end of several sessions, this offender was able to keep the green light on in 100% of the trials.

The value of the plethysmograph in such cases is not only to teach the *behavior* of self-control but to encourage the patient to develop the *concept* of self-control as well.

Such biofeedback, completing the feedback loop from the machine to the patient, is generally best accomplished during the first active phrase of treatment, especially for those offenders who are at high risk of reoffending soon. However, this work carries with it a hidden danger: the message that the goal of treatment is *better control*. It is preferable instead to aim for the primary goal of *elimination of deviant sexual arousal* rather than the ability to control it better. Plethysmograph biofeedback can be seen as one step toward that goal. However, in reality, a number of offenders, though a minority, must settle for enhanced control combined with a marked lowering of deviant arousal. In both cases, plethysmographic biofeedback is a valuable and powerful technique and almost always is incorporated into the battery of treatment methods for the sexual offender.

Masturbation Techniques

Imagery during masturbation and intercourse is of paramount importance in the understanding and treatment of the sexual offender (Abel & Blanchard, 1974; Evans, 1968; Hackett, 1971; McGuire, Carlisle, & Young, 1965). Fantasy sustains urge; thus gaining access to fantasies is often a Rosetta stone for interpreting sexual desire, action, and reaction (MacCulloch, Snowden, Wood, & Millis, 1983). However, the use of fantasies was suspect for a time because these phenomena were not manifested in observable events. The plethysmograph had become the only assessment technique trusted in the behavioral literature on treatment of the sexual offender.

More recently, cognitive covert responses have been reevaluated (Meichenbaum, 1974). Evidence has been presented that the subjective experiences of the sexual offender are of value in formulating a treatment program (Tollison, Adams, & Tollison, 1979). However, masturbation fantasies remain a private reserve to which the patient may grant access only when full trust is established. Of all fantasies, these may be the last to be shared. The very act of masturbation has been a private one. Even the broadening acceptance of masturbatory behavior as normal and universally practiced has not made the act of self-stimulation one that can be easily shared.

Therefore, the masturbation techniques to be described must be approached carefully after building firm rapport and trust with the patient. As the patient begins to divulge this material, the therapist must proceed cautiously, at times even encouraging him to make certain he is comfortable before sharing this private material. To many offenders, verbal rather than written accounts of this material are preferable. Complete confidentiality must be insured.

In the following description of masturbatory techniques, fantasies during masturbation are the focus of treatment. Sexual fantasies at other times, such as during intercourse or daydreaming, can also be employed to assist therapy and are dealt with in Chapter 6 on operant techniques.

Masturbatory Satiation

This technique, often also termed *orgasmic reconditioning*, makes use of masturbatory fantasies at critical periods during self-stimulation (Marshall, 1979; Marshall & Lippers, 1977). The fantasy/masturbation cycle can be conceived as beginning with masturbation and involving increases in sexual pleasure as the act proceeds. Immediately following orgasm and ejaculation, the sexual drive is reduced to its lowest ebb (Barlow & Abel, 1981; Berlin, 1983). Therefore, the time of the least sexual drive occurs just following an ejaculation, and this technique makes use of this phenomenon.

In practice, the patient is asked to masturbate to nondeviant fantasies until ejaculation. Then he is asked to continue to try to masturbate to deviant fantasies for a variable time thereafter. Marshall (1979) recommended one hour, but often the offender finds this excessive and may tend not to comply. A 30-minute period may be easier for the offender to accept and may thus be completed more faithfully. The patient should be asked to perform this technique each time he masturbates or at least three times per week. At times, case reports have indicated eradication of deviant sexual arousal with this technique alone, although that is not a common occurrence.

A recent addition to this technique involves the use of tape recordings. The patient is asked to record his fantasies using an audiotape cassette recorder while he masturbates. He is asked to begin with a fantasy of consenting adult heterosexual activity; following ejaculation, he is asked to continue the recording while describing deviant fantasies. The taping procedure allows the therapist to gain entry into the offender's fantasy world while at the same time ensuring better compliance with the treatment procedure (Abel & Becker, 1984). Parenthetically, some workers believe that the highest sexual pleasure occurs when an offender speaks of his own fantasies aloud.

This type of reconditioning relies on the belief (not yet objectively verified) that sexual drive is lowest just after ejaculation. Masturbating at that time, the sexual offender begins to associate deviant fantasies with a low sexual drive. Indeed, *to have to* masturbate then is quite likely an aversive event. Some workers stress the boring aspects of enforced masturbation after ejaculation and require offenders to repeat the same deviant scenes in their fantasies again and again during this period of lowest sexual drive (Abel & Becker, 1984). If this is true, the postejaculation masturbation period should be prolonged to enhance the boredom, extinction of, or aversion toward deviant arousal.

Such satiation techniques can be applied to a wide variety of disorders of desire:

- An exhibitionist was asked to masturbate three times each week to adult heterosexual fantasies. Just following ejaculation, he was asked to continue masturbating to exhibitionist fantasies for another 30 minutes. The patient reported no ability to achieve another erection. Instead, he felt his penis was only irritated by this practice, and a number of negative sensations were thus conditioned to the exhibitionist fantasies.

Although fantasies are usually the manipulated variable, the use of actual materials such as photographs with be even more dramatic:

- An unemployed welder, aged 32, with an 11-year history of heterosexual pedophilia, was asked to masturbate to pornographic pictorial material involving adult heterosexual consenting couples and to tape-record his fantasies as he did so. Just after ejaculation, he was asked to continue masturbating but switch to pornographic pictures involving sexual activity between an adult male and a young girl for the succeeding 30 minutes and to continue recording his fantasies. Although a

number of aversive techniques were used in his treatment program, he
believed this to be the most effective.

Although historically included among the reconditioning techniques, masturbation satiation would seem to be another form, albeit
covert, of aversive conditioning. Perhaps it is, but, if so, it possesses
additional elements: This technique not only forces the sexual offender to masturbate to deviant fantasies at a time when he is least
aroused but also asks him to masturbate to normal nondeviant fantasies first. What if the patient were merely asked to masturbate at a
certain frequency (as yet undetermined) to nondeviant fantasies?
There is some evidence that this procedure alone is effective (Bem,
1972). Moreover, another technique, that of alternating masturbation
to deviant fantasies with masturbation to nondeviant ones, has also
been reported as effective (McGonaghy, 1971; Vanceventer & Laws,
1978). However, not all reports are sanguine (Reston & Yamashita,
1983). The data are too tentative, as yet, to reach definite conclusions.
In summary, masturbatory satiation techniques may harbor two
components, both of value:

(1) masturbation to nondeviant fantasies at the time of maximal arousal
(2) masturbation to deviant fantasies at the time of minimal arousal

Further work is indicated to separate and test each component.
However, from a clinical point of view, these procedures have proven
quite effective and are generally included as part of the standard
repertoire of treatments for the sexual offender.

Masturbatory Fantasy Change

In this technique, the patient is asked to masturbate to deviant
fantasies until the point of ejaculatory inevitability is reached. At that
immediate point, he is asked to switch abruptly from deviant to
nondeviant fantasies (with or without pictures or tangible stimuli),
thus associating sexual climax with nondeviant material. In subsequent masturbatory sessions, he is asked to make this switch slightly
earlier each time, until he has masturbated to nondeviant stimuli
entirely (Conrad & Wincze, 1976; Lande, 1980; Marquis, 1970;

Vanceventer & Laws, 1978). As with the masturbatory satiation technique, the patient can also be asked to tape-record these fantasies so the therapist can gain additional information and ensure patient compliance (Abel & Becker, 1984).

Occasionally, such a switch can be too severe, and intermediate steps must be employed:

- A 13-year-old boy had attacked two 8-year-old girls in his neighborhood. He could get aroused with normal heterosexual stimuli as well as those connected with forcible sex with young girls. He masturbated daily. Thus he was asked to masturbate to fantasies of his two attacks but, just before reaching climax, to switch to scenes involving forcible sexual activities with consenting teenage girls or adult women. Gradually, he was able to change those fantasies to ones involving consenting activities with appropriate-aged females. He was able to make that switch and to make it earlier and earlier each time he masturbated. Within three weeks, he was successfully masturbating to consenting heterosexual, nonviolent fantasies exclusively.

This technique involves greater participation and control on the part of the patient than the satiation technique described above. The patient must make an often difficult leap across a wide gap and, as in the two cases described above, a bridge of gradual steps may need to be constructed. This difficulty underscores the inherent risk that, in assigning masturbation techniques, the patient may simply not perform them or, worse, may perform them inaccurately. Although it has been helpful to have the patient describe how he uses the technique, the stratagem of requiring tape-recorded masturbation sessions has provided an invaluable window into the offender's fantasies while providing the reassurance of compliance but with privacy maintained. Because these techniques rely on the patient's private experiences, actual or verified follow-through cannot as yet be measured. (For example, the patient can provide a falsified tape.) They should, nonetheless, almost always be included in a comprehensive treatment package. When performed correctly, they are extremely powerful methods of altering sexual arousal.

Direct Masturbatory Conditioning

It is sometimes possible to attempt modifications of these masturbation techniques in selected offenders who cannot follow through with these methods or refuse to do so:

- A 30-year-old garage mechanic could not discontinue his practice of bestiality, even though it repulsed him after each such act. After experiencing difficulty with routine masturbatory techniques, he was asked to masturbate to zoophiliac fantasies but, on ejaculation, to look at a number of pictures from veterinary journals of various animal lesions, stimuli that had already been demonstrated to reduce his sexual arousal. He was then asked to start looking at the explicit pictures earlier and earlier during masturbation. He could not sustain an erection while doing so but he was instructed to keep masturbating, even so. He lost any sexual pleasure associated with animals and had no recurrences.

- A widowed pensioner, 63, moved to a trailer court after his wife died. He began to make the acquaintance of many young girls who lived there, bringing them candy, taking them to the movies, and so on. He was reported for this suspicious activity and entered treatment voluntarily. He reported severe embarrassment in following through with masturbatory techniques, especially when tape recordings were to be used. He was asked, therefore, to speak aloud a sexual fantasy involving a young girl as he was masturbating in private with the recorder present but not turned on. He then agreed to do the same with his tape recorder on. He thus recorded three different fantasies involving young girls. However, he was not asked to share these with anyone until he felt ready to do so. Finally, he and a family member listened to the tapes three times, an aversive experience. In addition, he was asked to record three such tapes, speaking aloud, but gradually changing from deviant to normal heterosexual fantasies. This technique was believed helpful in his overall treatment program.

In the future, audiotapes and even videotapes of masturbatory sequences might be used to assist in the treatment of the sexual offender. However, this material is so sensitive and private that trust building of a high order must first occur. The offender must grant informed consent in writing; he must be assured of confidentiality; his tapes must be guarded with great care and should be erased when no further treatment benefit can be gained from them.

These masturbatory techniques bring into sharp relief some general issues in the treatment of the sexual offender. Some reliance must be placed on follow-through with homework assignments, yet many offenders may wish their therapists to believe that they are doing homework when they actually are not. It helps to have the offender explain and even demonstrate how he performs his assignments. Some offenders can be asked to do homework assignments in the therapist's office so they can be observed and coached in proper technique:

- The therapist for a homosexual pedophile doubted he was following through with assisted covert sensitization homework assignments. He asked the offender to come to his office three times each week in addition to his treatment sessions. At those times, the therapist made a treatment room available to the patient with a lounge chair, tape recorder, and one-way mirror. The therapist told the patient he would occasionally look in through the mirror to make certain he was performing the assisted covert sensitization procedure correctly.

A number of sexual offenders, when asked to practice these techniques, refuse to comply on moral grounds. They may insist that masturbation is either against their religious principles or that masturbation with deviant fantasies is objectionable. While this may appear hypocritical, and, indeed, some sexual offenders seem almost too conveniently to embrace religion after their offense is discovered, there is no doubt that many others turn to faith and prayer in sincere atonement, guilt, or grief. Fortunately, there is no shortage of helpful techniques to treat the sexual offender. Thus masturbation need not *always* be forcefully assigned. Many offenders will follow through with such methods after treatment is in progress, even if they hesitate at first.

Such cases, however, emphasize how the issues of patient compliance, informed consent, and voluntary entry into treatment must be considered in the total treatment program. Many, if not most, sexual offenders are partially if not entirely involuntary patients (Maletzky, 1980b), though this might also be said of many patients in general psychiatric practice. Informed written consent and written as well as verbal information should be given to the patient and his family where appropriate (see Appendix C). To some extent, these procedures can be suggested to the patient and, in the therapist-patient exchange, modified to suit the individual situation. The patient should not only feel that he is a party to treatment decisions, he should also actually be so.

Summary

The reconditioning techniques, including fading and the masturbatory fantasy methods, have formed powerful additions to the standard aversive therapies in the treatment of the sexual offender. They appear to be quite useful, but their implementation usually must occur only after trust is built as they are, at times, the most difficult techniques to apply. It is likely that they will be the basis of research yet to come on the role fantasies play in igniting sexual urge and keeping it aflame.

These techniques also bring into sharp focus the ethics of treatment, the role of the patient in shaping his own treatment program, and the extent to which private events can be employed in the treatment of the sexual offender. These issues will reappear in most of the succeeding chapters because they are integral to the total treatment program for the sexual offender.

5

Positive Respondent Conditioning Techniques

Although the aversive conditioning techniques, both by themselves and in conjunction with reconditioning methods, have produced excellent early results (Evans, 1980), there has been a more recent move to combine positive with negative conditioning methods (Adams & Sturgis, 1978; Adams, Tollison, & Carson, 1981; Josiason, Fantuzzo, & Rosen, 1980). This movement has reached a stage in which some proponents have suggested elimination of aversive techniques altogether (Adams & Sturgis, 1978; James, 1978). Indeed, some preliminary results indicate that positive conditioning, occasionally in combination with electric shock aversion or reconditioning methods as adjunctive techniques, produces excellent results (Abel, 1984; Josiason, Fantuzzo, & Rosen, 1980).

Certainly, many therapists are drawn to the idea of avoiding the use of negative stimuli, such as electric shock and foul odor, because of poor patient acceptance. A minority, but a significant one, of prospective sexual offenders refuse certain techniques of aversive conditioning. This is particularly true when electric shock is presented as

Table 5.1 *Anonymous Compliance Questionnaire: Question 1*

How helpful were the following parts of your treatment program? Answer on a -1 to 4+ scale, where -1 is harmful, 0 is no help, and 4+ is extremely helpful.

Modality	-1	0	1+	2+	3+	4+
				Percentage		
Foul odor aversion	7	10	19	31	14	19
Electric shock aversion	13	17	11	19	20	20
Foul taste aversion	6	12	17	24	32	9
Covert sensitization	0	24	19	18	31	8
Aversive behavior rehearsal	16	0	4	28	18	34

NOTE: N = 100 randomly selected sexual offenders of all diagnostic types.

part of the treatment plan (Fookes, 1969; Rachman & Teasdale, 1969a). To some extent, the other aversive stimuli, such as foul odor and taste, were developed to enhance patient acceptance.

To learn more about the issue of patient acceptance and compliance, a questionnaire was developed and distributed to 100 randomly selected sexual offenders with a variety of diagnoses as they were ending treatment. Tables 5.1 to 5.4 present the questions asked and the responses given. All questionnaires were returned anonymously. Patients were clearly cautious in endorsing the use of aversive techniques when compared with reconditioning and positive conditioning methods. Although the majority would again submit to

Table 5.2 *Anonymous Compliance Questionnaire: Question 2*

If necessary, how likely would you be to undergo the following treatments again? Answer on a 0 to 4+ scale, where 0 means you would not undergo that treatment and 4+ means you would definitely undergo that treatment.

Modality	0	1+	2+	3+	4+
			Percentage		
Foul odor aversion	12	15	37	29	7
Electric shock aversion	29	31	24	8	8
Foul taste aversion	9	21	46	18	6
Covert sensitization	3	27	24	30	16
Aversive behavior rehearsal	37	42	13	7	1

NOTE: N = 100 randomly selected sexual offenders of all diagnostic types.

Table 5.3 *Anonymous Compliance Questionnaire: Question 3*

Would you prefer positive conditioning techniques, such as desensitization and social skills training, to aversive methods of treatment?

Answer	Percentage
Yes	77
No	23

NOTE: N = 100 randomly selected sexual offenders of all diagnostic types.

aversive conditioning, they would do so only if absolutely necessary and, even then, after reconditioning and positive conditioning techniques had proven fruitless. The majority of these offenders were in mandated treatment programs, yet they were still hesitant about aversive conditioning methods, apparently even if noncompliance led to incarceration.

Almost 30% of these offenders would apparently elect to refuse aversive methods if required a second time. In practice, however, over 75% were undergoing some form of aversion therapy at the time they completed the questionnaire. (It is certainly possible that offenders were more courageous on paper than in a real treatment situation in asserting they would refuse mandated treatment techniques.) Offenders reserved their most negative responses for electric shock aversion therapy and aversive behavior rehearsal. Although 72% of the respondents had received some electric shock conditioning, the

Table 5.4 *Anonymous Compliance Questionnaire: Question 4*

How regularly did you carry out the following homework assignments? Answer on a 0 to 4+ scale, where 0 is not at all and 4+ is faithfully.

Modality	0	1+	2+	3+	4+
			Percentage		
Foul odor aversion	12	20	31	26	11
Foul taste aversion	19	11	47	13	10
Covert sensitization	9	16	39	21	15
Masturbation techniques	21	19	37	10	13
Desensitization	7	29	31	19	14

NOTE: N = 100 randomly selected sexual offenders of all diagnostic types.

majority of these men indicated a reluctance to again enter a program that employed shock aversion. Similarly, 57% of these men had been treated with aversive behavior rehearsal, yet approximately 80% indicated they would refuse this procedure if it were offered again. Those responding to the questionnaire indicated greater acceptance of positive techniques as opposed to negative ones and better acceptance of olfactory aversion when compared with shock. All patients were receiving olfactory aversion at the time.

In this anonymous questionnaire, many offenders frankly admitted noncompliance with homework assignments, particularly so with aversive techniques when compared with reconditioning and positive methods. More work is indicated in either enhancing compliance or improving the strength of positive conditioning techniques for homework assignments.

Perhaps these men simply did not want to be exposed to painful stimuli—not an unexpected response. However, a number of these respondents were voluntary patients already receiving such stimuli. Discussion with these offenders brought forth another possibility: There was a predominant theme that positive conditioning methods produced better results; thus such conditioning was not only less aversive but somehow stronger as well. It is not surprising that this view is also championed by some workers in this field, as a wealth of data from the operant conditioning literature bolsters the view that reward and social modeling approaches, rather than punishment, are preferable routes to acquiring new skills (Kazdin, 1978).

There remains, however, no a priori reason to assume that respondent or classical conditioning *must* also be more effective when utilizing positive as opposed to aversive stimuli. Indeed, the literature thus far can be used to support the opposite premise: Aversive conditioning techniques have produced the best outcome data thus far (see Rooth & Marks, 1974, for a sample comparison study). It appears, however, that positive conditioning techniques are becoming more popular, and optimistic reviews in this field have been published (Adams, Tollison, & Carson, 1981). In practice, a combination of these two methods would now seem preferable, and most conditioning programs for the sexual offender use both simultaneously (Abel, Lewis, & Clancy, 1970; Josiason, Fantuzzo, & Rosen, 1980). Parallels can be found in a combination of flooding and desensitization for phobic disorders or in the combined use of cognitive therapy with chemotherapy in the affective disorders.

Many offenders, their families, and the general public can harbor profound misunderstandings in this area.

- A 45-year-old elementary school teacher was arrested for indecent liberties involving several of his 8-year-old female students. Following full disclosure of prospective treatment methods, he adamantly refused to undergo electric shock aversion because he believed it produced brain damage with memory loss. He relented only with great hesitancy, finding it difficult to believe that electric shock aversion was not related to electroconvulsive therapy for depression.

As demonstrated in this case, electric shock is the most difficult of the aversive techniques for patients to accept or understand, with the possible exception of aversive behavior rehearsal. Not only is electric shock confused with electroconvulsive therapy, it is also associated in offenders' minds with barbarism, torture, and medical experimentation. Sexual offenders and their families may also associate electric shock aversion with the term *punishment*—often, but imprecisely, used to describe all forms of aversive conditioning. When describing programs to patients and their families, it is probably best to list electric shock aversion as just one of several aversive techniques. It is also helpful for the therapist to administer the electric shock to him- or herself before employing it with the patient.

No matter how the aversive techniques are described, however, they should be just one weapon among many in the arsenal employed to treat the sexual offender. The inclusion of positive respondent conditioning therapies makes eminent good sense for a number of reasons:

(1) They are effective when used in combination with reconditioning and aversive conditioning techniques (Adams, Tollison, & Carson, 1981; Josiason, Fantuzzo, & Rosen, 1980).
(2) They are more acceptable to patients and their families.
(3) They may enhance the efficacy of conditioning therapies employing other methods, perhaps in a synergistic fashion.

- Although referred by the court for mandated treatment, a 27-year-old general contractor with homosexual pedophilia refused to undertake any treatment associated with aversive conditioning. He claimed such techniques should be relegated to the past and tied them directly to nefarious processes such as "brain-washing and concentration camp tactics." He was successfully treated with desensitization and success imagery (described below) without recourse to aversive methods.

• A 57-year-old lay minister in the Church of Latter-Day Saints, referred for heterosexual pedophilia, refused any electric shock or olfactory aversion, explaining that viewing the pornographic materials associated with these techniques violated his religious principles. A combination of positive conditioning techniques, however, was only minimally successful. He was persuaded by the treatment team, in conjunction with his minister, to add aversive methods to the treatment protocol and achieved elimination of deviant sexual arousal with this combination.

These cases demonstrate the necessity of not only having the capacity to administer a wide variety of conditioning techniques but also possessing some flexibility in employing them as well to help the offender maximize treatment potential.

Desensitization

IN VITRO DESENSITIZATION

Although desensitization was one of the first clinically useful techniques to emerge from the behavioral sciences (Quinsey & Marshall, 1983), it has seldom been mentioned in the academic literature as a treatment approach for the sexual offender. Perhaps this is because of its association with, and success in, treating specific phobias. Behavior theorists, interested in desensitization's mode of action, were not likely to apply it to the maladaptive sexual approach disorders because of the very different clientele they were treating: patients with classical phobias or students in analog studies frightened of snakes or public speaking.

Even today, desensitization is not commonly thought of as a treatment approach for the sexual offender, although this stems more from a lack of use and familiarity than from any negative-outcome studies. Although not numerous, positive reports are present in the literature. Videotaped desensitization to heterosocial and heterosexual scenes has been used with positive effect in homosexual patients (Caird & Wincze, 1977), although the male homosexual may surreptitiously identify with the female in these scenes, thus engendering "backward conditioning" (Tollison, Adams, & Tollison, 1979). Purely imaginal desensitization has been demonstrated, via the plethysmograph, to enhance sexual arousal to heterosexual stimuli in a group of strongly homosexual men, but, in this study, additional aversive therapy was necessary to reduce homosexual arousal at follow-up (Bancroft, 1970). Similarly, in vivo desensitization has been employed in combination with chemical aversion (Cooper, 1963), and covert sensitization (Gray, 1970), to enhance appropriate sexual arousal. Desensitization has occasionally been successful, even without such combinations, as reported in two single-case studies (Barlow & Agras, 1973; Wickramaserka, 1972) and in one comparative study with electric shock aversion, which used the anticipatory avoidance paradigm (James, 1978).

The sexual offender is often frightened of heterosexual adult interactions, social as well as sexual. Desensitization of these fears makes good sense. Moreover, the offender should already be acquiring the basic skills to accomplish desensitization by his participation in aversive conditioning—relaxation exercises and imagery techniques.

- A 14-year-old boy had attacked and raped three preadolescent girls within a span of one year. He had never dated and felt awkward around girls his own age. He was taught relaxation techniques, and then a list of scenes was drawn up, with his participation, of fearful social situations. A hierarchy of such scenes was established and, beginning with the least fearful, he was asked to imagine under relaxation the easiest scenes first. After imagery without anxiety, progressively more difficult scenes were imagined under relaxation. As these elicited less and less anxiety, he was asked to begin practicing social situations with his sister while relaxed and, later, to initiate conversations with girls his own age.

There are three requirements thought to be necessary for any desensitization procedure:

(1) adequate muscular relaxation
(2) clear imagination of a given scene
(3) a hierarchic presentation of scenes beginning with easier scenes and progressing to more difficult ones

As first formulated, these requirements had to be combined: It was believed that the patient had to imagine being within a scene while simultaneously being relaxed (Wolpe, 1969). This formulation of desensitization, however, may well be too rigid. Some studies show that desensitization can produce beneficial results even without formal relaxation training (Marks, 1981a). However, in this report, the patients were informally relaxed by instruction and implication. No study required its subjects *not* to be relaxed when imagining scenes.

Moreover, the requirement that scenes be imagined in exact sequence, never progressing beyond the patient's limit of anxiety, is probably not essential (Stang, 1974).

- An attorney referred a 34-year-old welder for molesting two young stepdaughters during a five-year period. His wife was in the process of divorcing him, and he was frightened by the thought of having to meet women and date again. Along with aversive conditioning, a plan was devised to desensitize him to social situations involving age-appropriate women. Table 5.5 lists the scenes used. These were constructed without an attempt to precisely rate anxiety levels and thus order the scenes in strict hierarchic fashion. After several weeks of relaxation practice (also employed in aversive conditioning work), three early scenes selected from this list were presented for 60 seconds each with a 30-second interval in between. Tapes of the entire process were made for the patient so that he could perform the technique at home four times a week. As progress was gained, additional sets of three scenes were recorded, roughly advancing from easier to more difficult scenes but without any attempt to rate the anxiety coincident with any one scene. During a 12-week period, the patient became less apprehensive about social situations and asked several women at work for a date.

- A 47-year-old gardener exposed himself almost daily. He was extremely shy and had never married. He had experienced several homosexual liaisons but was dissatisfied with this orientation. During aversive conditioning, his difficulties in initiating actions with women became apparent. He and his therapist constructed a list of scenes involving socially appropriate behaviors of increasing difficulty. However, the patient reversed the intended order to the hierarchy in a misunderstanding. Nonetheless, he rapidly gained confidence socially and, following treatment, reported more ease with women in general and eventually a satisfying relationship with a woman.

Table 5.5   *Examples of Scenes (abbreviated) Used to Desensitize a Sexual Offender to Approaches to Women, Without a Strict Hierarchy*

Scene	Content
1	Idiosyncratic pleasant scene: watching ocean waves breaking over rocks
2	Passing a familiar woman in hall at work; smiling, making eye contact, and saying "Hi"
3	Being introduced to a new woman employee at work
4	Having female cousins to dinner at house
5	Being introduced to a new woman supervisor at work
6	Talking with two women friends at a party
7	Being introduced to an attractive woman at a party

Lest these examples create a misimpression, a number of cases are not such obvious successes. Failures have occurred for a variety of reasons, including a scene sequence that was too rapid, poor follow-through on homework assignments, insufficient time spent with positive techniques (aversive techniques have usually been heavily emphasized with these offenders), and perhaps too strong an avoidance response. One conclusion from these examples and a number of similar cases is clear: A strict hierarchy is not necessary. This finding echoes that found using desensitization in the treatment of phobias (Stang, 1974). There is less certainty about whether formal relaxation procedures need to be taught. This is often a superfluous issue in the treatment of sexual offenders as relaxation is usually initiated soon after entry into treatment in order to employ aversive imagery procedures as described in Chapter 3.

Despite similar success stories in the literature involving case reports (Barlow & Agras, 1973; Wickramaserka, 1972), desensitization has not been truly tested as a treatment technique for the sexual offender in its own right. It is thus uncertain whether desensitization alone is an adequate treatment for the sexual offender, even one in whom heterosocial phobias predominate. This is an area neglected in the world literature to date, yet one that is testable. If, as some contend, the core etiology in the maladaptive sexual approach disorders stems from deficient social skills and/or heterosocial and heterosexual avoidance behaviors, desensitization alone should exert a clearly beneficial result in the population being treated for sexual offenses.

It is also possible that desensitization can be of help even if a phobia is not the basic disorder in a sexual offender.

- A 15-year-old boy developed an excessive fear that sperm leaking from his penis might inadvertently impregnate his mother or sister through contact with their underclothing, as in the washing machine. He developed a compulsion to make certain this would not happen by separating their underclothing from his. In the process, however, he developed sexually pleasurable feelings derived from contact with their garments and soon began to steal them from his mother's and sisters' rooms and masturbate while fondling them. While aversive conditioning eliminated any sexual pleasure from these undergarments, desensitization was necessary to reduce and then eliminate the obsession about contamination. A hierarchy of scenes was constructed and a 10-week program of relaxation associated with these scenes removed the impregnation obsession.

The timing of desensitization will vary with each individual. Relaxation can be taught within one to two weeks, especially with home practice via cassettes tapes. Several sessions generally suffice to review scenes. Scene presentation should occur both in the office and at home with a tape recorder. In those patients for whom compliance is questionable, it often helps to ask the offender to come to the office two to three times per week to listen to tapes.

In producing tapes for desensitization, it is often preferable to start with brief (60-second) relaxation instructions followed by an idiosyncratic pleasant scene for another 60 seconds. Examples of such scenes should be drawn from the patient's memory. Often, seacoast, mountain, vacation, or childhood scenes are constructed with the patient, and those that help him to relax most are used. Such scenes should be paired with taped relaxation instructions.

Figure 5.1 presents a flowchart of a typical desensitization program, although the timing of the requisite steps is only approximate. One must be flexible and listen to the patient: He will tell the therapist how rapidly to proceed or how long to delay with the scenes. Typically, desensitization programs are initiated with two to three introductory sessions and then proceed through six to twelve weekly sessions, one-third of which can be devoted to desensitization procedures, leaving the remainder of time to focus on other techniques such as aversive conditioning. Tapes can be prepared directly within the session or privately later. These should not be unduly long, as many patients' attention can wander with tapes longer than 15 minutes. Typically, brief relaxation and pleasant imagery is followed by three desensitization scenes of 60 to 90 seconds each, with total time in a taped or live session not exceeding 12 minutes. The therapist is wise to use the patient's own language and to inject suggestions concerning calm and mastery during the scenes.

In work with the sexual offender, desensitization is generally used in combination with aversive conditioning. Because the aversive methods were applied to these disorders first, they were believed to be the major ingredients in a successful treatment recipe. From a specific point of view, however, it could be as likely that a combination of the two techniques, or desensitization alone, is the truly effective procedure. However, case reports and experience more often show aversive conditioning to be effective when used as the sole treatment technique, whereas desensitization by itself is rarely associated with the termination of deviant sexual arousal (Bancroft, 1970; Gray, 1970). Unfortunately, no partially or completely controlled studies have explored the efficacy of desensitization alone for these disorders. Such research might boost the status of the positive conditioning techniques in the treatment of the sexual offender; should the results prove inconclusive, such a study would nonetheless publicize the use of desensitization in this area, even if only as an adjunctive technique.

Following successful in vitro mastery of scenes (that is, lacking significant anxiety), in vivo practice should be implemented:

- The 47-year-old exhibitionist gardener in the example above was asked, in the midst of desensitization, to frequent a local tavern twice each week, to go to his library twice each week as well, and to practice relaxation in both locations. His next assignments included initiating eye contact and smiling at any female he passed on the streets or in shopping malls, or individual shops, all the while using relaxation covertly. At the same time, he was progressing through matching in vitro scenes on tape. As his mastery grew, he was asked to initiate conversations, store up anecdotes to relate, and share his experiences with others.

The relaxation procedure using a tape is necessary when initiating therapy but cannot be accomplished in day-to-day situations evoking tension. To assist with generalization, the patient can be asked to

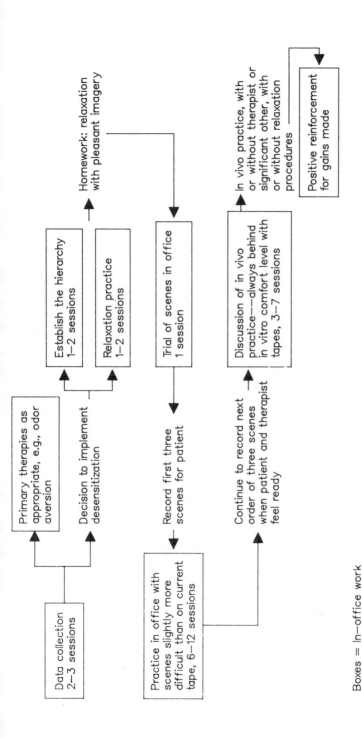

Boxes = In—office work
Out of Boxes = Homework for patient and therapist

Figure 5.1 Flowchart Depicting a Typical Desensitization.

practice relaxation two to three times per week but with eyes open and/or in a seated or standing position. The technique can thus be generalized to real-life situations and not be associated solely with a lying down, eyes closed, situation.

Desensitization can, of course, be extended beyond the office or hospital as the above case example illustrates. In vivo conditioning has had an increasingly valued position in the treatment of phobias, and, again, the treatment of the sexual offender can benefit from some of these techniques. It would seem that the closer such conditioning approximates day-to-day incidents and settings, the more powerful it would be in increasing desirable social and sexual behaviors. Although data confirming this supposition are scarce, literature exploring in vivo techniques is still in the seminal state and does not match the extensive documentation of desensitization in vitro. Encouraging early studies (Barlow & Agras, 1973; Cooper, 1963; Gray, 1970; Wickramaserka, 1972) and one comprehensive review (Adams, Tollison, & Carson, 1981) do exist, however, and it appears that a trend favoring in vivo techniques is building. Table 5.6 presents a succinct comparison of advantages of each type of desensitization as a guide to the following discussion.

Although it appears, at first, more natural to employ real surroundings in positively conditioning new behaviors, it does not necessarily follow that in vivo techniques will always be superior to in vitro ones.

- When a 52-year-old supermarket manager was referred following his apprehension for molesting young boys, he expressed twin goals: to eliminate sexual arousal to young boys and to build a fledgling interest in adult men. Although he had some interest in men, he had been embarrassed and frightened to venture forward into a homosexual life-style. He had little sexual interest in women. The patient was, therefore, asked to attend several meetings of a local homosexual rights organization, practicing relaxation covertly when he did so. At the second meeting, however, he was suddenly asked to venture an opinion on a controversial topic. Taken aback, he was speechless and thereafter refused to enter into other homosexual activities.

This patient was perhaps pushed too quickly into a real-life situation without adequate imaginal preparation. The case demonstrates that in vivo methods cannot always ensure positive reinforcement for desired behaviors. A more gradual introduction to a homosexual

Table 5.6   *Advantages of Both In Vitro and In Vivo Desensitization Methods*

Advantages of Desensitization	
In Vitro	*In Vivo*
1. Gradual exposure to imagined scenes resulting in less risk of traumatic or "backward" conditioning	1. More rapid improvement claimed in some studies
2. Fearful stimuli more easily controlled to prevent undue anxiety	2. Better approximation to "real-life" situations; enhanced opportunity for generalization
3. Greater patient acceptance	3. Greater potential for significant reinforcement to occur from successful trials
4. Can be used to gradually acclimate patient to in vivo desensitization	4. Opportunity for therapist or significant others to observe the situation directly
5. Easier to vary stimuli to promote generalization	5. Substitutes directly observable behavior for "mental events" such as imagery
6. Timing and number of sessions more easily controlled	6. Substitutes an active mode of self-control for the passive role of listening to therapist-presented scenes
7. More thorough research and clinical evidence supporting use	7. Possibly less expensive

life-style through classical imaginal desensitization might have produced better results. In addition, real-life situations were used from the outset; the construction of hierarchic steps did not occur. Although, in theory, a gradual hierarchic presentation of in vivo situations could be built, actually enacting it might prove to be difficult:

- A 21-year-old heterosexual pedophile with chronic subassertion and social avoidance behavior was asked to attend, in order, first an evening social with his family, then a picnic with friends, and then a cocktail party with people who were mostly strangers. He had little difficulty with the first assignment, but at the picnic, as he was talking with two young women, he spilled some wine on both of their dresses. They were understandably upset, and he was mortified and fled; he could not be induced to practice social approach behaviors for several months thereafter.

It is thus possible for a situation to become out of control. Neither the therapist nor the patient can exert as great an influence over the stimulus configurations, or the reinforcing qualities, of in vivo situations. In addition, there is little chance of directly observing the assigned tasks. Moreover, the number of times a behavior can be practiced cannot be directly controlled.

Nonetheless, in vivo techniques are gaining favor rapidly, despite this lack of control. Intuitively, practicing desired behaviors in actual situations would seem to be "closer" to real life and hence better generalized:

- When charges of sexual abuse were brought against a 42-year-old elementary school teacher, he admitted to a string of molestations occurring over a number of years. He was immediately suspended from his job and later barred from teaching in the public schools. Following protracted suits, he won the right to teach in a private school, but only at levels above the eighth grade. However, the private school where he was hired also contained children from kindergarten through the eighth grade. Among other therapies, he was asked to walk past the classrooms containing these younger children and use relaxation to block any sexual arousal that occurred. This began with the classrooms of older children and progressed to grades one, two, and three, his most difficult age groups. Finally, he was asked to sit in on some of these classes and supervise outdoor recreation, but always under an administrator's watchful eye. Again, he was asked to use relaxation to block any sexual response. He reported an absence of sexual arousal to this age group during the year of such practice.

In this patient, sexual arousal was described as a "tension," and relaxation was helpful in substituting an opposite state. In some ways, this parallels the therapeutic use of opposite affective states; anger, for example, might be fostered to combat depression. This patient's circumstances helped dictate the use of in vivo conditioning and probably contributed to the efficacy of the techniques employed.

Along with enhanced generalization, in vivo techniques offer the possibility of greater reinforcement as well.

- A 16-year-old voyeur had acquired a nightly habit of prowling his neighborhood, looking for sexually exciting scenes through windows and patio doors. He had never dated and had avoided most sexual contact with girls, yet he demonstrated no sexual arousal to boys or men. Masturbation fantasies were adult heterosexual, but, frequently, watching was preferred to participating. Following relaxation training, he was given assignments to approach girls his own age, first with task-oriented nonsexual comments such as help on an assignment. Gradually, he was asked to increase the social nature of his approaches such as giving a compliment to a girl or, finally, asking for a date. On his second approach, however, a girl he admired actually asked *him* to take her out. The value of that single event seemed sufficient to enhance his self-esteem and markedly accelerated his approaches to girls in many stimulus settings.

The real-life situations that in vivo techniques involve generate greater risks and fears, but the benefits can be enormous, as the above example shows. In addition, these techniques offer the advantage of directly sharpening social skills without the distancing or distorting effects that imagery can cause. Although there is some loss of control with their use, there is also a certainty that, if carried out, conditioning is occurring directly, without intermediary cognitive steps.

Moreover, in vivo conditioning involves active rather than passive modes of behavior change. If it is valuable to involve the patient to a greater extent in his own therapy, the more active techniques may be preferable.

In actual clinical practice today, in vivo and in vitro techniques are often combined.

- A 30-year-old bank teller was arrested for masturbating in his car while watching co-eds practicing soccer at a local university. Recently divorced, he was frightened to approach women socially, fearing they would somehow learn of his inappropriate sexual behavior. Following relaxation training, he was asked to imagine a series of heterosocial settings and interactions that were increasingly difficult for him. Once each scene had been practiced for several weeks, he was asked to actually put it into practice using relaxation to help him. Within several months, he reported little anxiety in such situations and was actively dating his future wife.

Thus imaginal procedures can flow into real-life ones as the patient progresses. This combination allows treatment to be more flexible, and, with each session, estimates of anxiety and progress can be used in a dialogue with the patient in considering when to advance in therapy step by step.

Success Imagery

A technique related to, and partially overlapping, desensitization can be variously termed *success imagery* or *positive suggestion*. It relies heavily upon relaxation and imagery skills.

- A 22-year-old college drama student complained of ego-dystonic homosexuality with only minimal sexual arousal to females. Along with aversive imagery techniques, he was given relaxation training and then asked to imagine, during relaxation, a picnic with the most attractive woman he could visualize. The therapist set the scene: "You are in a beautiful meadow with a stream coursing through it. Wildflowers are everywhere. It's a beautiful day and the girl is laughing quietly with you. She really sparkles. She likes you. You lie together in the meadow, breathing the fresh mountain air and holding each other, just enjoying her touch and the smells and the sounds of the meadow and the brook, very close to her and very happy." Similar scenes were presented with increasing sexual content. The scene presentations were believed to play an integral role in increasing sexual attraction to women.

It should be clear that this "success imagery" is very close to desensitization. However, its suggestive content is stronger, and no attempt is made to compose a hierarchy of scenes. In addition, it is based not on overcoming fears as much as presenting the *distinct possibility* of a positive outcome.

- Referred by his probation officer for therapy, a 42-year-old homosexual pedophile with an extensive history of molestations and resultant incarcerations reported no interest in women of any age but a faint attraction to adult males. He chose to attempt an increase in arousal to men rather then a complete switch to arousal to women. In association with electric shock and olfactory aversion techniques, he was asked, under relaxation, to imagine increasingly sexual interactions with adult males. Following treatment with these combined techniques, he felt comfortable enough to frequent homosexual bars, at first with his therapist, then by himself. He began to participate in homosexual organizations, met a partner at these meetings, and has had no residual sexual attraction to boys.

These examples demonstrate that success imagery, like desensitization, forms part of a treatment plan but is rarely expected to produce the abolition of deviant sexual arousal by itself. From these examples, it can be seen that success imagery can be distinguished from desensitization not only by the presentation of the likelihood of success but also by the *absence of a target fear*. The man trying to increase his arousal to adult men as opposed to young boys does not fear men but only wishes to become more aroused by them.

Success imagery is actually targeted at increasing positive sexual and social approach behaviors rather than deconditioning maladaptive sexual approach disorders. (Compare with social skills training, discussed in Chapter 7.) Along with desensitization, it nonetheless deserves a wider acceptance in practice. Both techniques have without doubt helped a number of offenders to experience greater comfort and pleasure in appropriate social and sexual relationships.

Orgasmic Conditioning

It is likely that orgasm and the acts leading to it constitute one of the most potent reinforcing events in human experience. In the search for powerful therapeutic techniques to overcome deviant sexual arousal, appropriate sexual arousal with masturbation and orgasm should be used. In Chapter 4, orgasmic reconditioning techniques were discussed. Masturbation and climax can also be used to directly stimulate and reinforce appropriate heterosexual urges and fantasies. In theory, an individual who masturbates exclusively to heterosexual fantasies cannot or should not experience any sexual urges other than normal ones (Bem, 1972). From this theoretical stance, it could be logically assumed that, if a patient has already masturbated occasionally to homosexual fantasies (as an example), but more often to normal heterosexual ones, his homosexuality can be reduced or eliminated by masturbating solely to heterosexual themes (McGonaghy, 1971).

In practice, this does not, unfortunately, always occur.

- Following his family's increasing awareness that a 52-year-old jeweler was molesting his two young nieces, he applied for treatment prior to any legal charges. His masturbation fantasies consisted of three types:

(1) fondling young girls' genitals while they uttered certain words of profanity;
(2) performing cunnilingus on young girls; and
(3) participating in consenting heterosexual activities with adult women.

   The patient was first asked to eliminate the weaker pedophiliac fantasy, the second one; following success at this over a period of one month, during masturbation he was next asked to eliminate the first fantasy while increasing the third fantasy. By the end of another month, he reported not only the ability to eliminate all fantasies involving young girls during masturbation but a marked decrease in urges to molest young girls as well. In addition, he reported an enhanced ability to become aroused by adult heterosexual scenes and a greater real-life interest in adult women. However, plethysmograph recordings did not reflect these self-reports. Only following the institution of aversive conditioning techniques did the plethysmograph begin to show a reduction in deviant sexual arousal.

Successful cases, however, are not difficult to discover.

- A 37-year-old, unemployed, married bricklayer was accused of two rapes during a two-month period yet was allowed access to outpatient treatment from a work-release setting. He gave a history of masturbating to sexually aggressive fantasies approximately 75% of the time with the remaining percentage devoted to heterosexual fantasies of consenting adults. Aggressive fantasies consisted of tying up women, shaving their heads and pubic areas, and forcing them to commit fellatio on him. He was simply asked to gradually (over a period of two months) reduce the percentage of masturbation to these rape and bondage fantasies and increase the percentage of consenting heterosexual adult fantasies, focusing particularly on mutual pleasure. By two months, he reported an 80% reduction in aggressive fantasies and a concomitant increase in normal fantasies, an estimate supported by the plethysmograph measurements.

The "orgasmic conditioning" in this last case seemed so essential and obvious to almost be considered an adventitial effect. Nonetheless, a recent report from a large ongoing study of treatment for aggressive sexuality is encouraging (Abel, 1984). This technique deserves further study, if only for its simplicity. In a field expanding as rapidly as that of the treatment of the sexual offender, techniques that are easily, conveniently, and economically employed should be explored with vigor.

Moreover, such techniques emphasize the importance of fantasies in the building and maintaining of sexual urges and behaviors. It is often fantasy that initiates sexual activity and fantasy that accompanies genital stimulation with mounting sexual tension, followed by the pleasure of release. Fantasies at the time of this release are often so intricately associated with orgasm that they may be not only stereotyped but obligatory as well. On no account should such important cognitions be ignored. Fantasies involving appropriate heterosexual behavior should be associated as often as possible with orgasm.

It is important, however, to avoid several pitfalls common in such work. If a patient is encouraged to masturbate "often" to heterosexual fantasies, he might attempt such masturbation enough to actually be performing masturbatory satiation and hence begin to associate heterosexual fantasies with low, rather than high, arousal. In addition, the therapist has no direct access to these fantasy techniques and must rely upon the patient's accuracy and honesty in reporting homework completed and levels of arousal attained. By adding masturbation tape recordings, however, as described in Chapter 4, some scrutiny of this work can occur.

Despite these caveats, the orgasmic conditioning technique cannot be overlooked. Within a program of positive and aversive conditioning techniques, it can form a convenient, effective, and inexpensive addition to the therapeutic arsenal.

Positive Olfactory Conditioning

Although a variety of aversion techniques have become familiar to many therapists treating the sexual offender, classical conditioning using positive stimuli remains a largely uncharted province. From a theoretic point of view, it could be as effective to increase desirable behaviors with pleasant stimuli as to diminish undesirable ones with unpleasant stimuli. From a pragmatic point of view, however, several obstacles present themselves when exploring the use of such stimuli.

One problem is a lack of data on the value of positive stimuli in the treatment of the sexual offender. This does not indicate that negative data exist, only that no data are at hand thus far. Also, clinical experience, so extensive in the use of aversive stimuli, is meager as yet in the use of pleasant ones. There is also an impression, yet unverified, that positively reinforcing stimuli are more variable, idiosyncratic, and difficult to apply than aversive stimuli.

The sole "positive" stimulus for which a literature exists is the cessation of an aversive stimulus. Studies have demonstrated that "shock-off" or "shock-prevented" situations ("anticipatory avoidance") are effective in the treatment of homosexuality to some extent (Abel, Lewis, & Clancy, 1970; MacCulloch & Feldman, 1967; MacCulloch, Waddington, & Sanbrook, 1978), although large reports are lacking. Such escape or avoidance studies do not actually use a discrete positive stimulus. Moreover, therapeutic effect can only be changed by varying the power of the negative stimulus rather than by changing any characteristics of the positive one.

Aside from electric shock, the chief aversive stimulus in the treatment of the sexual offender has been a foul odor. While there is no known positive electric stimulus (except perhaps a direct stimulation of primary reinforcing centers in the brain), pleasant odors are not unknown. In some mammalian species, pheromones, or sexually exciting odors emitted by a female animal, represent the chief or only known stimulus to initiate male sexual interest and behavior (Berlin & Coyle, 1981). Though this does not appear to be true in primates, the case has not been studied widely. It is possible, though unlikely, that subliminal odors directly excite central nervous system sites, thereby eliciting sexual arousal.

With the use of odor-assisted aversion, cessation of foul odor is a positive stimulus, but direct conditioning to a patient's favorite odors, delivered through a pump-activated reservoir, can also occur. Such examples as cedar needles, roses, and cologne have been employed in this fashion.

Most subjects report certain odors as pleasant; others as chemically irritating, such as ammonia or hydrogen sulfide; and others as foul, such as rotting tissue, mold, mildew, feces, or vomitus. Of interest is the relative dearth of neutral odors; even odors occasionally encountered, such as newly mown grass, seem to carry some affective valence. Because equipment to produce and deliver odors is available within a number of centers treating the sexual offender (Nadelson,

Nothan, Zackson, & Gornick, 1982), some experience with positive conditioning using pleasant odors has accumulated.

- An elderly attendant at a local amusement park spent increasing amounts of time watching children roller-skating at the rink where he worked. He began to give "free lessons" in skating to some of the young girls and to give them lessons in a "hands-on" fashion, progressing to frank sexual touching. In obtaining his history, it was learned that he especially enjoyed certain odors, some of which were associated with the amusement park, such as popcorn and the smell of the grease used on the equipment. These odors were produced in the treatment laboratory using the original ingredients and presented via an odor reservoir and pump through a nasal cannula, as described in Chapter 3 and Appendix D. These pleasant odors were presented in association with escaping or avoiding sexual activity with young girls and, eventually, with images of appropriate heterosexual activity. Such olfactory conditioning was believed to achieve the major part of his persisting improvement in sexual orientation during a follow-up period of seven years to date.

The odors that prove pleasing to many individuals can be shared as well as idiosyncratic and can usually be reproduced in the treatment setting. These odors can include food and plant materials. Equipment to present such odors need not be elaborate.[1] Hopefully, further experimentation can occur and experience gained in the application of positive olfactory conditioning may one day equal that of the aversive conditioning techniques already in force.

Amyl Nitrate Enhancement

Aside from the use of pleasant odors, positive olfactory conditioning can also employ substances that directly enhance sexual feeling. Evidence from the animal literature indicates a direct effect of pheromones, which travel directly from the nasal mucosa to forebrain areas, exciting the male animal into sexual activity (Miller, 1980). Although, as noted above, no comparable literature exists for humans, anecdotal reports do indicate that certain street drugs increase libido in males and females alike.

- A 23-year-old dental student was arrested on campus for sexually assaulting a female student. In giving a history, he mentioned some experiences with amyl nitrate ("laughing gas") of a recreational nature. As a dental student, he enjoyed easy access to the substance. He recalled that he experienced enhanced sexual desire when under the influence of the gas, an experience shared by many of its users. In olfactory conditioning, ampules of amyl nitrate were crushed into an odor reservoir and delivered via a nasal cannula in association with escape from sexually aggressive scenes and with entry into heterosexual scenes. The patient indicated that the addition of the gas to the standard olfactory aversion technique was an important factor in producing long-lasting improvement.

- A 46-year-old ego-dystonic adult homosexual elected to change his orientation to heterosexual after his wife learned of his homosexual activities. He experienced less sexual pleasure with women than men. In addition to odor aversion, he was presented with slides, videotapes, and movies of sexual activity with women, accompanied by descriptions of heterosexual activity and associated with amyl nitrate, presented by crushing two ampules into an odor reservoir and pumping the vapors through a nasal cannula attached to the patient's nostrils. The patient experienced a sexual "rush," which enhanced plethysmographic and sexual arousal to females.

With the current state of research in this area, there is no way to be sure of the contribution amyl nitrate has made to the elimination of deviant sexual arousal or the increase in appropriate arousal in individual cases. As a discernible odor, however, it is usually undetectable and hence its effect, if any, is probably not due to perceptual processes as with the scent of a favorite food or flower. This vapor may have a stimulating effect on the brain's sexual centers, particularly those involving the olfactory tracts just anterior to the limbic system, an area thought to be involved with the perception of pleasure in the initiation of sexual responses. Certainly, these anecdotal observations beg for experimental verification. If such a direct stimulating effect exists, can certain odors, tastes, or other stimuli directly condition or decondition sexual preferences? Can and should compounds be not only identified but manufactured? Will such substances be harmful in any way? These questions have, as yet, barely been considered but may be important in future research on the most effective and safest methods of treatment for the sexual offender.

Summary

Positive respondent conditioning techniques are becoming increasingly important in the treatment of the sexual offender. They have clearly been helpful in a number of cases and offer therapy under more pleasant conditions than those surrounding aversive conditioning. Care must be taken, however, to accurately identify for whom therapy is aversive or pleasant. It may be that aversive conditioning is as unpleasant for the therapist as for the patient, but this cannot determine what techniques need to be used. In this sense, however, the aversiveness of therapy is important to consider: If patient compliance is proven to be enhanced through the use of positive conditioning, especially with homework assignments, these techniques will have earned an important place in the treatment of the sexual offender. Larger and better controlled studies will be necessary, however, before these methods can be as widely applied as are the aversive conditioning techniques. There is little doubt that such studies will be forthcoming.

Note

1. For information, contact MECTA Corporation, 7015 McEwan Road, Lake Oswego, Oregon 97035.

6

Operant Conditioning
Techniques

Although operant conditioning techniques have been applied to behavioral problems almost as long as have respondent techniques (Thorndike, 1935), their literature, and, consequently, their use in the treatment of sexual offenders, has been almost completely neglected. Perhaps this neglect stems from a concept of sexual behavior as *respondent* to a constellation of unconditioned and conditioned stimuli. Certainly, the importance of innate stimuli in eliciting sexual response has an honored position in the behavioral literature of animal and human sexuality: Odors, sights, and sounds are powerful initiators and modifiers of sexual behavior.

However, there is no reason to suppose that there is an *intrinsic* superiority of respondent conditioning over operant conditioning in diminishing undesirable behaviors or increasing desirable ones.

- When police investigated reports that a 27-year-old automobile mechanic was exposing himself to young girls in his apartment complex, they discovered that he had an extensive history of similar behavior in three neighboring states over a period of 13 years. Odor aversion was producing a sluggish improvement when the therapist introduced the idea of a graph of self-reports of overt and covert exhibitionist behaviors and penile plethysmograph results weekly. One copy of the graph was to be placed on the patient's refrigerator and another over the therapist's desk. The patient then showed a more rapid recovery, and he expressed the belief that the graph spurred him on, noting, "It helped to see the results and I was proud of the improvement."

- A 45-year-old man with a long history of molesting young boys insisted he could not use slides and movies or pictures of pornographic material or even listen to sexual scenes "for religious reasons." He enjoyed just talking with his therapist instead. A compromise was proposed: He was given five minutes of talking time for every five minutes he agreed to view pornographic material. Therapy progressed more rapidly and in a less contentious manner thereafter.

The principles of operant conditioning seem so self-evident as to appear trivial. Nonetheless, significant changes in problematic and well-entrenched symptoms have yielded to operant conditioning techniques in a variety of areas. The lack of rigorous studies or even anecdotal reports should not prevent an application of these methods to clinical problems of sexual abuse.

In a sense, operant techniques have already been applied to the treatment of the sexual offender, as they are an inseparable element of several respondent techniques. In aversive paradigms, such as aversive imagery, they are incorporated in several ways. The therapist responds with positive social reinforcers such as praise when the patient completes a homework assignment or demonstrates improved sexual control in plethysmographic biofeedback. In addition, the escape from a deviant sexual scene during assisted covert sensitization is associated with fresh air or pleasant odors, thus reinforcing operant behavior (such as leaving the deviant situation) with an unconditioned stimulus.

However, there are ways to use operant techniques by themselves in addition to employing them as an aid to other methods.

Positive Conditioning Techniques

The several examples given above involve the use of positive reinforcement. However, it occurs almost as an integrated part of the respondent techniques described rather than as a planned approach on its own. There is no reason that such techniques cannot be applied in an overall plan for a patient.

- An elderly heterosexual pedophile was making tedious progress with aversive conditioning. He spoke with great emotional depth, however, about missing his family. An arrangement was established with his probation officer: He could earn increasing time at home for decreases in his plethysmograph readings. Progress was appreciably more rapid thereafter.

Thus, if positive reinforcement is to be used, it is also crucial to examine what stimuli are reinforcing for the individual patient.

Many examples of positive reinforcement contain an element of negative reinforcement as well. It is reasonable to suppose that the withholding of positive reinforcement functions as a negative reinforcer just as the giving of it functions as a positive one. Although this difference is largely semantic, it is best to present a treatment plan in a positive rather than a negative manner. An analogy from outside the sexual abuse literature might help demonstrate the differences:

- An 11-year-old boy is told he must complete all his homework each day or else he will not be allowed to watch TV that evening.
  The same boy is told that he can earn the privilege of watching TV each evening if he completes all of his homework that day.

The procedure in both cases is the same, but the manner of presentation is different. A positive set, or expectation of reward, is generated in the second example, a negative one of fear of punishment in the first (Meichenbaum & Turk, 1976). The positive set confers two advantages:

(1) It is usually more effective.
(2) It casts the parent or therapist in the role of a provider of reward rather than a purveyor of punishment.

Also, individualized programs of reward should be employed. Most helpful have been monetary reinforcers, especially money deducted from the patient's bill for therapy. Deductions can be enacted

for reductions in plethysmograph levels, but, at times, positive reinforcement may be necessary on a more immediate basis.

- When a positive reinforcement system was established for a 33-year-
  old transvestite in which decreases in his plethysmograph levels were
  rewarded with reductions in his bill, the expected boost in the efficacy
  of treatment did not occur. Instead, a reduction in his fee was made
  contingent upon homework sessions (associating garments with foul
  odors) under his wife's immediate supervision. She kept a record of
  the reduced fees where he could see it daily. More rapid progress, as
  validated by plethysmograph recordings, occurred upon institution of
  this approach.

Another positive reinforcer especially helpful in this area is the use
of increasing amounts of time with the therapist, especially if it is
free. Even so, a number of offenders have responded to this positive
reinforcer even when they had to pay for it. At times, the therapist
may be able to arrange special circumstances and particular rewards
for an offender in this regard.

- The therapist spent extra unbilled time with the wife of an offender in
  some of his sessions and purposely detailed to her the patient's successes in treatment. The patient appeared to be much more responsive
  to such praise in her presence than when it occurred in private sessions.
- An adolescent offender, with the help of his therapist, established a
  "luxury fund" of bonus money added to his regular allowance for
  completing homework assignments and for decreases in his
  plethysmograph readings. He could save or spend this sum for any
  reasonable article he wished.
- During a meeting with an offender and his corrections officer, the
  therapist was able to arrange a system wherein the patient would earn
  one day off his work-release center sentence for every 2% reduction in
  his plethysmograph weekly.

These programs, while sometimes difficult to establish, may have
an advantageous side effect: They can change what is essentially a
negative experience in therapy into a positive one. Unexpected rewards come to be associated with treatment, and therapy can be
viewed not only as an experience to endure but, perhaps, an interesting and challenging one as well.

In addition, these positively reinforcing additions to treatment tend to more actively involve the patient in his own therapeutic program. The offender quite often is a passive recipient of therapy, especially if aversive conditioning techniques are used exclusively. Not only is much of the treatment session devoted to aversive stimulation but, within it, the patient has little control over the provision of conditioned and unconditioned stimuli. As the therapist adds these positively reinforcing techniques, he is including the patient in the discussion of what is positively reinforcing to him. The patient and therapist cooperate to devise a program of reinforcement. The patient may thus not only accelerate his rate of improvement but may enhance his investment in treatment as well.

In an effort to deliver positive reinforcers in the most effective manner, the therapist may wish to use a positive reinforcement schedule demonstrated, thus far, to be the most resistant to extinction: the variable ratio schedule (Ferster & Skinner, 1957).

- The therapist for a middle-aged heterosexual pedophile agreed with the patient that his fee for each session of therapy would be reduced by 10% for each 5% reduction in the plethysmograph readings for that session. Following six sessions, the patient was arrested on a charge stemming from a sexual incident with a young girl that had occurred prior to the initiation of therapy. Following a brief incarceration, he was again referred for treatment. During this second period, his bill was again reduced by 10% for decreases in plethysmograph readings, but it was accomplished randomly, according to whether a number chosen from a random numbers list was even or odd. Plethysmograph readings declined rapidly and, following active treatment and through six years of follow-up, no reoffense occurred.

In this example, it is, of course, uncertain whether the practice effect, due to the greater number of treatment sessions, or the inhibition a second arrest might have caused were additional variables. With experience, it has seemed, however, that variable ratio schedules of positive reinforcement have been at least equal to regular reinforcement schedules in effectiveness and superior in maintaining a good response during follow-up. Only large-scale controlled group research can shed any objective light on this issue, however.

Apart from these techniques of positive reinforcement, there is a simple positive reinforcement procedure not to be overlooked: direct social reinforcement such as praise by the therapist for gains made.

Although such praise may be most effective in front of peers or relatives, it should not be neglected in any session, even if no one else is present. The effect of the therapist's approval and congratulations can be greater than imagined.

- In observations and audiotapes of a particular therapist's treatment sessions with a variety of offenders, negative and neutral statements outnumbered positive ones five to one. When given this feedback, the therapist was able to reverse this ratio; his efficacy, although not strictly measured, appeared to improve.

Thus it is not only the patient's actions that must be monitored and discussed within the session but the therapist's behavior as well. It has proven most helpful to videotape some sessions or, alternatively, to observe sessions through a one-way mirror, with the patient's consent, to provide therapists with timely feedback.

Negative Conditioning Techniques

If positive conditioning methods are rarely mentioned in the literature, the use of negative conditioning in an operant sense is reported on even less. Currently, only single- or multiple-case studies exist, most involving children or the intellectually handicapped (Reid, Tombaugh, & Heunel, 1981; Richmond & Bell, 1983).

- A 14-year-old deaf and retarded youth had forced sexual relations upon a number of younger boys in the dormitory of the state School for the Deaf. He was to be evicted, though no comparable facility existed in the area and he and his parents strongly hoped he could stay in the school. A diagram was, therefore, constructed in which molesting behaviors were colored in as pieces of a pie. When the entire pie was colored in, he would have to be expelled. Such graphic visual information appeared to have a perceptible and beneficial effect on his behavior during and following his therapy.

It is difficult, with the current state of knowledge, to predict whether any patient will respond better to positive as opposed to negative conditioning. For example, in the above case, the patient could have been told that every day that passed without molesting behavior would earn him points that were required to purchase more time in the school. However, to reward the passage of time without an operant response is often difficult. In practice, trial and error with these operant techniques inevitably occur.

As with positive conditioning techniques, the therapist's own behavior in each session can be used as a method of positively and negatively responding to a variety of behaviors. At times, a therapist can ignore certain verbal behaviors while differentially paying attention to others. Often, a therapist can signal, in an unobtrusive fashion, interest, enthusiasm, even pleasant surprise, while manifesting indifference to negative material. The therapist's time and attention are often powerful stimuli to be used in extending the helpful effects of therapy.

- Under observation, a therapist practiced increasing his verbal response latencies to negative information from a patient, such as complaints about therapy and about his probation officer. Conversely, the therapist reduced his latencies and brightened his countenance when the patient described successful efforts to complete assignments or when he made positive comments about results of therapy. These techniques increased trust and rapport, seen as essential in working with this offender, who chronically denied any deviant sexual arousal despite plethysmographic evidence to the contrary.

This example demonstrates a potential problem with the use of negatively reinforcing techniques in working with offenders: They can diminish the cooperation of the patient. Hence negative methods are often combined with positive ones to prevent the development of a polarized situation in which the offender must constantly defend himself. For this reason, operant conditioning using negative stimuli should often be subtle and understated, if at all possible, while positive techniques should be made more obvious. Slight changes in the therapist's demeanor can be used to shift attention from negative to positive statements. At the same time, praise, financial reinforcers, and graphs can be used to more obviously focus on positive behaviors.

In any discussion of negative operant conditioning techniques, the distinction should be drawn between such methods as delaying latencies and ignoring certain material and the aversive respondent techniques more fully described in Chapter 3. Those techniques can be thought of as punishing a response, but they more often deliver the aversive stimulus in association with a deviant sexual stimulus such as a slide, movie, picture, or story related to the deviant sexual arousal, *regardless of the response*. In these classical aversive conditioning paradigms, the offender receives foul odor or shock whether or not he demonstrates arousal on the plethysmograph. In fact, more aversive sessions are more typically run without the plethysmograph than with it, as the instrument itself may inhibit arousal (Abel, Blanchard, Murphy, Becker, & Djenderedjian, 1981; Freund, Char, & Coulthard, 1979; Harbison, Quenn, & McAllister, 1970).

However, the patient can play a more active role in therapy with an avoidance technique.

- A 23-year-old restaurant manager was arrested for voyeurism in his own neighborhood. In the initial phases of treatment, all stories and slides depicting voyeurism were followed by electric shock, randomly interspersed with foul odor. Following a reduction in plethysmograph levels and in subjectively reported feelings of arousal, the patient was presented with an aversive stimulus in association with voyeuristic stories and slides but could turn off the sexual stimulus, and hence avoid the aversive stimulus, by depressing a signal button connected to the therapist's console. At first, the aversive stimulus was delivered only if the patient failed to turn off the deviant sexual stimulus within five seconds of its presentation. Later in treatment, the patient was required to turn off the deviant stimulus within one second to avoid shock.

Work completed in such "anticipatory avoidance" situations documents the effectiveness of this technique (Abel, Lewis, & Clancy, 1970; MacCulloch & Feldman, 1967), though there are dissenting opinions (James, Orwin, & Turner, 1972; Thorpe, 1972). Such techniques fall midway between positive and negative conditioning paradigms: The patient progresses through a passive respondent conditioning phase, then through combination phases, to arrive at a more active operant conditioning phase. Perhaps one of the most beneficial techniques in such progression is a message to the patient that he is an active participant in his own therapy and can control his progress therein, at least to a certain extent.

Summary

The positive and negative operant conditioning techniques are in their developmental phase. Case reports and anecdotes have been presented, but there are no group results or controlled comparisons. However, it seems likely that such techniques can contribute to the overall effectiveness of a combined treatment approach. The history of operant techniques in psychology demonstrates that they are most often applied to a population already under some environmental control: children and adolescents, the intellectually handicapped, and the chronically psychotic. Offenders are often under probationary control, however, and there is no inherent reason why such methods could not be employed in the treatment of sexual offenders at several levels:

(1) within a controlled environment such as a prison, halfway house, or work-release center,

(2) within a partially controlled environment such as a closely supervised probationary period in which the offender might have to report to his probation officer every weekday, or

(3) within a partially controlled environment in which the offender would be supervised by a significant other.

The provision of positive and negative reinforcers in one form or another has been presented as an adjunctive technique rather then a central one. In most treatment programs, these techniques have only been added to the respondent conditioning methods described earlier. Although this may be a function of popularity rather than effectiveness, it nonetheless appears that these operant methods, in themselves, would be insufficient to completely eliminate deviant sexual arousal. Sexual behavior is now viewed as so powerfully a product of respondent conditioning to a variety of conditional and unconditional stimuli that the respondent conditioning techniques have been almost exclusively tested and reported in the literature. It will take strong evidence to convince the majority of therapists that operant conditioning alone can match the results of aversive respondent conditioning thus far.

7

Adjunctive Techniques

While the sexual offender is often discussed in the literature as if he possessed a standard personality type, clinical experience indicates that sexual offenders can be as diverse in personality patterns and behavior habits as many other large diagnostic groups. Just as there is possibly no all-encompassing single type of "criminal," alcoholic, or schizophrenic, there are no agreed upon or scientifically verifiable persistent traits or behavior patterns in the sexual offender (Bonheur & Rosner, 1980; Jason, Williams, Burton, & Rochat, 1982; Smith, 1980). It follows that no single inflexible treatment scheme can or should be applied in the treatment of all such offenders.

Thus, although there is evidence that behavioral methods are effective in treating sexual abuse, no safe treatment approach should be rejected if it offers a possibility of aiding therapy. If techniques derived from any school or philosophy are respected as helpful, and if these techniques make sense to apply and are safe in their application, the therapist is obligated to include them in the treatment plan—based, of course, on a reasonable estimate of their potential benefit and the costs involved in their use. While such an eclectic approach is doomed to confound treatment variables, thus obscuring the part each single technique plays in effecting improvement, in clinical practice there is an obligation to efficiently pursue the goal of rapid elimination of the diagnosed condition. Certainly, such a practice will not suffice for the researcher intent on examining the contribution a single technique offers to the patient. There is no question that such research is necessary and that it must be carried out under strictly controlled conditions so that clinicians can learn about differential effectiveness. The clinician must be aware of both the state of academic research and the available clinical reports and experiences of those treating sexual offenders day-by-day.

A number of ancillary techniques have been found helpful in the treatment of the sexual offender. Such techniques, with rare exceptions noted in the text, have been applied here and there, without a plan to examine their individual effectiveness. Many such techniques have been discussed in anecdotal fashion in the literature, and some have hardly been mentioned at all. Nonetheless, they have all been found useful when combined with the behavioral methods of treatment already discussed. Their help in this fashion has probably been supplementary rather than primary; patients often improve without the addition of such techniques. In the experience of many clinicians, such methods on their own have not yielded measurable improvement; thus frequency and plethysmograph data rarely show improvement with these techniques alone. They seem, however, to have enhanced the quality of the improvements seen with behavioral techniques, particularly in the area of positive social approach behaviors.

- A 15-year-old bright, but socially backward, youth had attacked two younger girls in a park near his home. Standard conditioning techniques such as assisted covert sensitization were helpful in decreasing deviant sexual arousal to aggressive sexuality, but he continued to manifest an awkward manner with girls his own age. Placement in a group of male and female adolescents gradually led to several successful dates with girls his own age.

The discussion that follows attempts to describe the application of adjunctive techniques, such as group therapy, to the sexual offender rather than to provide a detailed review of the history and literature regarding the techniques themselves. Scattered references, however, should provide access to more complete descriptions and reviews for those who are interested.

Trust Building

The first adjunctive technique to be discussed, trust building, can hardly be considered ancillary as it forms an important basis for all of the other approaches. Trust not only must be established in the early phases of treatment but must be *maintained* throughout the course of treatment as well. One approach to trust building is the therapist's nonjudgmental manner, especially in the initial sessions. The therapist generally first sees the sexual offender at a time when his self-esteem is low and his defenses high. The patient may well expect further interrogation or ridicule during his early sessions, especially when he has to reveal sexual information to a stranger. It is imperative that the therapist impart a feeling of acceptance and a message that the patient is not inherently of low worth because of one set of behaviors. Focusing on the patient's assets and accomplishments early in treatment has been helpful in this regard.

- When a member of the town council of a small community was accused of molesting a young stepdaughter, the news was prominently displayed in the local newspaper. Before that, some progress in treatment had been made, but thereafter the patient became disconsolate and considered leaving his home of many years. The therapist asked him to compile lists of positive traits and achievements as well as to list things he had accomplished at the end of each day. In focusing on positive qualities and deeds, the patient developed not only an enhanced self-esteem but a closer bond with the therapist as well. He ultimately decided to remain within his community and was supported in doing so by most of its members.

Other techniques designed not only to increase self-esteem but to build trust include requiring the patient to say something good about himself for each negative self-statement and assigning him volunteer functions such as participating in a charitable organization's activities or helping in a church or community action program.

Trust building, however, need not be confined to self-esteem measures. Trust is usually built slowly by the therapist's demonstration of concern for the patient. While the therapist cannot condone the sexually offending behavior, he or she can acknowledge positive traits and behaviors and positively reinforce the patient's attempts to change. Particularly helpful have been the active listening skills already elucidated in the counseling literature (Heimberg, Madsen, Montgomery, & McNabb, 1980). The practice of paraphrasing and summarizing demonstrates the therapist's attention to the patient's messages rather than a preoccupation only with what the therapist considers important. Behavioral observations and perception checks show the therapist's concern about nonverbal behaviors. The therapist also needs to be aware of potential accusatory statements and phrase any observations or directions in a nonaccusatory fashion.

Discussions with the patient's relatives and friends as well as with his attorney or probation officer can also demonstrate concern. Such contact should be fully revealed to the patient. At times, sessions with wives, girlfriends, or parents can be most valuable in providing additional information. It is often best to speak with these individuals without the patient present to provide the freest atmosphere for information exchange. However, if private sessions occur, the patient needs to know that this is to facilitate information sharing rather than to foster secrets between family, friends, and the therapist. The judicious combination of these techniques, usually already used by counselors in a variety of subspecialties, should greatly assist information collection, ease the burden of the patient and his family in troubling times, and prepare the way for what could otherwise become a rocky road of treatment if there were no basis of trust in the therapist-patient relationship.

Social Skills Training

To accompany some of the positive conditioning techniques described in Chapter 6, practice or rehearsal of socially appropriate behaviors has often been of great benefits.

- In the midst of conditioning therapy for a young heterosexual pedophile, the patient was asked to initiate three conversations with girls his own age every two weeks. When this task proved too difficult, the therapist spent a five-minute portion of each session in modeling the appropriate initiation of verbal contact with girls and having the patient mirror this behavior. The patient was able to feel increasingly comfortable with such behaviors, practicing, then putting into practice, a variety of new behaviors: recounting interesting anecdotes; discussing current events, books read, and movies seen; and speaking about shared experiences, such as weather, traffic conditions, and news events. As sexual arousal was decreasing in response to heterosexual pedophiliac scenes, the patient reported decreasing tension and increasing success in maintaining female relationships.

• A 37-year-old office worker had exposed himself to young girls for a number of years. While assisted covert sensitization and aversive behavior rehearsal were effective in eliminating deviant sexual arousal, he remained shy and introspective and contemplated entering an adult homosexual life-style. Before implementing that decision, he was asked to construct a hierarchy of social and sexual approaches to women. Ten minutes of each session were spent in reviewing his hierarchy and recording, under relaxation, new scenes from it. Following seven such sessions, the patient began dating a young woman and reported ambivalence about homosexuality. While still considering this option, he held open the possibility of fully accepting a heterosocial and heterosexual life-style.

These examples describe a number of techniques that can be employed to assist the patient in increasing heterosocial and heterosexual behaviors and thus to increase the chances of success in mutually consenting adult relationships. Such techniques can include the following:

(1) *Modeling*: Examples of effective interactions with women can be demonstrated to the patient by the therapist or viewed on videotape (Barlow, Reynolds, & Agras, 1973; Lewinsohn, Biglan, & Zeiss, 1976; Reckers & Vasni, 1977; Whitman & Quinsey, 1981).

(2) *Behavior Rehearsal*: The therapist can introduce the practice of initiating and maintaining conversations and relationships using role-playing techniques (Curran, 1977; Twentyman, Boland, & McFall, 1981). A female therapist introduced for assistance in this area has been most helpful.

(3) *Desensitization* (Cooper, 1963; Gray, 1970):

   (a) *In vitro*: Relaxation practice can be followed by imagery of specific social and occasionally sexual situations (Barlow, Abel, Blanchard, Bristow, & Young, 1977; Conger & Farrell, 1981; Lipton & Nelson, 1980; McFall, 1982; Twentyman, Boland, & McFall, 1981). Two reports have specifically applied these techniques to the sexual offender with some benefit (Brownell, Hayes, & Barlow, 1977; James, 1978).

   (b) *In vivo*: The use of relaxation in real-life situations can be helpful as well. Chapter 5 presents a number of examples.

These same techniques can be applied to another goal, although one likely to be controversial: mutually consenting adult homosexual relationships:

- When a 45-year-old homosexual pedophile presented for treatment after being placed on probation, he showed little enthusiasm for or positive response to attempts to turn his sexual orientation to adult heterosexuality. Following further trust building, the patient admitted he would rather try to increase his small sexual attraction to men, particularly those in the age range of 18 to 25. A careful program combining aversive conditioning to sexuality involving boys with a fading-in technique of positive conditioning to sexuality involving men (see Chapter 4) gradually yielded an increasing arousal to adult males (see Barlow & Agras, 1973). Following treatment, the patient met, and moved in with, a 23-year-old man and initiated a relatively long-lasting relationship with him.

Is it ethical to try to establish or strengthen homosexuality, even that involving two consenting adults? Is it even possible to construct a treatment scheme so precisely engineered as to decrease sexual responses to males up to 17, yet increase sexual responses to men over that age? The answers are possibly "yes" to both questions, but with some hesitations. Some case studies (Geary & Goldman, 1978; Hayes, Brownell, & Barlow, 1978) and a research report (Harbison, Quenn, & McAllister, 1970) demonstrate that quite specific sexual arousal patterns can be conditioned or deconditioned. However, although arousal to different types of stimuli can be precisely controlled, a differentiation according to age is probably more ambiguous. The homosexual pedophile can be treated to reduce arousal to young boys and increase arousal to women, but can a heterosexual pedophile be taught to differentiate girls 13 to 14 from those 15 to 17? Similarly, can any homosexual pedophile differentiate boys of 16 or 17 from those of the consenting range of 18 and above?

Clearly, further research is needed to answer such questions. However, given the current state of knowledge about the treatment of sexual offenders, it does appear likely that such age distinctions can be grossly, but not exactly, drawn. Thus it is safest, employing positive conditioning as an adjunctive technique, to err on the side of conservatism and draw the negative features of a deviant stimulus and the positive features of the nondeviant stimulus in sharp contrast, with recognition of a "gray zone" in between.

- A 32-year-old lumber mill operator was arrested after molesting two children of a friend: a boy, 13, and a girl, 16. While a variety of aversive techniques were used in the deconditioning of sexual response to children and adolescents of both genders, positive social approach behaviors were practiced with adults clearly over the age of 25 to reduce any ambiguity about the ages of individuals in the stimulus presentations.

Such ambiguity exists even with heterosexual adults in which a positive sexual arousal pattern can occasionally be seen with provocative material featuring girls of 13 to 17 who are well developed. However, it does appear *possible* to build in sexual responses to relatively narrowly defined age ranges or different gender groups.

The remaining question, that of ethics, cannot be answered or perhaps even addressed here. In practice, the patient, usually a homosexual pedophile, is asked to ponder the question of eventual sexual choice as trust is built. Every option can be explored while aversive conditioning is begun. Alternatives and consequences are reviewed, and the patient is encouraged to discuss these choices with family, friends and pastoral counselors, especially with an eye toward any residual guilt likely to occur. If the patient firmly decides upon an adult homosexual course, then the therapist can choose positive conditioning methods combined with the social skills training mentioned here.

Anxiety Reduction Techniques

Although it has been surmised that some offenders may experience an increase in deviant arousal when anxiety mounts (Abel & Becker, 1984; Jones & Frei, 1977), no empiric research has demonstrated this relationship. Nonetheless, it has occasionally proven helpful to incorporate stress-reduction techniques into an overall treatment program for the sexual offender.

- A 19-year-old student had repeatedly placed obscene telephone calls to co-eds on his college campus during the school year. He gave a history of increasing urges to do so, however, around examination periods or whenever important term papers were due. He believed that tension surrounding these events increased sexual arousal in general and, secondarily, increased urges to make obscene telephone calls. Along with standard conditioning techniques, a program of anxiety management training was initiated:

— daily practice of relaxation training with an audiotape
— use of relaxation in tense settings
— self-initiated "muscle inventory" daily to detect tension building early (Meichenbaum, 1974)
— desensitization to scenes of taking tests or preparing term papers (Wolpe, 1969)

Progress was rapidly made in reducing overall tension and specific school-related anxiety as well; such progress possibly contributed to the eventual elimination of urges to place obscene calls.

Such anxiety-reduction techniques as desensitization have been extensively described in the behavioral literature. Relaxation training, a starting point for many of these techniques, has usually already been taught to the offender for better visualization of scenes in aversive and positive conditioning. Thus it would be relatively simple to add these techniques if it appears they would be beneficial.

A more extensive technique, formally called *anxiety management training* (Goldfried & Tsier, 1974; Suim & Richardson, 1971), has proven helpful in several cases in which intensive work needed to be done to reduce anxiety.

• Progress in treatment had been slow for a middle-aged heterosexual pedophile when further analysis revealed that he was experiencing severe anxiety about being exposed to any aversive stimuli such as odor and electric shock. He was asked to practice at home imagining exposure to both stimuli for three minutes twice each day and to vividly experience the anxiety *without running from it*. He was instructed to heighten the anxiety at these times by immersing himself in it, imagining the most frightening aspects of odor and shock possible. For two minutes thereafter, he was instructed to lie down, breathe deeply, and practice deep muscle relaxation with pleasant imagery. Following three weeks of this practice, he was able to again participate in aversive conditioning without undue apprehension.

At first, such anxiety management training might appear to be a technique quite opposite to desensitization. However, both techniques share a common and perhaps crucial element in addressing anxiety: exposure to a feared stimulus. As with flooding or implosion

(Stampfl & Levis, 1968), anxiety management training forces the patient to experience the stimulus without escape, perhaps extinguishing the fear of response. The technique can also be viewed, perhaps more simply, as rehearsal of a new skill, that of reducing anxiety. It gives the individual practicing it some sense of control by being able to increase, then decrease, an unpleasant emotion.

Care must be taken, however, in employing such techniques, helpful though they may appear. Most offenders coming to treatment suffer anxiety as a result of being apprehended and identified. Moreover, many will have experienced tension secondary to guilty feelings, marital stress, or other concomitants of their inappropriate sexual behavior. Much time and energy could be devoted to general counseling or more specific anxiety-reduction techniques at the risk of ignoring the probable major source of the stress: the offending behaviors themselves. Hence anxiety reduction should be employed only in cases in which the tension itself prevents reasonable progression in treatment, in which anxiety is overwhelming, or in which there is evidence that stress increases the probability of deviant arousal.

Assertiveness Training

During the last decade and a half, assertiveness training has blossomed into a well-respected technique for a multitude of ills (Heimberg & Becker, 1981). Some clinicians believe it is used almost indiscriminately; its literature often fails to specify the conditions it addresses, thus buttressing that view.

Nonetheless, there remains a legitimate role for assertiveness training in the treatment of the sexual offender, and several reports mention its use specifically in such a population (Gilmour, McConaich, & DeRuiter, 1981; Langevin et al., 1979). Many offenders not only lack social skills in general but seem to be inordinately afraid of, and sensitive to, the effects their behavior has on others. Many are frightened at the thought of anger or rejection and conform their behavior to what they believe others desire. Some theorists believe that such subassertion fosters internal tensions that become subverted and emerge as inappropriate sexual behaviors, while others believe this is an intuitive leap not yet supported by objective data. Still, assertiveness training has appeared to be helpful to selected offenders.

- A 21-year-old voyeur was especially timid with adult females. Although aversive techniques were successful in eliminating voyeuristic behaviors, he continued to lack confidence in social situations and, if anything, became more introverted as therapy progressed. He was referred to a local assertiveness training group and, within several months, was dating an attractive woman and had asked for, and received, a raise at work.

Often, but not always, assertiveness training and social skills training overlap. A number of sexual offenders are quite polished socially but generate increasing frustration by trying to analyze what others want, then bend to an enormous extent to provide it. Such patients have usually fared best in group situations where they can receive consistent feedback from peers as well as therapists in learning to recognize overly submissive, or overly compliant behaviors (Gilmour, McConaich, & DeRuiter, 1981; Mathis, 1980).

When the individual is treated for subassertion outside of a group setting, techniques of modeling, psychodrama, and bibliotherapy have been particularly helpful. The patient can be asked to read one of the popular assertion books (Alberti & Emmons, 1975; Smith, 1981) and make notes on how it applies to him and how he can apply this information to his own life. In addition, the patient can be given assignments to practice turning down requests (even if he wants to honor them) and on disagreeing with popular opinions (even if he really agrees). The *experience* of receiving positive reinforcement (acknowledgment, validation, respect) can often be the first step toward increasing confidence and successful interpersonal relationships.

Environmental Change

The sexual offender acts out his offense under the control of guiding or discriminating stimuli. For most such patients, the offense requires the availability of a victim, the absence of sure detection (such as being at home alone with the victim), and patient variables such as the level of general sexual arousal at the time. Only in the extreme would an offender molest, expose, or the like regardless of these variables. It follows that, as the patient can exert some control over these variables, he can reduce the probability of future sexual offenses.

- To reduce the chances of exposing, a middle-aged bank teller called his wife at the end of each workday to report that he was coming home. She knew the exact time the trip would take; an inordinate delay represented the likelihood of an attempt to expose.

- Another exhibitionist exposed from his car to women passing by; he knew they could easily see him at the driver's wheel. He traded this vehicle for a heavy pickup truck whose cab was so high he could not be seen from the street.

- A 50-year-old elementary school teacher had a two-year history of fondling several girl students during class. He was allowed to retain his position, and some measure of self-respect as a teacher, by switching to a nearby boys' private school.

The awareness of environmental variables and controlling stimuli are more recently spoken of as the "deviant cycle" for offenders. Emotional reactions, such as frustration, anger, or sadness, are believed in some cases to initiate a chain of behaviors leading to sexual abuse. Probably environmental stimuli, such as being alone with a victim, and psychological stimuli, such as time elapsed since last orgasm, are just as often sufficient to begin the process of offending.

Once the chain is initiated, each step becomes the stimulus for the next, leading almost inevitably to the act of sexual offense. Interrupting the chain early in its course is usually easier than stopping it later on: It would be much more difficult for a pedophile to stop himself from molesting a youngster whom he already has undressed than to never have been alone with that youngster in the first place.

Environmental changes can be simple, such as taking a different route home, or more drastic, such as moving away from a neighborhood or family or even obtaining a divorce. Out of consideration to an offender, and often to his family as well, the least disruptive changes should be considered first. Often, however, changes are enforced on the offender, such as the often necessary separation from the victim. Much has been written about the wisdom of such changes, but it appears that neither overall support nor indictment of this practice can be found in the literature because of the lack of objective studies (Jones, 1982). Judicial thinking on this issue currently emphasizes safety with separation. The therapist will become involved as he or she is asked to render opinions about whether and when an offender is safe to return to his family, an especially delicate issue if the victim is also in residence. A further discussion of factors indicating safety or danger in allowing an offender to be at large or to return to his family is presented in Chapter 10.

Marital and Family Therapy

In the experience of most clinicians, it is a rare family that is not fractured by the occurrence of sexual abuse. At the very least, information should be obtained through significant others about the offender and the effect he has had on the household. The therapist can be of service to the courts and to the offender and his family by trying to understand and communicate the impact sexual abuse has had upon all family members.

Detailed explications of marital and family therapy techniques will not be offered here; helpful reviews have already appeared in the literature (Mayer, 1983). All family members should be allowed to develop their points of view in an unhurried atmosphere and to discuss their feelings about the offender and his offense. In conjoint sessions, it is helpful to end by having each member say something positive about all others. Communication and decision-making techniques have also proven helpful (Heimberg, Madsen, Montgomery, & McNabb, 1980). A particularly crucial time for family discussion is when the offender is being reintroduced into the home. Honest emotions must be sought, and care must be taken not to become too enthusiastic an advocate of the offender's views. The therapist can understandably lose objectivity in working very closely with an offender over a number of months.

Cognitive Therapy

Although within the past half decade more has been written about cognitive therapy than almost any other branch of psychotherapy (Wells, 1985), there remain no controlled studies about this form of therapy for the maladaptive sexual approach disorders. This deficit may stem from the availability and efficacy of other behavioral techniques and the need, felt by all those working with the sexual offender, to quickly and effectively stop dangerous behavior using time-tested techniques such as aversive conditioning. However, studies using these techniques in treating the sexual offender would be welcome as they may represent an untapped resource for innovative additions to therapy in this area.

- When aversive conditioning measures had reduced, but not eliminated, exposing in a 35-year-old bartender, the therapist recalled an actual scene in which a female victim stared at the offender directly and said, with appropriate disgust, "You're sick!" The patient experienced a decrease in sexual arousal and erection immediately. Thus he was asked to continue imagining exposing scenes but to automatically hear those words in his "mind's ear." All urges to expose ceased within one month of employing this technique.

This example, however, could be considered alternatively as a case of covert sensitization, though the cognitive element would seem paramount. Such confusion underscores ongoing debate in the literature regarding the purity of cognitive as opposed to behavioral elements (Ledwidge, 1979). With the current level of knowledge, it is difficult to separate these components. The cognitive element is more clear, however, in another example.

- A middle-aged business executive had been molesting his 14-year-old stepdaughter for five years. He believed that he exerted substantially more power and control in this sexual relationship than with his wife, the girl's mother, and the therapist agreed. Thus, when urges to molest occurred, he substituted the conscious thought message: "You are losing control by molesting this girl and you will be placed in prison." The patient reported that this message became "automatic" when the urges occurred, and he was free of such urges within six weeks. However, several aversive measures were being utilized at the same time.

This case demonstrates the difficulty in evaluating cognitive techniques in the treatment of the maladaptive sexual approach disorders. No studies have yet attempted to separately examine the cognitive and aversive conditioning elements. From a clinical perspective, however, there is probably value in extending our thinking about the ways in which cognitive therapy can be put to use in these disorders.

Table 7.1 *Examples of Negative Cognitions Associated with Deviant Sexual Arousal and Their Positive Counterparts*

Negative "Old Message"	Positive "New Message"
I am powerless to direct and control my sexual urges.	I have a choice to control my sexual urges.
I can escape detection if I am quick, careful, and cunning.	I will ultimately be apprehended and go to prison.
It won't hurt just to masturbate to deviant fantasies.	Deviant fantasy is what hurts me by keeping these urges alive.
I would never do anything to hurt someone.	Victims can be permanently damaged by what I am doing to them.
I can exert power and control through these deviant sexual acts.	I will lose power and control by being discovered and sent to prison.

Table 7.1 lists some potential negative "old messages" upon perceiving an urge to molest (or expose or the like) with appropriate positive "new messages" substituted.

Cognitive errors or thinking distortions have also been proposed as perpetuating, if not generating, deviant sexual behavior (Abel et al., 1989). For example, many pedophiles believe that, if the child shows curiosity about sexual matters, he or she is interested in pursuing sexual activity. Others believe that, if a child does not immediately and forcefully resist early sexual advances, he or she actually desired sexual activity. It has been difficult for these offenders to think that a child might be so frightened of or confused about an adult sexual advance that he or she can offer little resistance. Some offenders may also believe that a child can offer sexual consent despite the child's lack of experience and an adult perspective with which to do so. In addition, an offender can believe that no harm will result from his crime; this delusion can be fostered by observations that a victim's problems may not be obvious at first but will only develop in teenage or early adult years. Indeed, some offenders portray *themselves* as the victims of their own crimes rather than the perpetrators of them. Although much of what an offender says about these issues, especially at early evaluations, may be self-serving he may repeat stories often enough to eventually come to believe them. These cognitive distortions can quite clearly lead to a perpetuation of offending unless vigorously challenged. Such challenges are often best made within a group setting where other offenders can recognize distortions and confront them forcefully.

Correcting cognitive distortions has become an increasingly used technique in the treatment of the sexual offender. It cannot be promoted as a sufficient method, in itself, to eliminate deviant sexual arousal, but it is a powerful tool within a program of various techniques for the sexual offender. This obviously will not be the last word on the use of cognitive methods for the treatment of the sexual offender. It seems unlikely, however, that cognitive techniques, in themselves, will completely replace the aversive and positive conditioning methods. The sexual response and its associated fantasies seem to be so deeply rooted that cognitive restructuring will probably be employed only as an ancillary technique, at least in the near future, in the treatment of the sexual offender.

Group Therapy

Early results using group therapy exclusively in the treatment of the sexual offender were mixed (Mathis & Collins, 1970a, 1970b; Witzig, 1968). Today, most therapists do not recommend group therapy as the sole treatment technique offered. However, group therapy exists in a multitude of forms, including supportive, behavioral, and confrontive groups. These may be helpful, particularly with selected offenders.

- Despite one year of intensive behavior therapy, a 52-year-old shopkeeper showed no improvement in plethysmograph readings associated with sexual activities with young girls. He continued to insist that he could not view pornographic materials or complete homework assignments because of his strong religious convictions. Placed within a group of heterosexual pedophiles, he quickly became the focus of the group as other members strongly confronted his ideas about treatment. When behavior therapy was reinitiated, he made rapid progress.

Despite such cases, most behavior therapists do not employ group therapy alone for the sexual offender, although, as in the above case example, some initial work in assigning homework in a confrontive setting has recently been reported (Adams, Tollison, & Carson, 1981).

Mention has already been made of group assertiveness training for the sexual offender (Gilmour, McConaich, & DeRuiter, 1981). Even in the example given above, the group process did not directly diminish arousal but set up a situation in which conditioning methods could finally be employed. Aside from a supportive role as mentioned above, however, some group behavior therapy might enable treatment to be delivered more rapidly and inexpensively to more offenders; seminal efforts in this direction now underway are to be applauded (Abel & Becker, 1984). It may be that offenders can be trained in relaxation, accomplish reporting of taped homework assignments, review cognitive distortions, practice assertion and social skills, and learn empathy in groups, thereby reducing the cost of treatment and gaining important group support.

An extensive discussion of group therapy will not be offered here (see the references above for more detailed descriptions), but it is of importance to note the types of groups and techniques felt to be particularly helpful to the sexual offender.

SUPPORTIVE GROUPS

Most therapists prefer that groups offering support to members be homogeneous. Thus a group could be composed of exhibitionists, homosexual pedophiles, and so on. However, although certain problems may be shared by each such subgroup, it might be advantageous to experiment with mixed groups as well. Often, bridging diagnostic lines can be helpful.

- A homosexual pedophile was placed into a group of mostly heterosexual pedophiles. The heterosexual pedophiliac patients, when learning of the new member's predilection, were generally negative and showed some repulsion at the acts he reported. However, the homosexual pedophile expressed equal distaste for relationships with young girls, though he was fully bisexual. The new member gained support from the group therapist while the older members received a new perspective on their molesting behavior.

Certainly, confrontation can occur within a generally supportive group; however, the overall purpose of these groups is to provide support, validation, and enhanced self-esteem as well as to share techniques helpful for individual members.

THERAPY GROUPS

The distinction between supportive and therapy groups cannot be sharply drawn. However, the major focus in therapy groups is not supportive or increasing self-esteem but exploring the genesis of each member's disorder. Mathis has been a leader in this area, particularly with groups of exhibitionists (Mathis & Collins, 1970b). Heterogeneous therapy groups are common, however, as tacit agreement is given to the notion that the form of the symptoms is secondary to their underlying cause. Behavior therapists have not been enthusiastic about this form of group therapy as it implies that uncovering and insight can eliminate deviant sexual arousal. There is as yet no demonstration of this assumption, but lively debate will probably continue.

BEHAVIORAL GROUPS

The intent of behavioral group therapy is to eliminate deviant sexual arousal rather than to foster increasing responsibility or uncovering motivations. Its procedures are likely to be quite different from other forms of group therapy. In such groups, offenders are often given relaxation training, then asked to imagine a series of individualized scenes of sexual abuse followed by depictions of negative images:

- The group of seven mixed heterosexual and homosexual pedophiles was given relaxation training followed by pleasant imagery. Following three such hourly sessions, each offender was seen in one individual session to construct a hierarchy of deviant sexually arousing scenes. Again, in group, each offender was instructed to relax and to imagine his own pleasant scene and then his "Scene 1," "Scene 2," and so on. Three such scenes were presented to the entire group each session for the next five hourly sessions. A pilot study examined these offenders' plethysmograph results, compared with a matched group of seven offenders treated in a similar fashion but on an individual basis. The study revealed slight but statistically significant differences favoring those offenders treated individually rather than in a group fashion.

Despite these negative results, behavioral group methods can still be helpful in the treatment of the sexual offender. Group relaxation techniques appear to be as effective as individual relaxation sessions and would be a more effective and less costly means of providing this basic treatment. Moreover, overt aversive stimuli such as foul odor or electric shock might prove as effective administered to groups as to individuals. On the other hand, the highly personal nature of such treatment, often requiring embarrassing self-disclosure, may indicate that treatment is best conducted in a highly protected and private manner.

CONFRONTIVE GROUPS

Group therapists may elect to employ confrontive group techniques in any type of group therapy. These techniques include use of a "hot seat" to increase feedback to an individual sexual offender; deliberate baiting or challenging; and the use of psychodramatic techniques such as mirroring, doubling, and role-playing (as in a confrontation between the offender and his victim). Although these techniques are not restricted to confrontive groups, it is in these groups that such techniques become the major focus of therapy. Such confrontations have proven more helpful than would have been at first surmised. Although initially they may engender resentment, the group format often helps in breaking through resistance. Other offenders can easily recognize some of the minimization and denial seen in the newly identified offender. With such confrontation, more rapid progress can often occur, as in the case examples cited earlier in this section.

Special mention should be made here of three self-help organizations composed of offenders alone and with no professional group leader but with group facilitators present in each session: *Parents United*, *Recovering Offenders*, and *Sexaholics Anonymous*. All three are attempting to serve a national audience. Parents United and Recovering Offenders have had more group experience in this area than many therapists working with offenders and often their assistance is valuable. Therapists should attempt to forge a liaison with these organizations and cultivate a good working relationship with their leaders. These groups generally maintain a confrontive approach although liberally mixed with healthy doses of faith and mutual support. In the experience of most therapists treating sexual offenders, an ideal situation is one in which these groups are combined with professional individual therapy. The nature of these groups often precludes collection of even retrospective data, but joint efforts in that direction should be encouraged.

Sexaholics Anonymous was originally proposed as a support group for patients with high sexual drive or low sexual impulse control, although currently a variety of offenders are accepted within it. In practice, its focus has been based on the 12-step program originally proposed for Alcoholics Anonymous. It often serves as an arena within which an offender and his family can express themselves and derive understanding and support. It has also been helpful in focusing on the often unique problems associated with the hypersexual patient and, should he have a family, the tormenting effects he has upon them as well.

In summary, many kinds of group therapy can be helpful in the treatment of the sexual offender. Based on the current state of knowledge, group therapy as a sole treatment method does not appear as promising as do combinations of group and individual approaches.

Impulse Control Training

The maladaptive sexual approach behaviors can be viewed as disorders of impulse control. However, this analogic leap is not overwhelmingly convincing: If molesting a young girl represented only a lack of impulse control, it would follow that most men have impulses to molest young girls but control them. Ongoing research demonstrates that presumably "normal" males do not generally show plethysmograph responses to deviant sexual stimuli (Farkas et al., 1979; Quinsey & Chaplin, 1988), although scattered variances exist (Freund, Char, & Coulthard, 1979).

On the other hand, there may be a type of sexual offender who is truly hypersexual, with a decreased threshold to sexual stimuli, or polysexual, with sexual arousal to a variety of stimuli such as young girls, boys, animals, and so on. This is especially true of adolescent offenders and those suffering some central nervous system damage (Langevin, Wortzmang, Wright, & Handy, 1989):

- A 15-year-old boy, injured in a gun accident, sustained damage to both frontal lobes. He then began to peek into windows in his neighborhood, attempted sexual relations with his 9-year-old sister, and molested several young male cousins. He was placed on a contingency program such that he was rewarded with points exchangeable for money for each day that went by without reports of inappropriate sexual behavior. In addition, he could earn points by viewing non-pornographic sexual material and not masturbating for increasing lengths of time. These procedures, used exclusively, seemed to eliminate deviant sexual arousal and no further sexual misbehaviors occurred.

- A 22-year-old unemployed male would masturbate in his car just after seeing a pretty woman walk by. He made some attempt not to be seen by parking away from other cars in large parking lots, but he was detected on three occasions and finally required to begin a treatment program. In addition to aversive conditioning, he was asked to view pornographic movies in the clinic then remain in the waiting room under watch of office staff and not masturbate for increasing lengths of time, beginning with one hour and progressing to 12 hours. When reporting some success in these techniques, he was asked to begin masturbation but stop after one to two minutes, then to stop at points closer and closer to ejaculation, to build better control.

As seen, these techniques can offer reinforcement, with point systems or therapist approval and self-satisfaction, for successfully fighting the sexual impulse. Only one report in the literature thus far details impulse control procedures specifically for the sexual offender (Snaith & Collins, 1981); this report is couched in terms of auto-hypnotic suggestion, although its procedures are similar to those already described in this section.

In some cases, *late in treatment,* a patient is asked deliberately to tempt himself so that he can practice restraint:

- A 62-year-old general contractor would follow girls home from a particular city park and engage them in sexually frank discussions, intended to initiate sexual contact. After eight months of aversive conditioning, the patient was asked to return to this park *with the therapist,* look for young subjects, and watch them leave but not follow them. After four such exercises, the therapist only accompanied the patient halfway for two more sessions, then requested that the patient visit the park four more times without him. At all times, the patient was instructed to look for victims and watch them leave without following them.

This procedure is usually combined with aversive conditioning by having the patient smell a foul odor, chew a bitter pill, or think aversive thoughts incompatible with molesting (see Chapter 3). Such techniques, of course, must be closely monitored for the sake of safety.

To many patients and therapists, the goal of treatment is to learn *control* over deviant impulses that will always be present to plague the offender. Behavior therapists have espoused a loftier goal: to eliminate deviant sexual arousal. In reality, there will always be patients who cannot eliminate the deviant arousal but who, through therapy, have achieved the twin goals of a marked reduction in deviant sexual urges coupled with an excellent control system. For these patients, the use of the plethysmograph as a biofeedback instrument assumes a major role in treatment.

Although the examples above demonstrate the practice of sexual impulse control, nonsexual impulse control can be practiced as well.

- In addition to assignments to view pornography and not masturbate, a 17-year-old public masturbator was asked to wait at least 30 minutes between feeling the urge to urinate and actually relieving himself. He was also asked to eat half his dessert with each meal and to buy a candy bar, eat half, and leave the remainder in view all day. In a similar vein, he was asked *not* to speak when he had something important to say in three entire hourly group sessions and to sit perfectly still in two of his seven classes per day. These techniques seemed to add to his general mastery over impulses.

One kind of sexual offender who may particularly benefit from sexual impulse control training is the hypersexual patient or "the sexual addict":

- A 43-year-old married business executive complained of leading a "double life." At once seemingly contented and successful, he reported that in reality his many "business trips" were often camouflages for sexual odyssies to houses of prostitution. His most satisfying fantasies included forcing two or three women to commit fellatio on him; he had come dangerously close to being reported to authorities for forcible activities with prostitutes. He had devised cognitive strategies to distract himself from the pressure of the sexual fantasies but these began to fade in their efficacy. He was treated with odor and electric shock aversion, but, in addition, a program of sexual impulse control was devised: He was asked to spend five minutes in his room, twice each day, dwelling on sexual fantasies without masturbating or having intercourse, then to leave his room and turn to other business. He was also asked to begin masturbation and then to discontinue it, at first, early in its course, progressing to discontinuing self-stimulation just prior to ejaculatory inevitability. These methods proved quite productive in teaching sexual control.

There is a growing recognition of such sexual addiction and its multiple risks: marital, legal, vocational, and financial problems as well as the acquisition of infections. Although hormonal treatment has been advocated for this condition, medication can often be used only temporarily due to either fear of permanent side effects or the termination of supervisory probation. Behavioral advances such as sexual impulse control training offer the sexual addict an opportunity to learn permanent control of his condition.

It is clear that these techniques fly in the face of what appears to be a basic tenet in present-day psychotherapy: to facilitate rather than inhibit expression of wants, needs, and the affective states associated with them. Nonetheless, these impulse control devices have been helpful in teaching mastery over impulses that could result in harm to others and to the patient himself. No overall philosophy is being espoused; techniques that seem to help must stand on their heuristic value rather than being viewed as building blocks in any theoretic model of etiology. Thus these impulse control techniques can be useful when *added* to a total treatment program, especially in the adolescent or the patient whose central nervous system is compromised. If they help even a few such individuals avoid harming others or prevent these offenders from the expense and potential harm of prison, they would be worthwhile additions to an overall treatment plan.

Empathy Training and the Clarification Process

It is of interest that many offenders, when asked if their offending behavior was wrong, reply quickly that it certainly was so; but, when asked why, they often fumble and respond in vague and moralistic generalities. Frequently, therapists hear: "It is against my principles." "The victims are too young." "It's sacrilegious." "It is against the law." Few consider the victim in their replies. When prompted, many offenders will eventually discuss effects their behavior might have had upon the victim, but they continue to be diffuse: "They are too young." "She might be harmed physically." "He might grow up to be a homosexual." Often, an offender is so caught up in his own troubles he can only perceive himself as the victim of the crime.

Often, the offender does not develop a concept of the potential harm his actions might have had. Perhaps often too, the therapist, in a desire to avoid being paternalistic and authoritarian, does not describe in detail the possible damage done, even though he or she is likely to be familiar with data indicating the frequency of distrust in men in general (Jones, 1982), the tension surrounding further sexual activity (Dimock, 1988), homosexuality (Dimock, 1988), poor interpersonal relationships (Jehu, 1939), a generalized increase in background anxiety (Caffaro-Rouget, Lang, VanSanten, 1989; Hampton & Newberger, 1985), and an increase in medical complaints (Cunningham, Pearce, & Pearce, 1988) seen in many victims of sexual abuse. Therapists may try not to overburden the offender with more guilt and lower self-esteem. Fortunately, there has been a rapid increase in services for the victims of sexual abuse and for affected families as well (Carte, Rosen, Saperstein, & Shermack, 1985). Still, the sexual offender may remain ignorant of the tragic harm his behavior can produce.

- A 14-year-old boy molested his 8-year-old sister and exposed to two more of his classmates near their school yard. He admitted to the charges reluctantly and participated minimally in treatment efforts. He was asked to prepare and deliver a talk to a fifth-grade class designed to warn youngsters about sexual advances. He also participated in a group of victims, chiefly female, 7 to 15 years of age, and was asked to prepare a report describing treatment for a group of women molested as youngsters. He subsequently became more invested in his treatment and showed a good treatment response within several months of these techniques being initiated.

- In the course of a routine patrol on Halloween night, police observed a 52-year-old man exposing himself to two groups of youngsters knocking on his door for "trick or treat." In addition to aversive conditioning, he was given the task of writing scenes for a play, to be actually performed in elementary schools in the area, warning children of sexual approaches. He was also asked to play the role of the victim of sexual abuse in several treatment sessions. In addition, he was asked to write two life scripts for victims of sexual abuse. He believed these empathy training techniques were instrumental in preventing any further episodes of exhibitionism.

It has also been most helpful to ask the offender to write a letter of clarification to the victim, explaining his responsibility, exculpating the victim from any complicity he or she may feel in the matter, apologizing, and expressing hope, if appropriate, for a healthier relationship in the future. When engaged in such a task, the offender can participate fruitfully in a discussion of the inability of a minor to grant sexual consent. The offender is frequently affected in a positive direction by reviewing victims' reports and police files, reading letters victims have written explaining the impact the abuse has had, and viewing videotapes of victims being interviewed about their experiences. Paradoxically, these techniques seem even more powerful when the victim is not the offender's own, perhaps because the neutral situation removes him from the necessity of an adversarial position.

In selected cases, it may be possible to conduct several sessions with an offender and his victim(s). In such a delicate situation, a victim's therapist might also be included. The clarification process then becomes an interactional one, with the victim encouraged to ask questions of the offender to try to sort out the complicated emotions he or she might have about the abuse. The therapist(s) in such a setting has a rare opportunity to help heal the wounds of ruptured relationships.

These empathy training techniques, previously described in other contexts (Becker, Skinner, & Abel, 1983), are always combined with other treatment methods for the sexual offender. Nonetheless, many offenders report a strong effect from these techniques on their subsequent actions. These techniques can also be incorporated into group therapy for the offender. It must be added that these methods have never been tested independently, and hence any final evaluation of their efficacy is premature.

As with impulse control training, empathy training appears to be of particular value in working with adolescents and those with some central nervous system deficits, although it certainly should not be limited to those subgroups. Although it is unlikely ever to become the dominant focus of therapy for the sexual offender, empathy training can be an effective ancillary technique, especially in groups where psychodramatic techniques such as role reversal and peer feedback can be used with good effect. Some therapists believe that such techniques should be mandatory in the treatment of the sexual offender.

Paradoxical Intention

At times during the treatment of the sexual offender, the therapist may be placed in a polarized situation as an extension of the judicial system, as when treatment is a required condition of probation or parole. Often, a paradoxical approach, as first proposed by Haley (1963), can be used to pry open a "stuck" situation in therapy.

- A 43-year-old disabled construction worker was convicted on a number of counts of molesting his four stepdaughters, 7 to 16 years of age. He immediately renounced his sexual misbehaviors and insisted that the arrest and conviction had helped him "find the Lord"; hence he could never conceive of molesting again. His therapist then asked him actually to plan to molest one of the girls again. He was repulsed by the idea but, under constant pressure, agreed to devise such a scheme and write it out. By examining the plan in detail with the therapist, the patient began to realize he was not as secure in his conviction that offenses could never recur, which led to a less optimistic but more realistic self-appraisal.

Again, adolescents and those with poor impulse control may be special candidates for such therapeutic devices.

- A 16-year-old boy with moderate retardation had molested several younger boys in an institutional setting. He denied the charges and vigorously opposed treatment; each session turned into a stereotyped drama in which the therapist would insist on treatment and the patient would deny the need for it. Finally, the therapist canceled the next office session and visited the patient at the institution. There, he encouraged the boy to discontinue therapy and recommended this to the boy's therapist as well. As these discussions proceeded, the therapist's message was clear: "I don't think you should receive treatment. If you really did molest those boys it will probably happen again. If you didn't, you don't need treatment." With this change, the boy asked for "one more session." He subsequently admitted to the problem indirectly and began to request treatment. Even then, the therapist expressed reservations but honored his requests. Eventually, the patient admitted that all the molestations had occurred, and he subsequently progressed well with conditioning therapy.

Despite these examples, however, concern must be voiced about the indiscriminate use of such techniques. In general, duplicity is to be avoided in treatment. In these cases, it was used to help the patient, but clearly such actions, and explanations for them, can be satisfying to therapists while patronizing to patients. As a most careful analysis of these situations is necessary, it would be judicious to include another therapist in a decision to use such techniques.

- A 14-year-old boy bound a 5-year-old girl with rope and proceeded to fondle her genital area and touch her nipples. He was placed in a semiclosed adolescent unit of a psychiatric hospital for safety and for assessment of treatment techniques. He had previously run away from several foster homes and had left the hospital twice within the first 48 hours of placement there. Upon apprehension and return, the hospital staff decided to give him the message that they expected him to run away and proceeded to help him plan it. He was told that his behavior was quite predictable. He was given full freedom of the hospital, left alone in the cafeteria and halls, and told in group that staff were glad he had not run yet but they expected he would do so soon. He remained on the unit without attempting to leave for the remainder of his hospitalization of 34 days.

In this case, paradoxical messages were used in association with reinforcement for not running. In theory, perhaps the most potent reinforcers for leaving were removed by the paradoxical procedure: shock, surprise, and noncompliance with adults' expectations. As seen in this example, such paradoxical approaches need not be restricted to sexual behaviors alone.

These paradoxical techniques have proven helpful in a minority of cases, but, if employed judiciously after review and consent by other therapists or parents and guardians, they can form part of an overall therapeutic program, hopefully built upon trust and mutual cooperation.

Deviant Cycle Awareness

If a single act of deviant sexual response is taken as a final culmination of a series of steps, offending can be broken down into a chain
of behavior that began with stimuli, external or internal (or both),
and led to new stimuli and responses. It is reasonable to analyze this
chain and determine its origins, sustenance, and endings. Although
most authors (Freeman-Longo & Bays, 1989) speak of a "cycle,"
implying an inexhaustible supply of beginnings with culmination
inexorably leading to reinitiation, it may be more parsimonious to
think of a chain, as external stimuli are not so predictable in guaran-
teeing the incessant and necessary regeneration of deviant behaviors.

The behavior literature indicates that a chain of addictive and
consummatory responses is most easily interrupted at its inception
(Martin & Pea, 1988):

- An alcoholic can more easily stop drinking behavior by never entering
a tavern than by entering one, ordering a drink, bringing it to his lips,
then putting it down and not drinking. (Admittedly, doing the latter
can be viewed as stimulus inoculation, or operant practice; however,
with sexual offenders, such practice is probably as much foolhardy as
it is dangerous.)

Each offender may have his own initiating and sustaining stimuli,
some of which may actually be the absence of self-controlling behaviors and taboos.

- A homosexual pedophile had been molesting young boys for over 30
years. He had organized a volunteer organization to help delinquent
youths and was admired for his efforts, which were often quite beneficial. Initiating and sustaining stimuli included
  (a) identification of a particularly good-looking boy between the ages
      of 12 and 15,
  (b) identification of such a boy who was also particularly despondent
      and passive,
  (c) beginning to spend increasing amounts of time with his victim,
  (d) purchasing gifts, doing special "favors" for the boy,
  (e) inviting the boy to his home to sleep overnight,
  (f) taking the boy on overnight camp-outs,
  (g) engaging in increasingly intimate physical contact,
  (h) engaging in increasingly frank sexual discussions,

(i) "teaching" sex to the boy, and
(j) engaging in frank sexual activity.

Attempts at recognition and disruption of this cycle in its earliest phases included

(a) keeping a sexual log,
(b) eliminating any association with the volunteer organizations,
(c) working out routes in driving to work and home to avoid schools, playgrounds, and parks,
(d) informing his minister of his whereabouts twice daily, and
(e) recording a videotape instructing him in covert strategies to reduce sexual desire for boys.

- An insurance company executive had molested his stepdaughter 20 years earlier, then molested two stepgranddaughters. An analysis of his pattern revealed the following steps:
  (a) receiving negative feedback from his company's president,
  (b) increasing muscular tension leading to headaches,
  (c) drinking alcohol to reduce the pain,
  (d) forgetting to take his blood pressure medicine when drinking,
  (e) feeling increasing pain,
  (f) lying in a dark room to reduce the pain,
  (g) experiencing increasing sexual fantasies as the pain diminished,
  (h) then calling his stepdaughter to offer to baby-sit, encouraging her and her husband to go out so he could be alone with his victims, and
  (i) molesting the children.

Treatment interventions included relaxation training for pain reduction, going to AA meetings, buying a pill-reminder alarm box, and being honest with his stepdaughter in a letter to her about his molestations.

Chains, or cycles, can be long and circuitous. In many offenders, there are a variety of controlling stimuli with subtle and indistinct variations. Areas to explore include adult relationships, financial problems, vocational difficulties, substance abuse and health problems. It often takes a number of repeated attempts to help an offender delineate these chains and then get beyond the denial, minimization, and rationalization commonly encountered in this work. Often, aborting a chain, or cycle, at its earliest steps is necessary, because for some habitual offenders, once several early steps are taken in the chain, a cascade of emotions and cognitions spill out and rush downstream too swiftly to divert the flow. Cycle awareness and diversion will continue to be important elements in the treatment of the sexual offender.

Response Prevention

Cognitive response prevention has been mentioned in the subsection on cognitive therapies in this chapter. Although forms of response prevention such as thought-stopping and thought-changing techniques have often been described in the literature (Lombardo & Turner, 1979; Wolpe & Lazarus, 1966), there has been no systematic attempt to apply them to the maladaptive sexual approach disorders. Nonetheless these techniques can and have been employed within this population with apparent success in some cases:

- Under court mandate, a 41-year-old janitor with a history of molesting several daughters and stepdaughters was referred for treatment. During aversion therapy, he continued to complain of urges to sexually molest one of his victims again. He was asked to contemplate this act during a clinic session, then suddenly the therapist shouted, "Stop!" The patient agreed that at that point his thoughts about molesting did stop. He was taught to practice this technique himself, and he reported it to be moderately helpful in reducing the frequency and severity of urges to molest.

- A 25-year-old exhibitionist could not avoid driving the same routes on which he had previously exposed because it was necessary in carrying out his job. A list was, therefore, constructed of competing thoughts that could help prevent urges to expose. These included thoughts of his parents and children, sports, and recreational activities. He found that, eventually, after sufficient practice, his thoughts would automatically turn from exposing to these competing cognitive responses.

The similarity of these approaches to those of cognitive therapy, mentioned earlier in this chapter, should be apparent. In addition, actual competing behaviors can be used almost as readily as competing thoughts.

- A 27-year-old transvestite was asked to have available pieces of masculine clothing (under- and overgarments) as well as his usual supply of feminine stockings and undergarments. With any urge to cross-dress, he was asked to write down the time, likely cause of the urge, location, and his response. In addition, he was asked to dress in the masculine clothing immediately thereafter. In association with aversive conditioning, these techniques were effective in terminating all cross-dressing within three months of initiating therapy.

Of course, not all such examples are unequivocal successes, but enhancement of therapeutic benefits is often seen when applying such techniques.

Relapse Prevention

While any treatment effort to reduce the risk of reoffending can be thought of as *relapse prevention*, this term has come to be used for a specific set of behavioral and cognitive strategies. A recent addition to the literature outlines in greater detail the steps usually incorporated into a successful treatment program (Freeman-Longo & Bays, 1989):

(1) An awareness of deviant cycles. Each offender needs to review, both in group and in individual therapy, the steps inexorably cascading toward an offense. Typical examples have been described in the above section on deviant cycles.

(2) A review of high-risk settings and situations.

- A 19-year-old student had committed three rapes during a period of four years. These always occurred while he was driving at night in residential areas. Part of treatment was an insistence that he forfeit his driver's license and sell his car.
- A 37-year-old man had molested his girlfriend's daughter. An exhaustive review of his deviant behavior yielded a clear pattern of molesting his victim after arguments with his mother, which, in turn, only occurred after he used alcohol. Contact with the victim could only occur after behavioral treatment, couple's counseling, and a monitored Antabuse[1] program.

Risk situations are usually both external and internal.

- A 15-year-old boy had molested three younger girls when baby-sitting for one particular couple but never at anyone else's house. In the offending situation, he had gained access to a large store of pornographic videotapes which he viewed at that house, leading to arousal and ultimately to the molestations.

(3) An analysis of options. Many offenders fail to evaluate all the choices available to them in an offending situation. Often, however, sexual gratification is too powerful to yield to cognitive restructuring. Nonetheless, at certain points in treatment, particularly following some aversive conditioning, the offender can profitably explore options if caught in a potentially dangerous situation:

- Two men had formed a "sex club" with three young teenage boys. The men would offer the boys gifts, alcohol, and money in return for sexual activity and posing for photographs and videotapes. One man was jailed while the other was placed on probation. This latter offender identified the following alternatives to pursuing sexual activity if he encountered a handsome boy:
  (a) turn physically away;
  (b) chew a bitter pill;
  (c) walk away from the situation;
  (d) actively fantasize his arrest, conviction, and imprisonment;
  (e) call a sponsor from his support group;
  (f) call his therapist; and
  (g) write about the experience in his log, including what was learned from the situation.
- A 45-year-old physician admitted to molesting several young girls, though none in his medical practice. While visiting his fiancée, a friend of hers arrived with two young girls. The ladies suddenly decided to go shopping and asked this offender to "watch the kids for a few minutes." While at first he protested that the situation unfolded so rapidly he could not have escaped it, he was able to see that this was a dangerous situation from the very first, and that he needed to leave immediately, even if it was awkward to do so.

Relapse prevention is often divided into two major components:

(1) the anticipation and avoidance of risky situations
(2) the presence of escape plans

In clinical experience, most offenders do manage to become engaged in potentially dangerous settings; it is often only with repeated negative experiences that they can learn to anticipate and avoid traps. It has proven helpful to ask the offender to keep an activities log and to write out "fail-safe" cards to carry with him, with reminders of helpful techniques and telephone numbers in case of emergent situations. Often, stapling a picture of his wife or girlfriend to these cards is a powerful reminder of what the offender might stand to lose unless he can control his behavior.

Potentially risky situations for many pedophiles include driving by or loitering around parks, playgrounds, schools, videogame stores, and fast-food restaurants. Baby-sitting, coaching, or teaching children and volunteering to help disadvantaged children are all obviously dangerous activities. Those for exhibitionists and rapists are, typically, visiting beaches or nudist camps, "cruising" in a car, entering pornography shops or X-rated movies, soliciting prostitutes, and loitering in parks.

In summary, relapse prevention has become a staple in the treatment of the sexual offender. Although it does not lend itself to rigorous experimental verification, it is employed in a wide variety of clinics with diverse theoretic underpinnings. It will no doubt remain a flexible, yet robust, technique that should become increasingly helpful during the next decade.

Substance Abuse Measures

While substance abuse probably accounts for only a small fraction of sexual abuse, one drug plays a predominant role among all others: alcohol. Within a large sexual abuse clinic, the frequency of men who offended *only* when under the influence of alcohol has been fewer than 5%, although this percentage increases to approximately 26% when the categories are broadened to include all those who offended occasionally when intoxicated.[2] Indeed, the majority (83%) of men who offended at times when drinking also offended when sober. At times, both these groups believed that alcohol was the root of their sexual problems. This is not very likely when one considers that many men in our society become intoxicated, but very few molest (expose, or the like) when under the influence.

There remains, however, a minority of men who will offend less or not at all if their alcohol consumption is controlled.

- A retired minister could not gain control of either his exhibitionism or his drinking. Aversive conditioning was helpful in eliminating exposing when sober; when he drank, however, he continued to expose. A monitored Antabuse plan was instrumental in helping him to not reoffend. With such a plan, he was given the usual warning that combining alcohol with Antabuse could cause a serious medical reaction. He was required to drink liquid Antabuse at a pharmacy every Monday, Wednesday, and Friday, and the pharmacy was instructed to contact his probation officer should he not attend. At that time, an automatic revocation of his probation would have occurred.

Unfortunately, it appears that treatments to reduce deviant sexual arousal have been more effective than treatments to discourage alcoholism. Although claims have been made for the effectiveness of self-help groups (Alcoholics Anonymous, 1978), conditioning therapies (Miller, 1983), and standard psychotherapy (VanDijk & VanDijk-Kauffman, 1973), controlled studies are often depressingly uniform in showing no method to have yielded more than a 50% abstinence rate with long-term follow-ups of six months to six years (VanDijk & VanDijk-Kauffman, 1973).

In such cases, action must be initiated by the therapist to assist the patient in remaining abstinent. The use of monitored Antabuse programs has been helpful, but such monitoring cannot usually be extended beyond the period of probation or parole. Groups patterned after Alcoholics Anonymous are helpful to some, while outreach programs help others. Recently, special Care Center inpatient programs appear to have achieved some impressive short-term results.

Summary

Adjunctive techniques such as social skills training, assertiveness training, family therapy, cognitive therapy, the group therapies, impulse control training, and empathy training may be supportive of major treatment techniques such as aversive conditioning or orgasmic reconditioning methods. However, in a number of cases, particularly in the adolescent offender or the offender with central nervous system damage, these techniques may actually allow conditioning methods to take hold better or may even surmount the established therapies in their importance.

The sexual therapist will need to be knowledgeable in, and technically proficient at, a number of these techniques, as it seems unlikely that only a few treatment approaches will prove sufficient in the treatment of any single sexual offender.

Notes

1. Disulfiram (Ayers Laboratories) combines with any alcohol ingested to cause an extremely unpleasant and sometimes physiologically dangerous reaction.

2. Figures are taken from records of the Sexual Abuse Clinic, Portland, Oregon, from early 1978 through mid-1990.

8

Somatic Therapies

It has only been relatively recently that practitioners of medical psychology have come forward with proposals to combine behavioral technology with medication. Psychologists cannot prescribe medicine, neither are they routinely trained in psychopharmacology. As a result, articles in the behavioral literature rarely mention chemotherapy, and medical texts touch only lightly upon behavioral techniques (Maletzky, 1981).

However, at a recent seminar on treatment of the sexual offender that was held in the Pacific Northwest (Maletzky, 1984a), a large section of the program was devoted to the use of depo-Provera and its incorporation into a sensible overall treatment approach. At that meeting, a proposed bill in the state legislature was discussed. The bill established a mechanism of providing depo-Provera to suitable sexual offenders but did not provide for any concomitant behavioral treatment.

Research reports on the combination of medications with behavior therapies are scarce and have only been sporadically described in recent years (Paykel, 1979). The relative lack of interest in this area in the past has been reversed recently and there are review articles in the literature (Marks, 1981a, pp. 249-287). This chapter will review the utilization of medications for the sexual offender but always with the intention of employing medications as *part* of the treatment program rather than as isolated treatment approaches in themselves. In this narrow focus, no attention will be given to

(1) the use of medications to treat a concomitant psychiatric illness such as schizophrenia or a major affective disorder,
(2) the use of antianxiety medications to reduce the tension commonly seen in the sexual offender under familial and legal pressures, and
(3) the use of medications to treat a concomitant physical illness such as diabetes or epilepsy.

It should be noted that certain psychotropic medications may exert profound effects on a patient's sexual life. Neuroleptic and antidepressant drugs commonly diminish libido and can produce impotence; such a "side effect" can be used to therapeutic advantage occasionally, as will be further discussed. Even nonpsychiatric medications can alter sexual desire and performance. For example, common antihypertensives diminish potency as do parenteral steroids and certain medications prescribed for cardiovascular conditions.

Of course, a number of medical illnesses themselves can reduce libido and potency. Diabetes, prostatitis, and arteriosclerosis come quickly to mind. Fortunately, many nonmedical practitioners today seek medical consultations if indicated, thereby enhancing a broad-based treatment approach for the sexual offender.

Medications to Decrease Male Sexual Arousal

NEUROLEPTIC MEDICATIONS

Although all the known medications effective for schizophrenia have been reported to diminish male sexual arousal, thioridazine (Mellaril) will be chosen for discussion here because it has been employed as an antiarousal drug more than others within this family. Moreover, it suppresses arousal to a greater extent than its sister drugs and does so more consistently (Burnstein, 1983). In fact, this "side effect" has often been a reason for medication refusal on the part of schizophrenic patients. While thioridazine also reduces sexual arousal in the female patient, its greatest antiarousal effect is usually seen in men:

- A 52-year-old mechanic had been molesting young boys for many years. He preyed upon youngsters in city parks in a compulsive manner, but after each sexual encounter he claimed to feel "nauseated" and vowed he would never repeat the act. Because of a history of nonmalignant breast mass (unusual in men) several years earlier, hormonal agents carried some risk. A dose of 100 mg of thioridazine at bedtime reduced frequency of erections (including nighttime and morning awakening erections), masturbation, and sexual fantasies, with deviant and nondeviant content, approximately 75%. Dizziness upon arising was a moderate problem; however, no falls occurred.

- On referral by his treating psychiatrist, a 29-year-old long-distance truck driver gave a history of exposing himself to women as he drove by various truck stops. He was under treatment at the time for a good prognosis schizophrenia and his medication, haloperidol (Haldol), had been gradually reduced. Because he could not control his urge to expose, medication was considered, at least for the initial part of therapy. Because he was already taking haloperidol, his dose was increased from 2 mg at bedtime to 5 mg at bedtime. He reported a marked decrease in actual exposing behavior and a lesser but measurable decrease in urges to expose. His reports were matched by declines in his plethysmograph readings to all sexual stimuli. He did not experience drowsiness while driving (see Comings & Comings, 1982).

Two factors are crucial in the decision to employ medications:

(1) A high probability of continuing to offend in the absence of measures to reduce the offender's contact with the community, such as incarceration, hospitalization, or detainment in a work-release center.
(2) A behavioral treatment program has been initiated but the rapidity of behavior change cannot be guaranteed.

The plan to prescribe medication should include a reasonable estimate of the duration and a statement about its discontinuance once behavioral measures have been demonstrated to decrease deviant sexual arousal. Because of long-term, occasionally irreversible side effects, attempts to reduce or eliminate the medication should be made from time to time.

If medications are chosen, an adequate dosage must occur. Generally, 50 mg to 150 mg of thioridazine can be prescribed. Dosage cannot be prescribed primarily on body size and weight but must be based largely on clinical response. These medications need only be administered once each day, preferably one or two hours before bedtime. Most of their side effects occur within the first two to six hours after each dose, hence the patient can be asleep throughout this time. The effect of decreasing libido, however, endures for many days.

Major side effects from the neuroleptic medications include the following:

(1) Drowsiness: The purpose of these medications is not to render the patient tranquil or sedated (even in schizophrenics). Every effort must be made to use the lowest possible dose to avoid this effect.

(2) Neuromuscular effects: The following occur very rarely with thioridazine:

    (a) muscle spasms, particularly of neck, jaw, and eye muscles;

    (b) tremors, particularly of the hands; and

    (c) Akathisia, restlessness, such as pacing, shifting position often, or not finding a comfortable position (this side effect can masquerade as "nervousness").

Other potential side effects include dry mouth, constipation, blurry vision, dizziness upon arising, sensitivity to sunlight, and reduced memory. Although none of these side effects is dangerous in itself, the effects tend to become so if the patient mixes alcohol with these drugs, drives when drowsy, or falls when getting out of bed in the middle of the night. A class of medications known as "anti-Parkinsonian" drugs (for example, Artane or Symmetrel) can eliminate the muscle side effects. Of greater concern, however, is the possibility of a late-blooming syndrome called tardive dyskinesia (Spohn, Cogne, LaCoursiere, Mazur, & Hayes, 1985). Although probably uncommon in men, some studies have found incidences of 5% to 20% among those who take neuroleptic agents for longer than two years. The syndrome, consisting of involuntary chewing and thrusting movements of the lips, tongue, and jaw (and, occasionally, arms or legs, although rarely the trunk) can be treated in recognized early, but untreatable cases have been reported in the literature. Paradoxically, this syndrome worsens when the offending drug is discontinued.

How effective is thioridazine in decreasing sexual arousal? No firm figures based on controlled studies are available. Clinical experience would suggest that this medication decreases sexual arousal (deviant and nondeviant alike) in approximately 70% of sexual offenders and usually does so to a moderate extent. The average patient taking thioridazine reports a 30% to 75% reduction (Burnstein, 1983). On plethysmograph tests, this medication has reduced levels of all sexual arousal an average of 20%. For some men, this figure approaches 100%. There are no data to discern which sexual offenders will respond best to the drug.

To summarize, all neuroleptic medications, and thioridazine in particular, reduce male sexual arousal to a moderate degree. As with all medications administered to sexual offenders, thioridazine reduces deviant and nondeviant sexual arousal alike. To achieve this result, it also produces, in most sexual offenders, a number of side effects; of chief concern are drowsiness and dizziness in the short run and possible long-term neuromuscular effects. Although the drug is not addicting, it, or others within its family, cannot be recommended. They generally are poorly tolerated and produce erratic effects. Their use has now been supplanted by the hormonal drugs, which will be discussed later in this chapter. However, there may be isolated cases in which it can prove helpful: the patient who is allergic to hormonal agents, who has had breast tumors (these can occur in males), or who also has schizophrenia.

HORMONAL AGENTS

Cyproterone acetate. In male primates, the magnitude of sexual response is mediated largely by circulating levels of the male hormone testosterone. Efforts to reduce testosterone levels, therefore, were forthcoming early in the treatment of sexual offenders (Blair & Lanyon, 1981), although there is no evidence that the *majority* of offenders excrete excessive amounts of male sex hormone (Bradford, 1983; Lang, Langevin, Bain, Frenzel, & Wright, 1989). Such efforts have been particularly intense in Europe, where biological concomitants of sexual abuse have long been of interest (Bártová, Náhurek, Svetzka, & Hajnová, 1979; Zbytovsky & Zapletálek, 1979). Research has centered on an analogue of one of the two female menstrual cycle hormones, progesterone. A synthetic form of this hormone, cyproterone acetate, has been shown to markedly reduce male circulating testosterone levels (Cooper, 1981). This medication has been used extensively in European studies; it is not available in the United States. Case reports and retrospective studies (Berlin & Coyle, 1981; Zbytovsky & Zapletálek, 1979), as well as one controlled study (Cooper, 1981), have documented a substantial reduction in male sexual arousal with the use of this drug.

Cyproterone acetate is given in oral form: Doses have ranged from 50 mg to 100 mg per day. Compliance problems can be minimized because reductions in plasma testosterone levels can be correlated with the dosage. It has only recently been produced in a long-acting injectable form. Side effects have been rare but include breast enlargement, tumors, and edema. In addition, dangerous side effects have been noted in women taking this drug (for menstrual irregularities or uterine bleeding) over periods of time from two to twelve months; malignant breast tumors, venous thromboses, and an increased hemorrhagic tendency have been reported as well (Zbytovsky & Zapletálek, 1979). Although these side effects are fortunately rare, their potentially serious nature cannot be overlooked.

Of equal concern is the question of feminizing changes induced by cyproterone acetate. Men have experienced embarrassing breast tissue proliferation and elevated voice pitch. Although these changes are believed to be reversible with discontinuation of the drug, there are reports of permanent changes in male transsexual patients taking the related hormone, estrogen (Cooper, 1981). Whether such permanent changes would occur with the use of cyproterone acetate is uncertain, but, with the information currently available, the temporary use of hormone therapy appears to be the wisest choice. Thus a three- to four-month use of a hormonal agent while behavior therapy is being initiated is recommended.

One side effect incidentally discovered with the use of such agents in the treatment of the sexual offender has been an antiaggression effect (Zbytovsky & Zapletálek, 1979). Offenders reported a "ceiling" placed on their angry feelings such that they were able to become angry at appropriate times but would not lose total control. This effect has not been widely studied but deserves attention as much for its theoretic implications as for its therapeutic potential.

Medroxyprogesterone acetate. This progesterone analogue, with the trade name "Provera," can be manufactured as a solution in an oily substrate; as such, it is called "depo-Provera" and represents the chief medication employed in this country for the treatment of the sexual offender. Its effect is not only to reduce circulating testosterone levels but to block end-organ response to this hormone as well (Freund, 1980; Gagné, 1981). This medication can be injected intramuscularly every one to two weeks, as it is absorbed into the bloodstream slowly from its deposition site in muscle tissue due to its oily base. Thus it has two advantages:

(1) It markedly reduces circulating blood testosterone levels.
(2) Its absorption into the sexual offender's bloodstream can be guaranteed.

- A 21-year-old homosexual pedophile was diagnosed as having mild mental retardation. Diffuse central nervous system damage was suspected; the patient had molested young boys, almost regardless of circumstances. His impulsivity and sexual predilection made repeated offenses likely regardless of consequences, but the court had already sentenced him to probation with required treatment and had not limited his contact with society aside from a prohibition against contact with males under the age of 18, a warning that had been of little consequence to him in the past. Because it would likely take some time for conditioning treatment to become effective, a depo-Provera program was recommended. The patient, his parents, and his probation officer agreed to this plan following several sessions in which the medication and its alternatives and risks were explained to all concerned and after each person read literature about depo-Provera and paraphrased its advantages, disadvantages, and alternatives. Written permission was then obtained from the patient and his parents.[1] A baseline plasma testosterone level was measured at 585 ng/dl, within the normal range. A dose of 200 mg of depo-Provera was then administered intramuscularly every two weeks for a total of four months. At one and a half months, circulating plasma testosterone levels were measured at 230 ng/dl, approximately one-half to one-third of the normal levels. The patient reported marked reductions in frequency of sexual fantasies, morning erections, and episodes of masturbation. As plethysmograph readings to deviant material declined, depo-Provera was tapered to 100 mg intramuscularly every two weeks for the fourth month of therapy and then discontinued with the full return of sexual fantasies and masturbation (but to nondeviant material only).

- When a 29-year-old unemployed construction worker was placed on parole after serving six years in prison for a total of four rapes, he had already been in treatment with a prison psychiatrist for the condition of chronic schizophrenia. An increase in his antischizophrenic medication (Loxitane) at parole did not reduce sexual urges. He was given 300 mg of depo-Provera intramuscularly every two weeks during the first three months of his behavioral treatment program with a consequent marked reduction in aggressive sexual urges during that time. Following a discontinuation of depo-Provera, behavioral treatment combined with social skills training continued to effect a reduction in, and finally an elimination of, urges to rape.

The last case is typical of one kind of offender often seen as needing hormonal therapy: A man who has committed aggressive sexual crimes and been incarcerated is then released on parole but has had no therapy up to that point. Such an offender is at high risk to the community, but, within the current judicial structure, most sexual offenders cannot be institutionalized indefinitely. Obviously, a different approach would be to have treated the offender with effective conditioning techniques while still in the institution, an alternative still only rarely employed.

The decision to use depo-Provera must hinge on a number of considerations:

(1) the probability of recurrent offenses during the early phase of treatment
(2) potential consequences of recurrent offenses to victims and to the patient
(3) the likelihood of behavior therapy to produce a rapid decline in deviant sexual urges
(4) the health of the patient
(5) the ability of the patient to render competent consent

Thus a patient with strong and frequent impulses to offend and/or inability to control these urges might be a suitable medication candidate. An important factor to consider is the offender's ability to control nonsexual as well as sexual impulses. Patients with evidence of central nervous system dysmaturation or dysfunction, with other behavior problems as well, or those in the younger age group should especially be considered.

Table 8.1 *Use of depo-Provera in Sexual Offenders: Characteristics of Medicated and Nonmedicated Populations*

Factor	Medicated Patients (N = 85)	Nonmedicated Patients (N = 4,915)
Average age (in years)	30.1	32.5
Average duration of offending behavior (in years)	13.3	7.2
Percentage with past convictions	45.7	33.2
Average number of victims	2.4	1.3
Percentage with primary or auxiliary diagnosis of homosexual pedophilia	29.4	16.9
Percentage who have raped	45.7	2.4

NOTE: All differences are significant at least at the p < .05 level.

Within one large practice, approximately 1.7% of offenders (N = 85) received depo-Provera to reduce the pressure of sexual impulses. Table 8.1 details certain characteristics of this population contrasted with offenders for whom the medicine was not recommended. The medicated patients were younger, more often had some central nervous system dysfunction, and were more frequently men who had raped or who were homosexual pedophiles. The latter is not surprising to many working in this field and reflects the belief that this subgroup of offenders is more difficult to treat. Although retrospective reviews of outcome do not unequivocally support this view, a trend has emerged that the homosexual pedophile may require longer and more intensive treatment (Maletzky, 1984b).

Another type of offender who often may benefit from hormone therapy may have had no legal problems whatsoever: the hypersexual patient (or "sexual addict"):

- A 33-year-old drug and alcohol counselor was admitted to a psychiatric hospital in an extremely suicidal state. He gave a 10-year history of promiscuous activity with prostitutes, the frequenting of pornographic book stores and movie theatres, and marital and financial instability. He lived in fear of contacting AIDS and was so troubled by the frequency and intense pressure of sexual urges that he requested immediate relief. Provera (the oral, not the injectable, form) was prescribed at a dosage of 10 mg each morning. With an almost immediate relief from the torment of sexual drives, he was better able to concentrate on behavior therapy, which included deconditioning in the seamier aspects of sex: for example, seeing gross infections in prostitutes, being discovered in adult book stores by relatives, and being arrested by an undercover policewoman.

Eventually, such a patient may well run into trouble with the law.

- A 47-year-old businessman frequented prostitutes often, received pornography from overseas regularly, and masturbated three to five times per day. While his fantasies were not deviant, he was beginning to masturbate in public. On one occasion, he paid a prostitute to commit fellatio on him in a public men's restroom. On another occasion he paid a prostitute to masturbate him under a table in a tavern. He was finally arrested on public indecency. A course of Provera was helpful in eliminating these inappropriate behaviors; he believed that his marriage was saved because of the medication, and it eventually had to be discontinued against his will following a course of behavior therapy. He was doing well at five years' follow-up without the medication.

Such patients often complain that the press of sexual urges is troublesome and, at times, agonizing. Oral Provera can be used in such voluntary cases where a court mandate does not exist. It is important to emphasize to such patients that the hormone represents a temporary solution and that behavior therapy will, hopefully, yield more permanent results.

This population of "offenders" has been recently described by Carnes (1984) as "sexual addicts," and a self-help group, Sexaholics Anonymous, has been chartered to help such patients in much the same manner as Alcoholics Anonymous can help with problem drinking (see also Chapter 7's discussion of groups). It has already proven beneficial, though quite probably its role will be a supportive and adjunctive one for these patients, who can be helped considerably by the combination of hormonal and behavior therapy.

Table 8.2 presents the experience of one sexual abuse clinic in the administration of depo-Provera over a period of 17 years. Although averaged data are given in the table, an adequate dosage of depo-Provera for any offender cannot be estimated based on body size or typical doses given to other offenders. Some authors have advised clinicians to depend upon the objective criterion of reduction in plasma testosterone. One goal, stated in the literature, is to reduce

Table 8.2 *Use of depo-Provera in Sexual Offenders: Dosage and Serum Testosterone Levels (N = 85)*

Description	Quantity
Average dose	275 mg by intramuscular injection every two weeks
Average predrug testosterone level	550 ng/dL
Average testosterone level during treatment with depo-Provera	240 ng/dL
Average length of depo-Provera treatment	4.7 months

circulating plasma testosterone to one-half of baseline levels (Gagné, 1981). However, others disagree and counter with the recommendation to suppress testosterone below prepubertal levels (Cooper, 1981). Average baseline values for an adult male typically encompass a range of 275 to 1,250 ng/dl while prepubertal values are usually less than 50 ng/dl. Following a typical dose of depo-Provera of 200 mg to 300 mg intramuscularly every two weeks, the patient's circulating testosterone will generally drop to one-half of baseline levels within a two- to four-week period of time. As packaged, the depo-Provera comes either as a 100 mg/cc or as a 400 mg/cc viscous fluid. The medication can be injected entirely in one intramuscular site but, if the amount of fluid exceeds 2 cc, two sites are preferable as this much fluid commonly causes irritation at a single injection site for several days thereafter.

The issue of when to discontinue depo-Provera must be addressed almost from its inception. Although some investigators consider long-term administration of Provera (over one year) to impose no risk (Berlin & Meinecke, 1981), there are cases of male-to-female transsexuals who have experienced irreversible effects: breast tissue growth and higher voice pitch. This issue will probably not be decided for several more years due to the lack of controlled research in this area and the rarity of the drug's long-term use. Because uncertainty exists about long-term or permanent effects, every effort should be made to discontinue the drug as soon as possible. In one large series, an average of about four months was felt necessary before behavioral techniques could take hold.

How is one to know how early in treatment this decision can be safely made? Self-reports and plethysmograph measurements can be helpful, but attention must be paid to the fact that treatment itself may be producing a falsely positive result. Provera can reduce libido and hence produce diminished reports of sexual activity and reductions in plethysmograph readings. However, it is rare that the drug *eliminates* sexual response. Thus the patient receiving Provera usually reports a decrease in the frequency of sexual daydreams, masturbation, and intercourse, but rarely their abolition, especially if the goal of treatment is to reduce circulating testosterone levels to one-half their original value rather then to produce a prepubescent level. Under these conditions, measurements of sexual response on the plethysmograph reveal reduction in levels of erection to all sexual stimuli of approximately 20% to 35%. However, adequate conditioning and the measurement of effectiveness should continue. It is not currently possible to know whether the *speed* of positive response to therapy under the influence of Provera is reduced. The final outcome is not weakened, however. Further, larger trials of men under treatment with and without Provera will be needed to properly address these issues. Nonetheless, it is reassuring to know that one can reduce the chances of repeated sexual offending while at the same time proceeding with behavioral treatment. In some cases, even were Provera to slow the progress of therapy, this might still be justified if the likelihood of repeated offenses is great. Studies documenting the magnitude of effect Provera exerts on the plethysmograph would be helpful in assessing this issue. Thus far, experience indicates that there is a rough correlation between circulating testosterone levels and plethysmograph response: With a 50% reduction in testosterone levels, the plethysmograph appears to register approximately one-third of its pre-Provera values for the same sexual stimuli.

Of course, these reductions in reported sexual urges and frequencies of masturbation and/or intercourse occur across the broad spectrum of sexual interest. Not only is sexual response to deviant fantasies and stimuli affected, but response to nondeviant fantasies and stimuli is reduced as well. This is unfortunate because often one goal in the treatment of the sexual offender is not only to reduce or eliminate deviant sexual arousal but to increase nondeviant arousal as well. With the current level of understanding, when using these drugs, it is not possible to selectively block arousal to one set of stimuli and not to other sets as well, and it does not now appear that such precision will be forthcoming in the near future.

As with any medication, there are side effects from Provera. These can include lethargy, headache, weight gain, and some feminization, including breast tissue enlargement, change in hair distribution, and increased voice pitch. However, these side effects are absent in most offenders, and only in an exceptional case is the medication discontinued due to side effects. One side effect, already mentioned for cyproterone acetate, has been a decrease in aggression, reported by approximately 40% of offenders taking these drugs. Such an effect is not wholly undesirable, however, in a population of men who have often forced their sexual urges onto others. A surprising number of offenders have welcomed this effect and report peace of mind found in the absence of troubling sexual and aggressive urges. No adverse effects of this reduction in aggressiveness have been described as were initially feared, such as a complacency in business affairs or an inappropriate passivity in interpersonal relationships.

There are nonmedical side effects from the use of Provera, however, that must be taken into consideration as well. The cost of the medication, the cost of trips to the doctor's office for injections if the "depo" form of the drug is used (self-injection is not advisable), and the cost of at least two plasma testosterone levels are not unsubstantial. In addition, the patient selected to receive depo-Provera may perceive that, by this selection, he is identified as a "problem case" and is not to be trusted at large. A special attempt should be made, if at all feasible, to include the patient in the decision to employ Provera, and efforts should be devoted to discontinuing it at the earliest possible time. Sometimes it is appropriate to taper the medication over a period of approximately one month, measuring plethysmograph levels to make certain that treatment effect is not reduced by discontinuing the medication. The effectiveness of ongoing behavioral treatment should be ascertained before completely stopping the medicine.

There are philosophical disagreements with the use of medication in any psychiatric condition, although, as mentioned earlier in this chapter, there has been a growing recognition of the good that can be produced with a combination of behavioral and medical treatments (Comings & Comings, 1982, Marks, 1981a, pp. 164-192, 249-287). Some writers are opposed to the use of antitestosterone agents such as cyproterone acetate or Provera and term their use "chemical castration." Of special concern are the reports that these drugs can induce a calming action and often reduce aggression (Berlin & Coyle,

1981; Cooper, 1981). However, it is also possible that these drugs, given only with the consent of the offender, may actually increase his degree of freedom by rendering him better able to control sexual urges (Berlin, 1981; Halleck, 1981).

Does the offender have a truly "free choice" if he is under some control and scrutiny by the legal system? Should the offender be offered the right to refuse somatic treatment and thereby be punished by incarceration (Bohmer, 1983)? It is impossible to give scientific answers to these questions (and, by their very nature, it may always be impossible), but, on an empiric basis, it appears that the vast majority of offenders who have received Provera believed it was of great help.

- A 14-year-old moderately retarded boy was referred for molesting 17 younger boys in his special boarding school. He was about to be evicted and, in his state, no suitable alternative school was available. With his and his mother's consent, depo-Provera was initiated along with an active aversive and positive conditioning treatment program. Rapid progress was made, but partial regression occurred when attempts to reduce depo-Provera occurred three months after the start of treatment. Further conditioning for two more months was followed by tapering and then discontinuing depo-Provera without recurrence of deviant sexual arousal. A five-year follow-up documented absence of deviant sexual arousal or feminizing side effects, and his education continued successfully.

Not all similar cases may need medication, however.

- A 34-year-old service station owner attempted to commit suicide by firing a revolver at his head after being arrested for molesting his two preadolescent nieces. Instead, he produced a lesion of his temporofrontal areas bilaterally. Following hospitalization and surgical debridement of the injured areas, he was found to manifest poor judgment and lack of impulse control. He committed several more molestations of young girls in his family. Medication was considered, but the patient and his legally appointed guardian refused permission. Therefore, an alternate plan was devised: He would live with his sister and brother-in-law, who guaranteed no supervised or unsupervised contact with minor girls. Behavioral treatment of his heterosexual pedophilia took over two years, but treatment gains were maintained over a three-year follow-up period.

Those philosophically opposed to the use of antitestosterone agents in these disorders have caused a necessary and detailed reexamination of the proper role drugs can play in the treatment of the sexual offender. As a result, guidelines for the use of such agents can be broadly defined:

(1) Antitestosterone agents should be employed only if there is
    (a) a substantial risk of repeated offenses in the period during which behavior therapy has been initiated but has not yet been effective or
    (b) a risk that any single offense will produce substantial harm to a victim as, for example, an act of child molestation as opposed to an act of exhibitionism.
(2) Such agents should be employed for as short a time as possible. Their use should be tapered once evidence is gained that behavior therapy is becoming effective.
(3) Such agents should be given at the lowest dose necessary to produce the required reduction of sexual drive.
(4) Such agents should be employed in cases in which continued monitoring of plethysmograph recordings and plasma testosterone levels can occur.
(5) Such agents should not be employed as the sole therapeutic approach.
(6) Such agents should only be employed in cases in which competent consent can be obtained or in which a guardian can approve their administration.

Some guidelines currently stem from experience rather than research at present. Nonetheless, given the current state of knowledge, they seem both reasonable and practical.

In summary, Provera has been used as part of a behavioral treatment program to reduce sexual arousal to all stimuli during the early part of therapy for noninstitutionalized dangerous sexual offenders. Although compliance problems are effectively eliminated because the medication can be administered in a slowly absorbed intramuscular form, potential benefits are compromised by the occasional occurrence of side effects, by the cost of the therapy, and by the uncertainties inherent in its long-term use. Possible reductions in self-esteem can occur but can also be addressed. It is likely that the use of Provera will continue into the immediate future, and, hopefully, this drug will be employed as a temporary agent and as just one facet of an overall behavioral treatment program.

Other Somatic Therapies

An estrogen (the primary female hormone) analog, diethylstil-besterol, should be discussed briefly. This drug has occasionally been used to produce an antitestosterone effect, but erratic responses and the possibility of thrombotic complications probably limit its utility in treating the sexual offender (Zbytovsky & Zapletálek, 1979).

Individual case reports describe the use of lithium (an agent for bipolar disorder) to decrease deviant sexual arousal (Bártová, 1979). Two surgical procedures have been employed, chiefly in Europe, for the sexual offender. The first, orchiectomy, or castration, is only of historical interest (Berlin & Coyle, 1981; Freund, 1980; Hein, 1981; Wille & Beier, 1989). The second, central nervous system ablation procedures, must currently be viewed as drastic and imprecise. There is an extensive, although somewhat dated literature in this area, chiefly from European sources (Berlin & Coyle, 1981; Freund, 1980; Schmidt & Schorsch, 1981).

Summary

Although there is healthy debate in this area, the use of medications in the treatment of the sexual offender has probably earned a definite, although limited, therapeutic role. The major medication to be considered is Provera, chiefly its depo form, although the occasional use of neuroleptic agents such as thioridazine may be justified. Provera has been found useful in difficult cases in which sexual offenders are at large who are almost certain to reoffend soon, regardless of consequences. For these offenders, behavioral methods will probably not eliminate deviant arousal quickly enough, and hence the temporary use of Provera, especially its depo form, should be considered. The number of such offenders is small and among them are many with central nervous system impairments, lack of impulse control, and offending behaviors of grave risk. In some research series, men who rape and homosexual pedophiles stand out as populations meriting special concern.

Medication should generally be used for a short period of time, averaging three to four months; its immediate goal is a marked reduction, generally to half, in circulating testosterone levels, accompanied by a similar reduction in deviant sexual arousal. Its ultimate purpose is to prevent offenses while behavioral measures are taking hold. As such, medication is a small but occasionally important part of therapy. Hopefully, the decision to employ medication should always involve the participation of the person most affected by its use: the offender himself.

Note

1. Appendix C contains a sample depo-Provera consent form.

9

Homework Assignments

Behavior therapists have slowly shifted from an emphasis on work accomplished during each session toward the recognition of the importance of work done between sessions. Several factors have combined to produce this gradual but steady change. It is becoming increasingly apparent, for example, that an hour spent alone with the therapist may not be as strategic or crucial as was originally believed within the traditional therapies. Indeed, the time and activities between sessions are now recognized as major factors in producing improvement in the maladaptive sexual approach disorders. Moreover, economy of time and resources is quickly becoming a major consideration in planning programs of treatment. Each treatment session with the therapist can be regarded, in this more recent view, as a time for the patient to report his progress, to review what has been helpful and what has not, and to plan further assignments and strategies.

In addition, the importance of treatment response generalization is increasingly being recognized. Are the beneficial results obtained within the treatment session retained outside it? To secure continuation of treatment results for increasing lengths of time and to enhance generalization results to real-life situations, at-home practice is evidently necessary.

Another factor in this growing trend is the recognition that the patient must participate in the planning and follow-through of his own treatment program. Homework assignments allow him to experience and report what works for him, thereby, hopefully, increasing his commitment to treatment goals.

But at-home practice may not necessarily suffice. Treatment must be practiced in a variety of situations that not only emulate but at times duplicate those situations that, in the past, stimulated deviant sexual arousal:

- Perceptible but slow progress was being made with a 37-year-old print shop foreman who had begun masturbating in public two years earlier. His habit had been to fondle himself while driving. Occasionally, he would be sexually stimulated by a passing woman to such an extent that he would masturbate through his open fly, his erect penis thus exposed. Because of his slow progress, less time was taken with actual conditioning in the office and more time was afforded to descriptions and demonstrations of several homework assignments:
  — He was to drive about town, searching out sexually provocative and risky situations and purposefully dwelling on sexual thoughts without masturbating for 12 hours thereafter.
  — During his trips to and from work, he was to immediately chew a foul-tasting propantheline tablet if he felt the urge to masturbate in the car.
  — He was asked to wait 48 hours before any masturbation or intercourse after driving in certain areas connected with a higher risk of encountering provocative situations (such as an area with many prostitutes or X-rated movies) and to practice containing his urge to masturbate in his car until he could arrive home and masturbate privately or engage in intercourse with his wife (see Maletzky & Price, 1984).

Although homework assignments must differ in their specifics based upon each offender's individual patterns, they usually share several common characteristics:

(1) They must match, as closely as possible, the set of stimuli controlling deviant arousal in real-life situations to effectively promote generalization.

(2) They must define for the patient, and others if involved, the situation and the responses to practice as specifically as possible to reduce confusion and the chances for errant or backward conditioning.
(3) They must be feasible enough to reduce obstacles blocking the patient's follow-through.
(4) They should be understandable to the patient as demonstrated by his ability to either paraphrase or practice the assignment within the treatment setting.

Not all assignments can fulfill those four criteria; however, they are valuable as guidelines in devising homework. In previous chapters, descriptions of homework assignments have been presented in the text and in case examples as a necessary part of treatment discussions. This chapter will describe types of homework assignments organized according to treatment technique, because the principles involved can be broadly applied. Case examples will again be utilized to demonstrate the successful, and sometimes unsuccessful, application of these principles.

Aversive Conditioning Techniques

COVERT TECHNIQUES

Within a treatment setting, the therapist has the advantage of environmental control. He or she can employ a number of covert or overt aversive stimuli at appropriate times during the session. It would be ideal if the patient were able to apply similar contingencies in real-life situations, but often it is impractical or impossible.

- Through a retrospective review, it was possible to identify a group of heterosexual pedophiles who exhibited marked plethysmographic response to electric shock as opposed to aversive imagery or aversive odor alone. Treatment staff worked with bioengineers to devise a portable electric shock generator to be worn inside a belt and controlled by the patient through his pocket. Field trials and patient reports were disappointing: Many patients honestly admitted that they would reduce the setting to zero or fail to use the device altogether.
- An equivalent experiment with patients who responded differentially to odor, but not shock, yielded a similar outcome, although for differ-

ent reasons: These patients did use vials of rotting tissues in some real-life situations, but the practice was cumbersome and unnatural. An exhibitionist could not uncover his vial, smell the odor, and imagine aversive consequences while driving his car at the same time; a homosexual pedophile complained that he could not uncover the vial when stimulated by boys in the park near his bus stop because there were too many others who could see him do so.

Although the use of real aversive stimuli is possible in many situations, it is not *always* so. Therefore, covert methods will form, in the foreseeable future, a valuable part of patients' homework assignments. Among these methods, covert sensitization has been most useful as a rapidly learned and easily practiced technique (Brownell & Barlow, 1976; Hayes, Brownell, & Barlow, 1978; Sajwaj, Libet, & Agras, 1974). In its earliest form, covert sensitization homework consisted of tape recordings made by the therapist, describing a brief relaxation technique followed by an idiosyncratic pleasant scene and then by one or more deviant scenes that contained three elements: building deviant sexual arousal, an aversive event or consequence, and (usually) an escape associated with removal of aversive imagery.

- A sample tape recorded for a homosexual pedophile began with 60 seconds of brief relaxation instructions (to improve imagery and provide relief with escape), enhanced over another 60-second period with a scene of rocking gently in a rowboat on a lake, followed by a scene of undressing and fellating a six-year-old boy. The sexual scene, which also lasted 60 seconds, ended with the boy urinating in the offender's mouth with suggestions of disgust, nausea, and vomiting. An escape was provided, however, with relief associated with escape from the boy, cleaning up, and breathing fresh air. The patient was asked to listen to this three-minute tape four times each week.

More recent forms of covert sensitization homework make the technique entirely imaginal by even eliminating the tape recorder:

- A transvestite was asked to caress women's stockings each day while sniffing his vial of foul odor. He complained that his wife objected because the smell lingered and was too strong. Although he accepted the suggestion to caress the stockings and merely imagine aversive consequences, his wife then refused to allow access to her garments. As an alternative, he was asked only to imagine the feel of these garments in association with *only the imagination* of a foul odor and nauseating scenes such as fecal stains on the garments. It appeared that this strictly covert procedure was partially responsible for his rapid improvement.

Such covert techniques need not be limited to imagery in a home setting. For example, a patient might be asked to purposely seek out places from which he had previously exposed and imagine exposing again with aversive imagery, such as being apprehended by police. In addition, the offender can be asked to simply imagine, vividly, adverse consequences whenever deviant sexual urge occurs. While the value of such techniques has not been rigorously assessed thus far, they certainly appear to possess potent therapeutic efficacy. However, they do not lend themselves to objective scrutiny: How is it possible to measure the role they play in causing reductions in deviant sexual arousal? Indeed, how is it possible even to know to what extent the patient is carrying out the assignments? Comments about these issues will be reserved for the end of this chapter.

OVERT TECHNIQUES

Contingent electric shock (Abel, Lewis, & Clancy, 1970; Evans, 1980; Quinsey, Chaplin, & Carrigan, 1980) and foul odor (Levin, Barry, Gambero, Wolfinsohn, & Smith, 1977; Maletzky, 1973b, 1974b, 1980a) have been demonstrated to reduce deviant sexual arousal when consistently applied within a treatment setting. Although it is difficult to apply these aversive stimuli outside of such a setting, these difficulties are not insurmountable and efforts should be made to combine overt with covert homework assignments whenever possible (Adams, Tollison, & Carson, 1981; Josiason, Fantuzzo, & Rosen, 1980; Maletzky, 1980a; Rooth & Marks, 1974).

Experience within a large outpatient sexual abuse clinic matches that of several in- and outpatient samples that demonstrate that homework assignments employing electric shock have not been as helpful as was initially hoped (Maletzky, 1980a; Stang, 1974). Even when an unobtrusive, small shock generator was employed, patients reported not administering the stimulus or, with variable dose units, not delivering a truly aversive shock. The electric stimulus itself is momentary; moreover, attempts to have patients deliver a series of brief shocks have not proven feasible. Further work with more sophisticated stimulus generators is in order, however, as there are certain patients who will demonstrate the greatest decline in deviant sexual arousal with this form of aversive stimulus.

While some therapists routinely ask their patients to wear a rubber band around their wrist and snap it upon encountering a provocative deviant stimulus setting, others believe this has little value. Neither side can rely on any controlled data thus far; however, while the negative impact of this procedure may be mild, it also offered the least obtrusive and possibly the most consistently followed aversive stimulus employed to date. It also serves as a reminder for the patient to be aware of potentially dangerous situations.

Foul odor has produced apparently effective results when used in homework assignments but has been difficult for the offender to apply in real-life situations. However, a good number of sexual offenders can work in conjunction with the therapist to devise a means of employing foul odor inconspicuously.

- Several exhibitionists were able to sniff foul odor unobtrusively while passing tempting situations in their vehicles as, for example, driving by a bus or van with an attractive woman inside. Several men who masturbated in public also found foul odor relatively easy to apply in their vehicles. A number of heterosexual pedophiles, however, could not apply the odor long enough to be effective: Their personal contact with victims made it unlikely they could use the odor inconspicuously.

As in other areas of treatment with the sexual offender, it appears that each situation may be unique enough to merit a detailed behavioral analysis and a flexible enough approach to learn from one set of experiences and shift to different assignments as necessary.

One relatively novel means of applying an aversive stimulus for homework assignments is the use of foul taste. A number of bitter substances can be concocted for such use. The behavioral literature contains references to concentrated lemon juice (Gold & Neufeld, 1965; Maletzky, 1980a) and quinine (Adams, Tollison, & Carson, 1981). The former may not be aversive enough for some, and it is difficult to conceal when applying it from the usual dispensers; the latter is a potentially cardiotoxic drug. As more extensively described in Chapter 3, experience with propantheline (trade name, Probanthine) has been generally favorable as it is universally perceived as bitter, especially when chewed; can be taken inconspicuously; can be safely swallowed or spit out to adjust for stimulus durations and hence contingent administration; and is relatively portable and inexpensive (Maletzky, 1980a).

- A 47-year-old garage mechanic with homosexual pedophilia was asked to carry five to seven propantheline tablets in a vial at all times. When encountering a provocative deviant stimulus in shopping malls, buses, or on walks about his neighborhood, he was to take one-half a tablet and chew it thoroughly for 30 to 120 seconds while trying to imagine sexual activity with a young boy that had nauseating consequences.

In this example, it can be seen that covert and overt assignments are combined. Again, trial and error will be necessary for many offenders to determine the most effective procedures. Results from plethysmograph recordings can help by revealing which combinations of sexual stimuli are most appealing and which combinations of aversive stimuli are most effective in countering this arousal.

Propantheline can be obtained with a physician's prescription and is available in 7.5 mg and 15 mg sizes. The lower dosage is quite adequate for purposes of taste aversion; the patient may be instructed to break the tablets into halves or quarters so that the taste is sufficiently vile with just a small amount. While the patient is instructed to chew the pills as long as exposure to the deviant stimuli exists and then to spit the contents out if possible, even swallowing two to three 15 mg tablets would produce no harmful effects. Higher doses would not be dangerous, but temporary side effects such as dry mouth, blurry vision, and constipation *could* occur. Those with glaucoma, bowel or urinary obstructions, ulcerative colitis, myasthenia gravis, or severe heart, liver, or kidney disease should avoid the drug. Even though there has been no report of toxicity with propantheline, a physician should always supervise its administration.

Aversive behavior rehearsal (see Chapter 3), another overt aversive technique, would appear, at first glance, to be limited to an office or rare hospital setting (Jones & Frei, 1977; Maletzky, 1984b; McGonaghy, 1972; Server, 1970; Wickramaserka, 1980). However, this technique can be used in selective cases.

- A 52-year-old exhibitionist, a lay minister in a fundamentalist order, underwent standard aversive behavior rehearsal with fair results.

However, this procedure could not be repeated when he was transferred to a physician in a distant rural community. He was asked to have two family members observe him exposing from his truck and to make no response for three minutes. He was to repeat this once each week for three consecutive weeks. He and his family members reported no further impulses to expose thereafter, despite the not infrequent opportunity to do so.

- A 23-year-old graduate chemistry student with a 12-year history of exposing was asked to expose to himself in a mirror twice a day for two weeks. He reported cessation of all urges to expose within three weeks of initiating this practice. However, a variety of other techniques were in effect at the same time. Still, this patient had been making tedious progress to that point. Plethysmograph tracings demonstrated marked lowering of deviant sexual arousal thereafter.

Although aversive behavior rehearsal is usually restricted to patients with exhibitionism, the technique is occasionally equally powerful in other paraphilias (see Chapter 3). A heterosexual pedophile might be asked to "molest" a large girl doll in front of a mirror three to four times a week. A transvestite could be assigned (with his permission) to cross-dress in front of a videotape camera, then view the tape himself or with family members; in any case, these powerfully aversive situations must be approached slowly and, always, with informed consent.

Clearly, these aversive conditioning methods enable the therapist to design a creative approach to each individual sexual offender's treatment program. As in the case of in-office aversion procedures, these techniques must be applied with a consideration not only of demonstrated efficacy in controlled reports in the literature but with an appreciation of individual differences and the feasibility, in the practical and financial sense, of that technique's application.

Reconditioning Techniques

Masturbation is and probably will remain for some time a private act. With the current level of knowledge and technical sophistication, it is difficult to measure the degree of erection during this act. However, the use of genital self-stimulation assignments can substantially undercut what some consider to be the roots of deviant sexual arousal: deviant sexual fantasies (Marshall & Lippers, 1977).

Chapter 4, in presenting the reconditioning techniques, has already provided a description of homework in this area. It would be helpful here, however, to review this important area so recently shown to be highly effective, especially in combination with other behavior therapy techniques (Marshall, 1979).

There are now two major techniques that use masturbation and fantasy to help reduce deviant sexual arousal.

MASTURBATORY SATIATION

In this technique, the patient is asked to purposely masturbate to nondeviant fantasies or material and, immediately following ejaculation, attempt to masturbate for varying lengths of time to deviant stimuli (see Chapter 4 for a more complete explanation). This compels sexual attention to deviant stimuli at a time when, theoretically, the offender's ability to become aroused is at its lowest. Moreover, it makes the offender masturbate to repetitive deviant fantasies over and over, thereby producing boredom and even aversion in connection with those fantasies. However, there are alternative ways of explaining the mechanisms by which this technique produces its beneficial effects (Marshall, 1979; Marshall & Lippers, 1977).

In practice, masturbatory satiation seems to work very well with some offenders and not at all with others, but there is now a frustrating lack of data with which to make this distinction beforehand.

- When a 52-year-old grocery clerk was sentenced to five years' probation for molesting young boys, he was required by the court to receive treatment in a sexual abuse clinic. His plethysmograph, however, demonstrated very little arousal to any stimuli and, accordingly, he admitted great difficulty in obtaining arousal in the treatment setting. He reported, however, an active fantasy life, especially during masturbation. Along with other assignments, he was asked to masturbate daily to scenes of adult, consenting, heterosexual relationships until ejaculation, at which point he was instructed to continue masturbating to deviant fantasies of sexual activity with young boys for 30 minutes more. Following 14 weeks of this assignment, he reported no further sexual arousal to young boys.

MASTURBATORY FANTASY CHANGE

In this technique, the patient is asked to abruptly change his fantasies during masturbation (or to change the actual stimuli being used, such as pictures) from deviant to nondeviant material at the point of ejaculatory inevitability. With each succeeding episode of masturbation, he is asked to initiate this change earlier and earlier until he is masturbating exclusively to nondeviant stimuli. Unfortunately, masturbatory fantasy change does not always proceed without difficulty.

- When asked to practice masturbatory fantasy change, a 32-year-old heterosexual pedophile with a 15-year history of sexual offenses insisted he was a "born-again Christian" and could not violate his principles by masturbating. He was able, however, to be convinced to use this technique during intercourse.

- A 24-year-old service station attendant was arrested for his second rape and sentenced to a one-year term at a correctional facility with daily passes to work. He demonstrated high plethysmograph arousal to aggressive sexuality but complained that he had no privacy to practice masturbatory fantasy change at the correctional facility. His therapist was able to secure a release for him to go home, under supervision, twice a week for masturbatory change practice.

- An elderly retired truck driver had been convicted of molesting a young girl living next door. He claimed he could not masturbate because he was a member of a religious faith that held masturbation to be immoral. A conference was arranged with the patient and his minister; following a thorough explanation of the goal of this technique, the minister helped persuade the patient to follow through with this assignment, granting a dispensation in his case.

Such outcomes are not always positive, and masturbation techniques, while powerful, cannot always be relied upon to help due to compliance factors and the very private nature of the act itself. More recently, attempts have been made to discreetly "view" at-home masturbation by asking the offender to tape-record his fantasies, spoken aloud, and then share these tape-recordings with the therapist as a check on compliance and to provide a focal point around which fantasies can be reviewed (Abel & Becker, 1984). Although such tape recordings have generally been employed in the satiation technique, they can also be profitably used for fantasy change procedures as well.

Although at first glance it would seem that such assaults on privacy would best remain within the confines of the therapeutic relationship, Abel and coworkers have used these recordings in a group format: Offenders listen to and critique each other's masturbation tapes (Abel, 1984). Such procedures are less costly than individual therapy, and future efforts will no doubt be directed toward applying group methods to what were considered areas appropriate only for individual work. Examples could include relaxation procedures, refining sexual scene hierarchies, and sharing masturbation tapes.

The limitations that masturbation techniques possess in their involvement with essentially private acts might also partly explain their efficacy in certain cases because they combine fantasy with the sexual pleasure of climax. Attempts to somehow study and quantify the process of masturbation must be made cautiously so as not to lessen its value as a treatment tool.

Positive Conditioning Techniques

DESENSITIZATION

Desensitization has been employed in behavior therapy longer than any other behavioral technique, chiefly for the classical deconditioning of phobias and for an increasing number of related disorders such as obsessive-compulsive illness and posttraumatic stress disorder (Freund, Scher, & Hucker, 1983). It is not unusual to view some sexual offenders as suffering from fear-related behaviors, although it is unlikely that a phobia of social interactions with women, for example, can wholly explain a particular patient's heterosexual pedophilia.

Nevertheless, in combination with other conditioning techniques, desensitization often forms an important weapon in the arsenal against sexual abuse. Chapter 5 describes its use in such cases, but additional mention here is warranted because it is also a technique that lends itself well to homework assignments. For example, relaxation exercises are generally incorporated into many behavioral approaches, and this is no less true in the treatment of the sexual disorders. While relaxation, in itself, is usually not the ultimate goal in these techniques, many patients employ relaxation to good advantage in day-to-day situations. However, it is usually included to enhance imagery during negative and positive conditioning. After presenting relaxation as a skill to be learned in the process of treatment, it can also be used in a desensitization program if indicated.

- A 14-year-old socially retarded boy had been arrested three times for molesting young boys in his neighborhood. To prevent institutionalization, outpatient therapy was requested. Evaluation indicated a high sexual arousal to homosexual pedophiliac stimuli, but the patient also demonstrated an almost phobic response to girls his own age. Attempts to use group and individual settings to practice social skills training were ineffective. Desensitization was attempted with relaxation followed by a hierarchic presentation of increasingly anxious situations with girls his own age. Tape recordings were made with relaxation, and three such scenes were recorded per tape with instructions to listen to the current tape five times a week. Because of scheduling difficulties, this part of treatment was already two months old by the time aversive conditioning was initiated. This afforded the opportunity to observe differential treatment effects. By this time, the patient was making gratifying strides in social approaches to girls his own age, but deviant sexual arousal was reduced just slightly. Completion of aversive conditioning led to elimination of deviant sexual arousal.

Desensitization is especially indicated in introverted, socially phobic patients but needs to be applied with sensitivity for individual patient differences. Across all sexual offenders, a select few will respond very well to this technique, but it is unlikely that desensitization alone will actually convert deviant to nondeviant sexual arousal. In addition, the sexual offender will require not only a hierarchy with personalized content but, occasionally, one with carefully attuned steps from one level of anxiety to the next. As has been amply demonstrated, construction of the hierarchy can be a crucial step in successful resolution of phobic behavior (Wolpe, 1969).

Operant Conditioning Techniques

Operant techniques are present in all human interactions. Although such processes often go unrecognized, they can be used systematically in the treatment of the sexual offender. In a clinical setting, a therapist can employ praise, time with the patient, and differential attention to positive statements as opposed to negative ones. But a patient himself, at home, can also attempt to arrange contingencies to enhance the likelihood of success with mutually approved goals:

- A 37-year-old bank officer kept detailed records of urges to molest girls and times of masturbation. In an office session, he and his therapist devised a graph, to be marked daily, to display frequency and intensity of urges, episodes of masturbation, and deviant fantasies. The graph was displayed in his bedroom at home, and an anonymous copy was placed on one wall of the therapist's office. The visual feedback was helpful in increasing energy and enthusiasm in treatment.
- A 15-year-old homosexual pedophile was making painfully slow progress in aversive conditioning and related techniques when a renegotiation of his treatment contract was made. Table 9.1 presents a detailed account of the new contract. It appeared that a major factor was a clearly defined contingency program with tangible and immediate reinforcers (tokens) tied to an eventual monetary reward for progress made. The table also documents the extensive cross-agency communication necessary, especially in the treatment of the juvenile offender.

While contracts can be devised with more or less detail and sophistication, the essential elements include cooperation in devising the program, flexibility in administering it, and the use of tangible and useful reinforcers. In different cases, appropriate positive reinforcers might be favorite foods, attention, luxuries, a trip, a nap, a club membership, dinner out, and so on.

Theoretically, when deviant behavior is negatively reinforced, the probability of its recurrence should decline. But sexual gratification, even if only in fantasy form, is so rewarding that most other contingencies may pale in comparison. In addition, it is questionable whether the sexual offender, already suffering psychological damage through the processes of legal exposure, guilt induction, and separation from his family, should be subjected to further verbal penalty in treatment. The provision of positive reinforcement not only can aid in the acquisition of new behaviors but boost a person's self-esteem and further encourage him to pursue mutually defined therapeutic goals.

Table 9.1 *Examples of a Contingency Program for an Adolescent Homosexual Pedophile*

Behaviors to be Reinforced:	Reinforcer[a]	Certifier/Witness
1. Attending each weekly treatment session	4 tokens	therapist
2. Listening to sensitization tape five times each week; self-administering foul odor	1 token each time	parents
3. Chewing bitter pill (propantheline) in two school yards previously associated with pedophiliac behavior	2 tokens each time	parents
4. Completing one written assignment each week: such as sexual history, overt and covert behavior logs, stimuli associated with pedophiliac urges, and letters of clarification to victims	3 tokens	therapist
5. Attending weekly meetings with probation officer	2 tokens	probation officer (juvenile division)
6. Asking teenage girl for a date	10 tokens	parents
7. Joining one extracurricular activity at school	10 tokens	school vice principal
8. Providing two hours of community service each week, such as performing errands for the Rape Victim Advocate's Office	1 token	Rape Victim Advocate's Office
9. Devising one new and sensible treatment plan for himself each month	10 tokens	therapist
10. Avoiding any drug or alcohol use each week	2 tokens	parents

a. One token = 50¢. Graph of cumulative tokens earned was displayed prominently in family kitchen; tokens were cashed in weekly.

Adjunctive Techniques

Homework assignments related to the adjunctive techniques described in Chapter 7 will no doubt suggest themselves to the therapist familiar with the clinical literature. Several such techniques have proven especially helpful in treatment of the sexual offender. Chief among these are *social skills training* (Barlow, Abel, Blanchard, Bristow, & Young, 1977; Conger & Farrell, 1981; Lewinsohn, Bigland, & Zeiss, 1976; Lipton & Nelson, 1980; McFall, 1982) and *assertiveness training* (Alberti & Emmons, 1975; Heimberg & Becker, 1981), both of which enjoy an extensive literature that will not be reviewed here. However, examples of some special applications of these techniques to the sexual offender may prove helpful.

- When a 19-year-old college student was first referred to a general psychology clinic, his chief complaint was "shyness." It was learned only later that he was also being charged with several counts of attempted rape, a behavior that seemed to contrast sharply with his seemingly passive introspective style. Although deviant sexual arousal was deconditioned to a moderate extent using aversive treatment techniques, he continued to manifest low social approach behaviors to appropriate-age females and still possessed some occasional, but stubbornly persistent, arousal patterns to stimuli associated more with aggression than with nonaggressive sexual stimulation. In coordination with social skills training in a group for sexual offenders, he was also given an assignment as part of his psychology class to research the pertinent literature of social skills training and devise a program of in vivo desensitization to initiating social interactions, including dating girls his age. He seemed pessimistic about this assignment, but reluctantly agreed, only to find that some tentative efforts on his part were moderately successful. This led to increased risk taking and a gratifying acceleration of response to aversive conditioning methods.

There is often a dilemma facing the sexual therapist in such cases: How much time should be allotted to what appear to be secondary treatment goals? Similarly, what portion of the patient's financial resources can justifiably be allocated to such "ancillary" techniques?

Some treatment decisions in these areas can be partially based on the extensive literature on the acquisition of social skills (Barlow, Reynolds, & Agras, 1973; Curran, 1977; Lewinsohn et al., 1976; Reckers & Vasni, 1977; Whitman & Quinsey, 1981). However, the role that such techniques might play in the treatment and rehabilitation of the sexual offender cannot currently be determined. It makes clinical sense to incorporate these techniques in an adjunctive manner so that they accompany other, more technical, methods of treatment.

A number of other homework assignments using ancillary techniques will suggest themselves to the therapist, especially in the area of *environmental change*. One patient may need to take a different route home to avoid passing a playground. Another may need to call his wife before leaving work so that she will know, if he is tardy, that he may have exposed on the way home. Still another may need to change his place of residence, because the associations between old environments and behaviors are strong. A homosexual pedophile should not continue to coach Little League, even after successful treatment; similarly, a transvestite would be encouraged to cancel his subscription to a lingerie catalog. While these situations might pose interesting challenges to the offender, they probably are not worth the risk of triggering any lingering tendencies.

Couples in *marital and family therapy* often need to practice better communication at home, such as paraphrasing, summarizing, perception checks, and behavioral observations. Alternatively, they may require feedback on their decision-making skills or need to learn to express feelings directly and to avoid accusatory statements. Homework assignments in these areas can proceed regardless of, and in conjunction with, conditioning therapies. While there appears to be value in therapist constancy here, there is also the growing conviction that specialists in marital, family, victim, and group therapies can be incorporated into the general treatment plan, provided one therapist assumes central coordinating control and all personnel involved communicate effectively.

Another technique often used in all forms of treatment is *bibliotherapy*. Although merely reading a book may occasion nothing more than intellectual arousal and curiosity, behavioral change can be fostered by emphasizing the *use* of information in written form. Books such as *Male Sexuality* (Zilbergeld, 1978) and *The Joy of Sex* (Comfort, 1972) can offer basic sexual education and enhance nondeviant sexual arousal. There are excellent texts for assertiveness training (Alberti & Emmons, 1975); the pamphlet "He Told Me Not to Tell" (Fay, 1979) among diverse others is an excellent source for helping with empathy training. However, reading assignments should be as clear as possible, with chapters and pages assigned, especially with the request that the offender keep notes regarding two questions:

(1) How does this material apply to me?

(2) How can I apply this material to my own life?

The therapist can review these written notes during succeeding sessions. In this manner, the patient may obtain some tangible benefit from his reading assignments.

Homework Compliance

Across all forms of homework, however, lies a shadow cast on this otherwise bright picture: reliability. Almost 90% of offenders responding to an anonymous questionnaire admitted that they did not complete some assignments and over 20% failed to carry out any techniques at home. Can therapists verify patients' reports? Can they trust what are, currently, private events? If the patient, under relaxation is asked to imagine a scene, can the process be made public, observable, and quantified? For that matter, can the state of relaxation be assessed? What is an offender truly thinking when a slide of a young girl flashes on the scene? What fantasies is he entertaining when he masturbates?

There are few studies to assist in answering these questions. It helps to know that clinicians using these same techniques in different parts of the world report similar self-report and plethysmograph data (Abel & Becker, 1984). It is also of some reassurance that patients report that such methods are helpful. Cross-validation of plethysmograph findings with multiple systems approaches via the polygraph promises to shed some light on these shadowy regions.

Even now, however, therapists can, in several ways, help to improve compliance with homework assignments.

(1) *Trust building.* Although it may sound trite, there is really no approach in this area that can help as much as fostering the subjective feeling of mutual respect and trust. The patient must be able to verify that he is not being stereotyped or denigrated. Even more important, he must feel he is a participant in the treatment course and that therapy is a joint learning experience. It is helpful to adopt a nonpatronizing approach and to use the patient's own vernacular in building scenes and understanding techniques.

(2) Verification. It often helps to frequently ask the patient to paraphrase homework instructions to make certain he has understood them. In addition, it is reassuring to patient and therapist alike for the patient to demonstrate, in the office, how he uses the foul odor while listening to a tape, how he chews a bitter pill, and so on. Paradoxically, trust is often seen to be built through such encounters. However, at times it may be necessary to test plethysmographic responses as a means of verifying compliance. Some offenders can be judiciously confronted if such objective data do not correlate with their reports of consistently following through with homework assignments.

(3) Reports of significant others. Friends and relatives can sometimes keep a patient "honest" by reporting frequency of homework practice; however, more often, they can help by participating in sessions designed to acquaint them with assignments. They can often encourage the patient to complete homework, and they can reinforce him when he does.

(4) Office work. In some cases, the patient can be invited to do homework in the office.

- A 35-year-old construction worker with a 15-year history of molesting young girls consistently reported listening to his tapes at home each day, but plethysmograph readings on deviant stimuli remained high. He agreed to visit the therapist's office three times a week to listen to the tapes in an empty interview room there. He showed more rapid progress thereafter.

Summary

Homework assignments have long been applied to almost all areas of psychology and psychiatry and are even blossoming in medicine as well (e.g., exercise and diet regimens). They seem particularly applicable to the behaviorial treatment of the sexual offender because of a need to enhance generalization from in vitro to in vivo modes and to guarantee safety being at large—especially crucial in an outpatient sexual abuse clinic setting.

There is no question that homework assignments form an integral part of the total treatment package for the consumer-patient who is a sexual offender. Although it is difficult, with the current state of knowledge, to foresee how some assignments can be verified and measured, it is also true that future research can help to identify the most beneficial factors in the homework package. With the current level of understanding, is seems that, if such treatment is to be as successful as possible, homework should be included in the treatment of every sexual offender. It is crucial, however, not to *rely* upon homework assignments to reduce deviant sexual arousal; noncompliance is quite high, especially for the aversive conditioning techniques. It seems prudent now to perform aversive techniques in the clinic setting with sufficient force and frequency *as if the offender is not completing any homework on his own.* Any homework completed will therefore strengthen in-office conditioning but will not be relied upon to alter behavior on its own.

10

Data Generated by an
Outpatient Sexual Abuse Clinic

The Sexual Abuse Clinic of Portland, Oregon, has been in operation as a distinct entity since 1978, although data to be presented here include results on patients treated beginning five years earlier. The clinic is not associated with any governmental agency but is a private fee-for-service organization. Patients are treated in six locations with similar facilities. Two are centrally located in an area of over 1.5 million inhabitants while four others are in moderately populated cities 45, 60, 90, and 100 miles from the central city. These latter serve wide areas of two adjoining states. Without these distant offices, patients would have to travel 200 to 300 miles round-trip for each appointment.

The very concept of an *outpatient* sexual abuse clinic implied an ability to ascertain whether a sexual offender is safe to remain at large. Fortunately, there is evidence that can be used for informed opinion on danger of being at large for various populations of offenders, although predictions in many cases remain imprecise (Maletzky, in press). Chapter 1 addressed this problem in general;

and there are more detailed data on this issue to be presented later in this chapter.

If the patient is determined to be at a high risk to reoffend within the community, referral to an inpatient sexual offenders' unit is mandatory. Assessment and treatment within such a unit may well include all the behavioral techniques already employed in outpatient care although usually on a more intensive basis than can be realized in the clinic setting. The overriding difference is in the security necessary to protect the community.

Once such a decision is reached and assignment to an outpatient program has been made, an assessment of which techniques will be most helpful can proceed. Information must be collected to determine which assessment techniques, therapeutic procedures, and homework assignments will be most helpful. Obviously, as treatment continues, more data will become available with which to evaluate each patient's progress. There are few patients for whom the therapist can predict, during the first few sessions, an entire treatment course. The collection of such data in a number of settings during treatment and on extensive follow-up, however, has provided valuable clinical information from which to learn more about the most effective treatments to employ in individual cases.

Such data can now be obtained from a variety of sources. This chapter will provide results of various treatment techniques at one sexual abuse clinic during a period of 17 years. The literature now available indicates that these findings are representative of a variety of other outpatient programs (Abel & Becker, 1984; Kroop, 1984; Slaughter, 1976; Wolfe, 1984). By critically examining the results of such work, intelligent choices can be made not only in selecting appropriate therapies and making sound recommendations to judicial agencies but in planning for prospective and well-controlled studies as well.

The Sexual Abuse Clinic staff includes five therapists at the doctoral level, two clinical social workers, four mental health therapists, and a psychiatrist-director (who devotes approximately 20% of his time to the clinic) as well as secretarial, business office, and reception staff. One psychologist, one social worker, and one therapist provide family, victim, and group therapies. The remaining psychologists and therapists provide complete treatment programs for their patients. To date, all personnel involved in actual conditioning have been male. However, two female therapists are in the process of preparing to perform conditioning and plethysmographic work. Female therapists have already been helpful in providing social skills training and a woman's perspective in empathy training and group therapy as well. In addition, these therapists have provided invaluable supportive and therapeutic counseling for victims and their families. The psychiatrist-director performs administrative and research functions, screens all new referrals, and performs supervision via weekly or biweekly meetings with each doctoral-level or master's-level therapist; through these meetings, all cases are reviewed.

Equipment found at all locations includes the penile plethysmograph, slide and movie projectors, videotape cameras and recorders, audiotape recorders, odor pumps, electric shock generators, biofeedback devices, and assorted electronic equipment necessary to combine the presentation of slides, movies, videotapes, and stories with aversive and positive stimuli. An extensive library of pornographic material in the form of slides, pictures, movies, and video- and audiotape recordings has been accumulated through the years through outright purchases, the production of material internally (generally drawings keyed to each patient's deviant arousal patterns), donations from offenders, and material collected by police or district attorneys' offices following confiscation.[1]

Physical separation of the patient from the therapist during presentation of stimuli is possible through partitions with one-way mirrors to allow (with the patient's consent) visualization of the treatment process. Appendix D describes in greater detail the equipment used and the physical setting in which it is employed. The Association for the Treatment of Sexual Abusers, a new organization, has established equipment and laboratory guidelines that can be obtained directly from the association.[2] Psychologists and psychiatrists may be unfamiliar with moderately sophisticated electronic instrumentation. While such devices may seem foreboding (see Figure D.1 to D.5 in Appendix D), in practice, the use of such equipment is easily learned and does not impair the human interaction necessary to all forms of therapy.

The time course of treatment varies considerably depending on offender characteristics and practical considerations. The *average* offender receiving outpatient treatment is seen once or twice a week for the first three to six months, then twice a month for several more months. Thereafter, the offender is seen monthly for another three to four months before booster sessions every three months are initiated.

Thus the average offender is in treatment one and a half to two years, although a certain amount of this time is occupied by infrequent sessions.

In the process of treating the sexual offender, it has become clear that the demands of a treatment session can fight against rigid time schedules:

- In the treatment of a heterosexual pedophile, hourly sessions were planned. However, the patient's plethysmograph readings were uniformly low regardless of the type of stimulus presented, although they increased slightly as the sessions progressed. This patient explained to his therapist that he only got "warmed up" after an extended period; lengthening treatment sessions to one and a half to two hours helped produce more valid readings.

- An exhibitionist complained of the opposite problem: He could become highly aroused initially but became satiated quite rapidly. By treating him in 15- to 30-minute sessions, with 10- to 30-minute rest intervals interposed, a steadier course was possible.

- A heterosexual pedophile, court-mandated to undertake treatment at the clinic, lived and worked in a rural community 250 miles distant. Weekend appointments were arranged, which consisted of two one-hour sessions separated by two hours all on a single day so as to obviate the need for weekly trips. With visits to the clinic only twice per month, he still made rapid progress.

It has become clear that flexibility is essential in arranging the practical aspects of treatment. This is also true in an area not often discussed in texts: the cost of treatment. Many (but not the majority of) sexual offender outpatients are in lower socioeconomic brackets. Long-term flexible payment arrangements ease the financial burden of therapy that is often imposed against the patient's will. The offender will appreciate whatever arrangements can be made in this direction, and therapy will no doubt be enhanced.

Again, more detailed descriptions of equipment found in a sexual abuse clinic are found in Appendix D. In addition, Appendix C presents some of the necessary forms employed in the workings of the clinic, including a standard progress note form, a patient information brochure/consent form, and a depo-Provera consent form.

Table 10.1 *Primary Sexual Diagnoses of All Offenders Treated in the Sexual Abuse Clinic (N = 5,000)*

Primary diagnosis[a]	Percentage	N
Heterosexual pedophilia	57.3	2,865
Homosexual pedophilia	17.1	855
Exhibitionism	15.4	770
Rape	2.9	145
Public masturbation	1.5	75
Voyeurism	1.4	70
Frotteurism	1.2	60
Transvestism	1.2	60
Fetishism	0.6	30
Obscene telephone callers	0.5	25
Sadomasochism	0.5	25
Zoophilia	0.4	20
	100.0	5,000

a. In cases of multiple diagnoses, a primary diagnosis was ascertained. For example, 7% of pedophiles were both heterosexual and homosexual in their arousal to minors; these men were always assigned a primary diagnosis of either heterosexual or homosexual pedophilia based upon their histories and arousal patterns.

Subjects

DIAGNOSTIC CATEGORIES

Outcome data have been routinely collected in the treatment of sexual offenders during the past 14 years. Thus far, results in the treatment of 5,000 offenders have been obtained and will be presented in the remainder of this chapter.

Table 10.1 (a re-presentation of Table 1.9) presents the primary sexual diagnoses of this large group, all of whom are male. The clinic has treated just 15 women thus far. Their data are not included in the current sample and neither are they presented as a separate group due to the small number of cases treated and the hazard thereby of overgeneralization.

In cases of multiple sexual offender diagnoses, a primary diagnosis was chosen, based upon the major offense. This distinction was difficult in only a few cases:

- On routine testing, a 16-year-old boy who entered treatment because of molesting two sisters, 5 and 11, showed high plethysmograph readings to sexual stimuli associated with both young girls and boys. Upon confrontation about these results, he also admitted to molesting several young boys in his school and to occasionally masturbating to fantasies involving young boys. Because the plethysmograph-documented arousals to young boys were fewer than those to young girls, and because the time spent in fantasies about young boys was less than time spent fantasizing about young girls, his primary diagnosis continued to be heterosexual pedophilia with a secondary diagnosis of homosexual pedophilia. He was treated, of course, for both conditions.

As in this example, the secondary diagnosis of homosexual pedophilia in heterosexual pedophiles proves to be the most common cause of multiple diagnoses and hence raises questions of etiologic significance that have not yet been addressed. On a practical level, routine testing for homosexual pedophilia should be included in the evaluation of each heterosexual pedophile and vice versa.

As with most other facilities treating sexual offenders, the majority of patients in this clinic have been heterosexual pedophiles. However, several trends in these data are of interest. Figure 10.1 follows the four major primary diagnoses over the 17-year span of these data and documents a striking trend: The lion's share of sexual offenders entering treatment during the earlier years were exhibitionists but, in more recent years, heterosexual pedophiles have come to dominate. A moderate increase in homosexual pedophiles of advancing ages is also seen along with a leveling of referrals for exhibitionists, while referrals of rapists have remained relatively stable. Throughout the years 1973 to 1977, the probability that any sexual offender entering treatment would be diagnosed an exhibitionist was 57%; for the years 1978 to 1990, the figure was 15%. Conversely, the likelihood an offender would be diagnosed a heterosexual pedophile in 1973 to 1977 was 32%; in 1978 to 1990, it was 68%. Because the number of offenders admitted to the clinic has increased each year, the data now to be presented come, in the main, from heterosexual pedophiles (N = 2,865). However, as seen in Table 10.1, sizeable numbers of homosexual pedophiles (N = 855) and exhibitionists (N = 770) have been treated. The numbers of offenders treated primarily for the remaining maladaptive sexual approach disorders—such as voyeurism, fetishism, and transvestism—are small, but the high correlations of

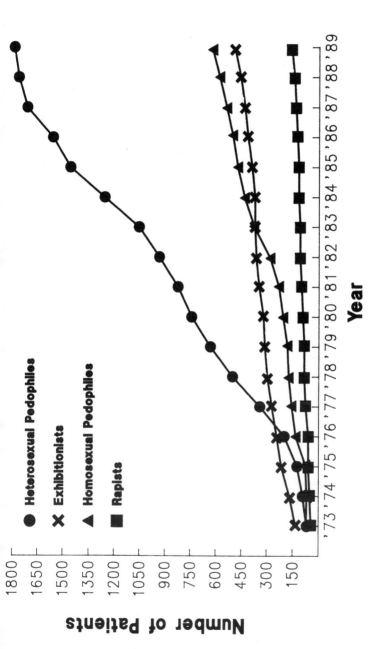

Figure 10.1 Cumulative Number of Patients with the Four Major Primary Diagnostic Categories Entering the Sexual Abuse Clinic, 1973 Through 1990 (N = 4,635)

219

outcome data among groups inspire some confidence in how well the results can be generalized.

This change in incidence of heterosexual pedophilia *relative* to exhibitionism has no doubt stemmed from the increasing awareness and reporting of sexual crimes against children. A broad spectrum of individuals involved with children have contributed their efforts to this endeavor: parents, other relatives, neighbors, pastoral counselors, school personnel, and governmental agency workers. All those working in this area need to continue their efforts at publicizing the positive outcomes therapy can produce. However, this increase is also most surely a dark reflection of changing social configurations: More families are now fractured, divided, reunited, and shifted about without the reassuring confines of marriage and a stable family structure. Stepfathers as well as live-in and drop-in boyfriends are currently commonplace. Girls may dash from bath to bedroom half dressed, naively unaware that the eyes of arousal belong to a man whose name they have just learned.

SOURCES OF REFERRAL

Despite the changing pattern of diagnostic categories throughout the years, sources referring these offenders have remained relatively constant. Table 10.2 lists the percentage of patients referred from major sources for the eight largest diagnostic categories. (Table 1.10 in Chapter 1 lists referral sources for all offenders, not divided by diagnostic categories.) The data do not reveal many sizeable differences across diagnostic groups. However, rapists were far more often referred by corrections officers after adjudication within the legal system, whereas the majority of pedophiles were referred when they were undergoing examination for trial or sentencing. The vast majority of offenders continue to be referred by officials and agencies rather than by themselves, their families, or concerned professionals, which underscores the reluctance offenders have in presenting themselves for treatment prior to discovery of their offenses.

Because offenders are referred so often by corrections divisions (probation and parole officers) and other governmental and private agencies, coordination and communication with these sources has been essential. Frequent telephone contacts and typewritten progress reports on a monthly basis have proven effective in the coordination of care. Although some workers caution that strict attention must be

Table 10.2 *Percentage of Referral Sources for the Eight Major Diagnostic Groups (N = 4,900)*

Referral Source	Diagnosis							
	Heterosexual Pedophilia (N = 2,865)	Homosexual Pedophilia (N = 855)	Exhibitionism (N = 770)	Rape (N = 145)	Public Masturbation (N = 75)	Voyeurism (N = 70)	Frotteurism (N = 60)	Transvestism (N = 60)
Attorney	40	36	38	25	40	36	17	11
—Before charge	7	5	9	6	20	5	11	8
—After charge	33	31	29	19	20	31	6	3
Probation/parole officer	35	47	36	71	24	29	22	46
District attorney	4	5	7	2	2	2	9	0
Police	2	3	10	0	12	5	2	0
Children's services division	3	5	0	0	2	2	0	3
Professional therapists	5	1	2	2	5	12	3	19
Pastoral counselors	4	1	1	0	2	4	2	6
Self	4	0.5	4	0	7	0	4	11
Spouse	1	0.5	1	0	2	7	0	0
Other relative(s)	1	0.5	0	0	2	5	1	3
Friend(s)	1	0.5	1	0	2	2	0	0

paid to confidentiality (Abel & Becker, 1984), such considerations must always be weighed against concerns for community safety. The clinic has generally reported any knowledge of a repeat offense, a parole or probation violation, or a potential risk to any individual. Judicial opinion is, as yet, not well settled on these complex, often sinuous, issues.

DEMOGRAPHIC CHARACTERISTICS

The 5,000 offenders from whom data are available constitute a relatively heterogeneous sample of men and boys. Table 10.3 lists a number of demographic characteristics for these offenders as a group. Table 10.3 is essentially a summary of Tables 1.1 through 1.8 in Chapter 1. As can be seen, this sample was composed of boys and men across a wide age range, although the majority were between 25 and 50 years of age. Although it is common to separate adolescent from adult offenders, a separate analysis revealed no differences in outcome measures; the adolescent offenders ($N = 170$) here are combined with adult offenders for outcome measures.

Many of these offenders were in the lower- to middle-class socioeconomic groups, had little secondary education, and had unskilled or physical labor jobs. It is hazardous, however, to seek generalized explanations for such behavior within a socioeconomic or educational framework. For example, it is commonly believed that many offenders were themselves victims of sexual abuse at an earlier age and may be acting out some unresolved conflict because of their own victimization (Groth, 1979b). Indeed, in a recent series, fully 59% of 83 rapists had been molested as youngsters (Petrovich & Templer, 1984). However, among the current sample of 5,000 offenders, just 29% were victims of sexual abuse. Although this figure seems lower than expected from the general experience of clinicians in this field, it also appears to be higher than one would expect in a general adult male population. However, there are no large-scale studies of the incidence of sexual abuse in the general population of adult males. A recent study reported that approximately 50% of male and female psychiatric patients had been molested as youngsters (Carmen, Reiker, & Mills, 1984). An astonishing consensus of a 30% victimization rate has appeared across a variety of studies recently among the general population of adult and minor females.

Table 10.3 *Demographic Characteristics of Sexual Offenders Treated in the Sexual Abuse Clinic (N = 5,000)*

Characteristic	Data
Age:	
Average	34.7 years
Range	13–79 years
Educational level:	
median level attained	11th grade
range	6th grade to doctoral level
Marital status:	
married	45%
living with a woman	12%
divorced	21%
never married or lived with a woman and over 21 years old	19%
never married or lived with a woman and under 21 years old	2%
widowed	1%
Employment:	
employed	76%
average duration—past jobs	3.6 years
Military history:	
previously in service	37%
receiving honorable discharge	89%
Psychiatric history:	
nonsexual diagnoses	29%
—sociopathic personality	27%
—alcoholism	14%
—mixed substance abuse	6%
receiving mental health care in the past	9.2%
Medical history:	
average prior hospitalizations	22.7%
taking medications daily	8.2%
Legal history:	
any prior charges	35%
type	
—sexual only	76%
—nonsexual only (non-driving related)	13%
—sexual and nonsexual (non-driving related)	11%
—alcohol-related only (including driving)	12%

One difference between the present population and others may be the definition of what constitutes sexual abuse.

- A 15-year-old youth had passed several notes to girls in his class at school of a frank sexual nature. He had begun to pat the buttocks of several other girls. At the age of 7, an uncle had begun to visit his house frequently and suggested an arrangement in which he would sleep with the boy. Frank sexual activity then began. The uncle fondled his penis and then forced him to commit fellatio on him. The uncle threatened the boy that, if he told, he would break up the family. The youth had only disclosed this information to his therapist in the midst of therapy.

- A 26-year-old sawmill employee reported he was molested as a boy. At the age of 10, a 16-year-old female baby-sitter undressed him and herself and initiated him into a variety of sexual behaviors. He enjoyed the activity and excitedly told his friends about it: Indeed, he began to encourage his parents to socialize more.

The difference between these cases of "molestation" would appear qualitative. In work at the Sexual Abuse Clinic, the first case example above would be classified as an offender who was molested as a child; the second would not.

It is unclear whether subpopulations of offenders (pedophiles as opposed to rapists, for example) are more prone to have been victims of sexual abuse. Although being a victim might more readily predispose an individual to offend, it clearly cannot be a sufficient factor to explain most abuse. In addition, the confounding factors of genetic contribution and family upbringing (Sugar, 1983) need to be further separated and explored before this issue can be objectively addressed.

Indeed, many adult men who sexually offend are married, not a few happily and for a long time. The vast majority have broken no law other than that for which they were referred. Similarly, the majority of these offenders who were at one time in the military had been honorably discharged; most were employed, did not abuse drugs or alcohol, and had no history of violence or prior psychological treatment. Although, to those working daily with sexual offenders, these findings are not surprising, they may be so to the public and the media. These facts should not be taken to deny, however, the harm sexual abuse causes to victim and perpetrator. Yet, it is still important to correct the frequent image of the sexual offender as a deranged, perverted, or potentially violent criminal. The clinic has treated bank presidents, school superintendents, ministers, transient drifters, attorneys, longshoremen, and physicians. No overall or easy attribution of deviant sexual arousal to single factors will probably be forthcoming, at least in the near future.

Table 10.4 presents an overview of the offending behaviors themselves among men with the eight most common primary diagnoses prior to treatment. Several factors stand out within these data as important in understanding broad patterns of sexual abuse. As a group, homosexual pedophiles have the highest number of covert actions (thoughts, urges, and dreams) per unit of time while transvestites and exhibitionists report the highest number of overt actions (for example, exposing or masturbating while wearing female underclothing) prior to treatment. This may seem surprising, as exhibitionism is a crime in which the perpetrator is often easily identified and subsequently apprehended. However, a number of exhibitionists who expose very frequently, although fleetingly, may have skewed these data to some extent. The high frequency of covert homosexual pedophiliac acts is of interest and may account for the longer average duration of treatment needed in this condition. Heterosexual pedophiles fell within the middle ranges for both categories. As expected, offenders who did not require the active, conscious participation of a victim, such as public masturbators and voyeurs, had a relatively high frequency of overt, as opposed to covert, acts at baseline.

Certain important data could not be reduced to objective tabular presentations. One such finding is the extent to which a patient would risk discovery in order to offend.

- A 65-year-old retired orchardist would hold his 5-year-old granddaughter on his lap, bouncing her on his knee. He would occasionally pretend to slip as he lifted her, his hand seemingly accidentally sliding to her crotch area. Often he would call her over to "tuck in her blouse," but in so doing would pull her pants out far enough to gaze at her genital area. At all times, he would try to camouflage the sexual intention of his actions. Indeed, he would only engage in this behavior when alone with the girl.

- A 27-year-old chemical plant employee began to molest his 4-year-old stepdaughter when his wife was at the store. Gradually, he grew bolder and started molesting her older sister, aged 7, and occasionally did so upstairs in her room, even when his wife was present downstairs.

Table 10.4 Symptom Profiles Among Sexual Offenders Treated in the Sexual Abuse Clinic for the Eight Major Sexual Diagnostic Categories (N = 4,900)

Referral Source	Diagnosis							
	Heterosexual Pedophilia (N = 2,865)	Homosexual Pedophilia (N = 855)	Exhibitionism (N = 770)	Rape (N = 145)	Public Masturbation (N = 75)	Voyeurism (N = 70)	Frotteurism (N = 60)	Transvestism (N = 60)
Average covert behaviors per week	14.1	22.7	13.7	3.4	4.7	6.2	21.3	7.7
Average overt behaviors per week	1.9	2.4	2.9	0.2	1.2	1.7	2.1	3.5
Average baseline plethysmograph arousal[a]	82.6	93.8	68.0	72.1	61.5	31.5	90.7	86.9
Average years of offending behavior	9.3	11.7	7.5	2.4	6.4	3.7	6.8	4.3
Percentage with prior sexual charges	30.4	36.5	42.5	24.1	11.1	14.3	44.4	11.0
Percentage with prior sexual convictions	22.5	29.7	35.2	22.7	4.4	4.8	44.4	5.5
Average years in custody	0.8	0.9	0.6	1.4	0.4	0.4	0.4	0.5
Average years on probation and/or parole	2.1	2.3	1.9	2.7	0.7	0.6	0.2	0.3
Average ratio of convictions/charges	0.67	0.7	0.57	0.8	0.46	0.29	0.54	0.75
Average age, in years of victims	10.8	11.4	N/A[b]	N/A	N/A	N/A	21.5	N/A
Average number of victims	1.4	2.6	14.3[c]	1.7	7.4[c]	N/A	11.7[c]	N/A

a. In percentage of full tumescence, for three deviant test stimuli.
b. N/A = not available.
c. Estimate.

Those offenders who became more brazen in their sexual approaches generally show a longer treatment course, although it appears that their eventual outcomes are as satisfactory as those for patients who are more cautious in their approaches to victims.

Another datum difficult to quantify is "severity." Although frequency data can be presented, it is still questionable whether this totally defines the extent of offending. Is it possible to rate how serious a crime is? Probably not; we may know how long a maladaptive sexual behavior has existed and what effects it may have had on the victim, but, as will be seen, these data do not correlate well with treatment outcome. It seems more "serious" for a homosexual pedophile to commit fellatio than to fondle a boy's penis, but the effect on the boy may be more damaging with the latter. It is best now to clearly state our ignorance in this area even though courts may expect firmer opinions.

Baseline plethysmograph values obtained just prior to treatment across all diagnoses for relevant deviant test stimuli are also presented in Table 10.4. While the highest initial readings were obtained for homosexual pedophiles, the difference between this group mean and that of the lowest group, voyeurs, may relate more to the difficulty in presenting adequate test stimuli to the latter group. This highest/lowest group difference was barely significant statistically ($p < 0.10$). Although intraindividual plethysmograph readings were highly reliable, interindividual ones were not. Thus one could not have discerned a diagnosis based upon plethysmograph readings alone.

The demographic variable producing the greatest difference across diagnostic group means was history of legal difficulties. Table 10.4 presents charges and convictions for all diagnostic categories. It can be seen that exhibitionism was a crime not easily camouflaged. Men who exposed were arrested, charged, and convicted of this offense almost one and a half to two times as often as heterosexual and homosexual pedophiles and ten times as often as voyeurs and men who masturbated publicly. Men who rape, however, had the highest ratio of convictions for charges. For example, this datum is approximately 74% for heterosexual pedophiles, 81% for homosexual pedophiles, 83% for exhibitionists, but 94% for men who rape.

Finally, of interest are a subgroup of handicapped offenders: There were 228 boys and men whose IQ was at "borderline" to "moderately retarded" levels; there were 11 deaf offenders who received treatment through lipreading or an interpreter using American Sign Language; there were 5 offenders who spoke no English and who were treated with interpreters; and there were 4 blind offenders. The results for all these groups were no different than for the remainder of the cohort (although there were too few handicapped offenders to perform any statistically meaningful comparisons) and, therefore, data will not be presented separately for them.

In summary, data collected at entry into the Sexual Abuse Clinic demonstrated that there was no easy way to categorize sexual offenders demographically, although some generalizations could be drawn from interdiagnostic comparisons on pretreatment offending behaviors: Homosexual pedophiles had the greatest number of covert behaviors while exhibitionists had the highest number of overt actions and convictions for their crimes. The potential influence these data have on outcome will be discussed later in this chapter.

Areas of Evaluation

As part of all offenders' ongoing treatment in the Sexual Abuse Clinic, evaluations were undertaken on a number of measures.

SELF-REPORTS

Each offender was asked to keep a written daily record of covert and overt maladaptive sexual approach behaviors, defined as follows. *Covert deviant sexual behaviors* are urges, fantasies, and dreams of deviant sexual activity. *Overt deviant sexual behaviors* are actual deviant acts or masturbation to deviant sexual fantasies.

Data collection was initiated at baseline and then at 1, 3, 6, 12, 18, and 24 months after the initiation of treatment, and at the end of treatment. Thereafter, data were collected annually at follow-up sessions. Data were reduced to frequencies of both types of behavior per week.

PENILE PLETHYSMOGRAPH

Plethysmograph recordings were obtained at the majority of sessions for all offenders. However, three "test stimuli" (slides and/or stories) were chosen by the therapist with the following criteria:

— The subject matter pertained to the offender's diagnosis.
— The subject matter elicited no less than maximum arousal minus 20% on at least three of four presentations.

Such "test stimuli" were never paired with aversive stimuli. Therefore, they served as indicators of the generalization of treatment effects.

Chapter 2 and Appendix D describe the plethysmograph itself and techniques for its use. Testing with the plethysmograph was performed at all active therapy sessions, then at 3, 6, 12, and 24 months after the initiation of treatment, then annually at follow-up sessions.

TREATMENT COMPLIANCE MEASURES

(1) The therapist's reports. The therapist was asked to rate the patient's behavior on a 0 (not at all) to 4+ (very much) scale regarding the following two questions:

(a) How much has the patient progressed?
(b) How well is the patient following through with treatment and homework?

These measures were taken at the same time intervals as indicated above for the penile plethysmograph.

(2) The observer's reports. One "significant other" was chosen by the therapist and the patient. It was preferable to choose an individual who lived with the patient (76% of all cases). The observer was asked to rate the patient's behavior on a 0 (not at all) to 4+ (very much) scale regarding the following two questions:

(a) How much has the patient progressed?
(b) How well is the patient following through with treatment and homework?

These measures were taken at the same time intervals as indicated above for the penile plethysmograph.

LEGAL RECORDS

A thorough search of all municipal, county, state, and national computerized police files was undertaken at the identical time intervals as given above for data recorded on arrests, charges, and convictions for sexually related offenses. Fortunately, clinic staff enjoyed good relationships with local authorities and were grateful for the privilege of sharing these records. Although these files were theoretically open to the public, in reality, coordination from authorities was necessary to gain access to them.

Polygraph tests were available for a number of offenders, but these results were not incorporated into outcome data because too few patients were tested and those who had been were preselected as more dangerous.

Admittedly, most of these data collection techniques were less than ideal scientifically except *perhaps* for the plethysmograph. Self-reports would be expected to be optimistically inflated as offenders wish to appear improved in order to both comply with probation requirements and shorten treatment. Observers can rarely be unbiased as many were spouses, parents, and girlfriends; even therapists' opinions could be skewed toward the sanguine end of the outcome spectrum. However, cross-correlations between self-reports, observer and therapist reports, and plethysmograph recordings were surprisingly high, a result reported previously (Maletzky, 1980a). Many offenders informed their therapists when they were not progressing. A number divulged potentially harmful information of continued deviant sexual behavior or criminal activities, such as visiting their homes when not allowed. Although it became increasingly apparent that one could not always assume an offender was trying to mislead his therapist, certainly frequent flagrant examples of deception occurred. Thus it was reassuring to have access to a *variety* of assessment techniques. It is possible that additional physiological responses correlated with sexual activity may be forthcoming through continued research. These possibilities include pupillography; polygraphlike measurements of autonomic responses such as the galvanic skin response, blood pressure, and heart rate; and perhaps even focal brain recording in the future. Researchers working with positron-emission techniques in the central nervous system have almost casually discovered that reports of sexual arousal consistently accompanied a specific hypothalamic pattern.[3] Should further research disclose a detectable, reliable, and valid CNS pattern indicating sexual arousal, clinicians and forensic experts may both have a window into the brain and a terrible responsibility to show that "mind reading" can be put to constructive use. (For a more complete discussion of assessment techniques, the reader is referred to Chapter 2.)

Each sexual offender is unique, and the time course of treatment can thus be described only approximately. As an average, treatment for this sample began with weekly sessions of one hour each for approximately three to four months then decreased in frequency to twice per month for several months before tapering to once per month for several more months. Thereafter, booster sessions were held once every three months two to three times prior to terminating treatment and entering the follow-up and evaluation phase. Hence the average offender spent approximately eighteen months in treatment, although among all 5,000 offenders, a range of four months to forty months was seen.

Methods of Treatment

All offenders for whom data were gathered were treated with the behavioral techniques of aversive conditioning. Although a variety of aversive techniques were employed, almost no patient went unexposed to an aversive conditioning method. At different times, controlled comparisons were conducted among a variety of aversive techniques such as electric shock aversion, aversive behavior rehearsal, covert sensitization, and assisted covert sensitization. At other times, the use of adjunctive techniques was investigated. Thus any individual sexual offender was not likely to be treated with exactly the same methods for identical durations as any other. Often, precisely controlled groupings were employed to compare techniques, although, at other times, patients were treated within the clinic using whatever techniques were judged appropriate to the situation. Moreover, the ordering of treatment approaches was not strictly controlled; some offenders were treated first with aversive techniques while others received positive conditioning or biofeedback first. As opposed to other reports (Abel & Becker, 1984), no impression of an important sequencing effect was perceived.

Such retrospective collections of results may carry value, although they are not a substitute for double-blind results: All these offenders were offered a program of the behaviorally based techniques that were thought generally to be indicated. The lack of controls was partly compensated for by the large size of the sample and by the fact that this population was treated using the same methods as would be employed in most behavioral treatment centers in this country. This is a typical population of sexual offenders treated by personnel with usual clinical backgrounds and experience and with techniques that are in common use. Although it deals with some subjective and retrospective data, it is an example of the state of behavior therapy for the maladaptive sexual approach disorders as developed during the past 12 years. These data help to pinpoint future areas of selective concern in which more restrictive, objective, and prospective controlled methods can be employed.

Table 10.5 lists the major treatment techniques used as a means of summarizing how they were disbursed over the major diagnostic categories. Some significant differences emerged: Homosexual pedophiles received more aversive conditioning and generally more adjunctive techniques, perhaps because of greater perceived treatment resistance in this group and their longer courses of treatment; exhibitionists and public masturbators were more often given instructions to use foul taste aversion in vivo, probably due to the greater certainty that such offenders would often happen upon typical situations that had provoked offending behavior in the past. Rapists were more often given empathy training and group therapy, the latter perhaps as a treatment response to counter perceived hostility, denial, and low self-esteem. All public masturbators were treated with impulse control training (sexual as well as nonsexual) as were most voyeurs, which underscores the clinical impression that patients in these groups often showed the labile emotional profile that reflects some immaturity.

Despite these overall (and occasionally weak) generalizations, however, most sexual offenders treated in this clinic received a variety of techniques that suited their clinical presentation. There was a wide enough overlap here that one could not predict diagnosis based upon type, duration, or intensity of treatment method.

Table 10.5 Percentage of Sexual Offenders in the Eight Major Diagnostic Categories Receiving Major Treatment Techniques (N = 4,900)

Referral Source				Diagnosis				
	Heterosexual Pedophilia (N = 2,865)	Homosexual Pedophilia (N = 855)	Exhibitionism (N = 770)	Rape (N = 145)	Public Masturbation (N = 75)	Voyeurism (N = 70)	Frotteurism (N = 60)	Transvestism (N = 60)
Conditioning methods:								
assisted covert sensitization	98	100	92	90	84	83	100	100
covert sensitization	100	100	95	95	93	100	100	100
electric shock aversion	92	100	88	100	82	75	94	100
aversive behavior rehearsal	57	48	78	90	11	10	50	83
plethysmographic biofeedback	96	93	57	100	78	33	61	81
masturbatory reconditioning techniques	92	94	63	95	91	76	89	86
foul taste aversion	78	90	100	59	100	83	75	56
desensitization	46	90	40	45	67	38	28	33
amyl nitrate conditioning	62	74	39	48	31	15	11	36
Adjunctive methods:								
empathy training	67	85	43	100	49	76	94	47
social skills training	55	87	80	87	93	10	22	78
assertiveness training	24	47	53	80	73	21	14	33
impulse control training	31	57	63	67	100	90	94	42
Counseling methods:								
marital/family counseling[a]	37	17	24	43	18	26	17	39
group therapy	4	7	13	92	11	5	11	61
Medication:								
depo-Provera	1	1	1	5	0	0	0	0

a. Many offenders were receiving counseling at other agencies. The above figures include only Sexual Abuse Clinic counseling.

OUTCOME DATA

Overall treatment results will be presented, keeping in mind that these data were pooled for all diagnostic categories; the selection of subjects was not rigorous; assessment techniques were partly subjective and retrospective; and application of treatment techniques was not always rigorously controlled. In balance, the data came from a very large group of sexual offenders. The assessment techniques were those commonly available for cross-validation and included some objective measures and cross-correlations. The treatment techniques were those that were in contemporary use. It appears that a combination of large clinical studies and smaller well-controlled projects may be necessary to prevent a triumph of technique over purpose.

All data to be reported were collected at standard time intervals of each month of active treatment, then every three months during intermediate and booster phases, and, finally, yearly when possible during a follow-up period as long as 17 years in some cases.

Self-Reports

Covert and overt deviant sexual behaviors. Figure 10.2 depicts the average deviant covert behaviors (urges, fantasies, and dreams) and deviant overt behaviors (actual deviant sexual acts or masturbation to deviant sexual fantasies and/or materials) by all offenders as a function of time in treatment and follow-up. It can be seen that only a minimal decline in self-reports of covert and overt behaviors marked the initial weekly treatment sessions. By the sixth and twelfth treatment sessions, however, a moderate to marked reduction occurred in these reports. There is thus little immediate change, and, based upon these data, sexual offenders in the clinic are warned not to expect rapid gains in treatment at first. In contrast, offenders who do not progress adequately by the eighth treatment session (typically after two months of treatment) should be reevaluated with attention paid to the quality of the scenes, slides, and fantasies being presented.

- A 49-year-old musician who had molested a number of young boys in his neighborhood, including several of his music students, was making poor progress despite having had nine treatment sessions. A repeat analysis revealed that a crucial element in his arousal pattern was

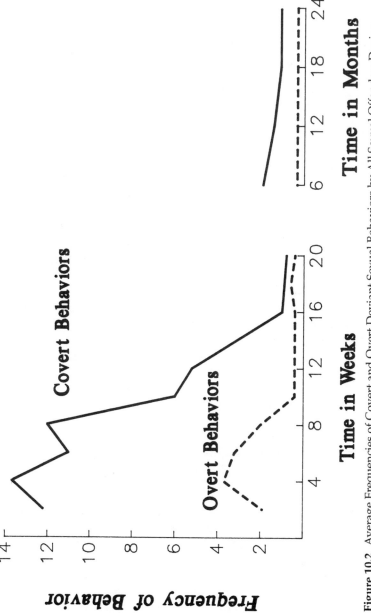

Figure 10.2 Average Frequencies of Covert and Overt Deviant Sexual Behaviors by All Sexual Offenders During Treatment and Early Follow-Up ($N = 5,000$)

235

missing: He had harbored a fascination, even a fetish, for weapons and achieved the highest plethysmograph readings upon repeated testing when homosexual pedophiliac slides and fantasies were presented in association with weapons. For example, a typical scene pictured a young boy holding a gun. Incorporating such stimuli into his slides and stories produced greater treatment gains.

- When progress in treatment was noted to be painfully slow, reevaluation of therapy was undertaken for a 21-year-old voyeur. Movies had been used to a great extent in his treatment program. A closer analysis revealed that this patient always attended movies with his mother as a youngster and was associating the sexual movies with her again, thereby reducing the impact of the stimulus. A switch to slides and stories produced satisfactory progress.

These data help in determining *approximately* when treatment gains are to be expected. Although an allowance must be made for individual variations in the progress of therapy, if the patient is not responding adequately after five to eight treatment sessions, a reanalysis is probably indicated.

In a population of sexual offenders who are to report the number of times they continue to offend, much bias is to be expected. It is surprising, however, that self-reports of overt acts, whether in vivo or in masturbation, correlated reasonably well with reports of covert behaviors and, as will be seen subsequently, with plethysmograph measures. In addition, these men sometimes reported such activities even when no suspicion was warranted.

- A 24-year-old heterosexual pedophile showed adequate reductions in plethysmograph measures during his first ten treatment sessions. In the eleventh session, however, he confided to his therapist that he had remolested, even though observer reports and plethysmograph data showed improvement. Further aversive and positive conditioning were helpful in eliminating deviant sexual activities.

Although the use of a variety of assessment techniques can help to pinpoint deficiencies in the treatment program, establishing trust with the individual patient can aid immeasurably in the acquisition of honest data. The correlation between covert and overt behaviors on self-report was 0.79, that between covert reports and plethysmograph measurements was 0.54, and that between overt reports and the plethysmograph was 0.62. If these correlation coefficients match those of data generated elsewhere in the treatment of the sexual offender, then a legitimate conclusion might be that the plethysmograph has added little value to our measure of treatment response. However, average data may be misleading.

- After 12 treatment sessions, a homosexual pedophile showed only moderately reduced arousal on the plethysmograph, yet he reported a marked decrease in covert and overt behaviors. When new stimuli were presented, however, his plethysmograph soared while he continued to insist no arousal was occurring. He was subsequently charged with molesting two more young boys and then admitted he had falsified his self-reports in treatment.

Thus, while it is to be expected that offenders will exaggerate their responses to treatment and deemphasize remaining deviant arousal, their self-reports still form one data pool from which to draw at least cautious conclusions and on which to base general recommendations.

Penile Plethysmograph Recordings. As detailed in Chapter 2, the plethysmograph is not infallible; hence a wide range of assessment devices are necessary for cross-correlation. This is especially true because a large number of offenders will attempt to minimize the extent of lingering deviant fantasies and urges. The plethysmograph lends some reassurance in the quest for objectivity and will continue to be the major device employed in the assessment of treatment for the sexual offender in the near future. At the same time, it must be kept in mind that approximately 30% of offenders will not manifest deviant arousal on this instrument. Thus the false negative rate is currently unacceptably high.

Several purely clinical observations may be helpful in increasing the specificity of the plethysmograph:

(1) Noting a *detumescence* immediately upon presenting an erotic stimulus: This reduction in penile circumference is thought to reflect lengthening of the penis without volumetric change as an *immediate* predictor of arousal. Data have not yet been collected to know whether this observation can be reliably measured in offender and nonoffender populations.

(2) Presenting normal heterosexual adult material, obtaining a strong erection, then measuring the rate of detumescence on being exposed to

deviant material: Observations indicate that it is easier to suppress an erection than to lose one. Theoretically, a nonoffender would lose an erection produced by depictions of adult consenting sexual activity when, for example, homosexual pedophiliac stimuli are presented. A homosexual pedophile also obtaining an erection with depictions of adult consenting sexual activity might not be able to camouflage his lingering arousal when stimuli associated with homosexual pedophilia are presented.

(3) Employing two strain gauges, one at the base and one near the head of the penis: Correlations between penile length and circumference could be measured directly to provide more objective data on sexual arousal, length, and circumference of the penis.

All 5,000 patients reported here were evaluated at baseline and during treatment with the plethysmograph. The experience gained with this number of patients had enabled clinic staff to acquire knowledge about a variety of maneuvers patients may use to deceive a therapist:

— manually stimulating the strain gauge
— looking away from a visual stimulus
— closing the eyes
— differentially excluding a spoken fantasy by concentrating on competing thoughts or fantasies
— masturbating or engaging in intercourse just prior to testing

Manual manipulation of the strain gauge produces an erratic tracing clearly not secondary to erection. Similarly, coughing, sneezing, and body motion can be detected. Figure 10.3 demonstrates some of these secondary patterns. Auditory stimuli help when the patient refuses to attend to visual stimuli. In addition, from time to time, a probe test has been useful to ensure that the patient is attending to the visual stimuli. One of the biofeedback lights, previously described, can be switched on at random during the slide presentation part of a plethysmograph evaluation session or during treatment. The patient is asked to press a button (or raise a finger) as quickly as possible in response to this light, thus demonstrating how well he has attended to and observed these stimuli. Often, patients will try to concentrate on competing fantasies when listening to sexual scenes; it is then helpful to have the patient recite his own scenes. Obviously,

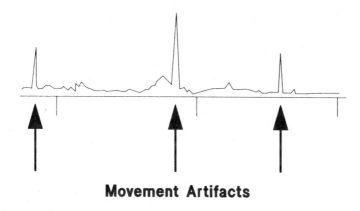

Movement Artifacts

Figure 10.3   Example of Artifacts in the Penile Plethysmograph

therapy would be easier if such patients showed more cooperation, but this is frankly not always expected in a population of sexual offenders; hence techniques must be devised to circumvent these obstacles. Perhaps it is building a solid base of trust and cooperation between patient and therapist that ensures the largest part of success in this vein.

The plethysmograph, in registering sexual arousal, generally manifests gradual erection and subsequent detumescence. Figures 10.4 and 10.5 demonstrate typical plethysmograph tracings before and after successful treatment in an offender with both heterosexual and homosexual pedophilia. The gradual rise and maintenance of deviant and nondeviant arousal can be easily distinguished from various artifacts in the figures. Normalization of the record with treatment is apparent.

Figure 10.6 presents averaged data on plethysmograph responses for all 5,000 offenders as treatment was progressing. Data are presented as responses to three highly rated deviant test stimuli never associated with aversion. Slower initial decline was followed by more rapid decreases in deviant sexual arousal with a gradual slowing as active treatment was ending. A further decline was seen after a typical increase in the initial booster stage as depicted in Figure 10.7,

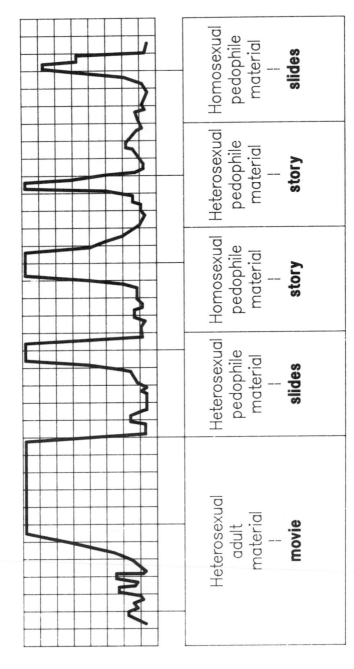

Figure 10.4 The Penile Plethysmograph Recorded During the Fifth Treatment Session for an Offender with Heterosexual and Homosexual Pedophilia

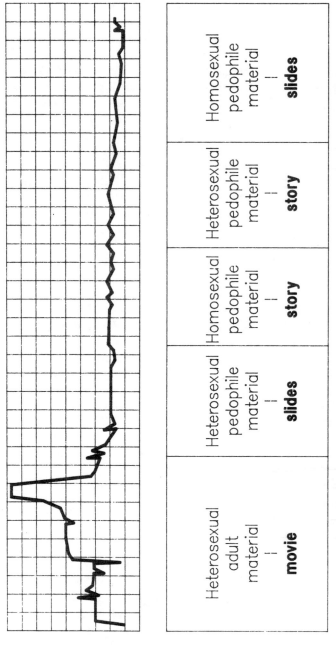

Figure 10.5 The Penile Plethysmograph Recorded During the Next-To-Last Booster Session for an Offender with Heterosexual and Homosexual Pedophilia.

which extends averaged plethysmograph data for 450 randomly selected offenders across all diagnostic categories over a period of five
years from the initiation of treatment. This increase may be due to
some (but not most) offenders who suffer a slight exacerbation during the early booster stage. At this time, it is not possible to identify
which, among all offenders, will relapse during this period. Booster
sessions are thus necessary as treatment is being terminated. Offenders can be given these sessions of aversive conditioning once every
three months for six to twelve months following the end of active
treatment. This frequency has usually been sufficient to maintain an
absence of deviant sexual arousal on follow-up for extensive periods
of time (Maletzky, 1977). An area begging research in this field is the
delineation of a characteristic patient profile that would help in identifying those offenders at risk for relapse so that booster-phase treatments can be intensified for those susceptible to recurrence of deviant arousal and reduced for those not likely to be at risk.

In evaluating treatment response from plethysmograph data, success is defined as attaining a criterion of reduced plethysmograph
ratings to three test stimuli, individually chosen based on each
offender's baseline records and never associated with aversion.
These stimuli have yielded between 80% to 100% of maximum erection, and must decline to under 20% of maximum erection upon
termination of treatment and follow-up. Figure 10.8 presents averaged arousal data, divided into four major diagnostic categories:
heterosexual pedophilia, homosexual pedophilia, exhibitionism, and
rape. Significant differences were found across these categories: Men
who raped had the poorest outcome ($p < .005$). Within all other
categories, ultimate success occurred within a gratifyingly range:
86% to 95%. Although numbers of men who raped were small in this
review compared with other diagnostic categories, the data seem
clear and indicate the possibility that these men may not share common characteristics with other offenders and may be a more heterogeneous group that is more difficult to categorize and—of even more
practical significance—to treat.

Excellent reviews discuss the merits of the plethysmograph (Laws
& Osborn, 1983). Again, it is helpful to employ multiple assessment
techniques so as not to rely upon a single device. Although use of the
plethysmograph might appear to be expensive and technical, skill in
its use is easily gained. It lends a reassuring objectivity to the mea-

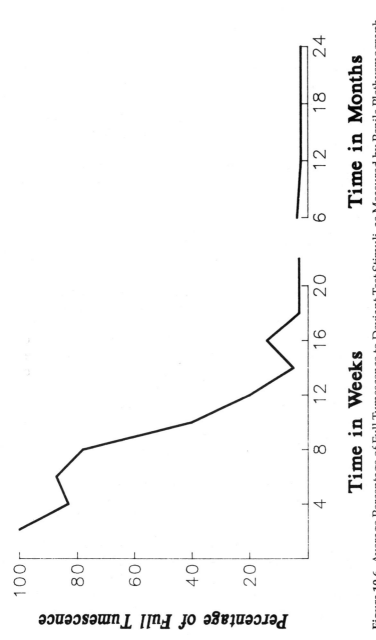

Figure 10.6 Average Percentage of Full Tumescence to Deviant Test Stimuli, as Measured by Penile Plethysmograph Recordings During Treatment and Short-Term Follow-Up, for All Offenders Treated (N = 5,000)

243

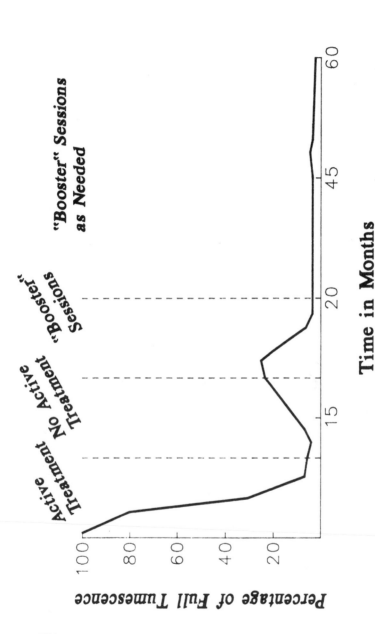

Figure 10.7 Average Percentage of Full Tumescence to Deviant Test Stimuli, as Measured by Penile Plethysmograph Recordings During Treatment and Extended Follow-Up, for a Sample of Offenders Across All Diagnostic Categories (N = 450)

244

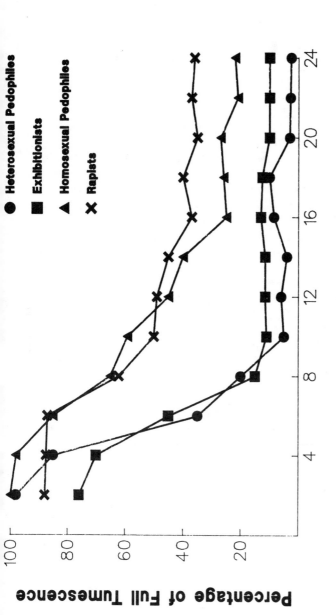

Figure 10.8 Average Percentage of Full Tumescence to Deviant Test Stimuli, as Measured by Penile Plethysmograph Recordings During Treatment, for All Offenders Within the Four Major Diagnostic Categories (N = 4,635)

surement of actual sexual response and will probably continue to be so employed for at least the foreseeable future.

Treatment Compliance Measures

CORRELATION COEFFICIENTS

The correlation coefficient between the scores and self-reports of average, combined covert and overt deviant sexual behaviors and the penile plethysmograph determination for the three test stimuli, computed for sexual offenders within the four major diagnostic groups, is presented in Table 10.6. It can be seen that this coefficient was relatively high for all major groups of offenders except one: men who rape. Several problems, however, occur in comparing this group with other categories of offenders. As noted above, the numbers of rapists treated was smaller than that of all other major groups; the numbers of covert and overt acts were lower than for any other group; and an outcome by diagnostic category comparison as shown in Figure 10.8 indicates a significantly poorer outcome for rapists when compared with all other offenders. In considering these differences, several possible mechanisms should be considered: The rapist generally commits his crime at a much lower frequency than all other offenders (see Table 10.4); he usually reports very few fantasies regarding the act; he often reports normal fantasies during masturbation and intercourse; and he often rapes as an apparent response to being denied sexual release elsewhere. It is possible either that basically different generative mechanisms operate in this group or, more likely, that men who rape form a heterogeneous group difficult to subcategorize at the current level of understanding.

OBSERVER'S REPORTS

Two questions were asked of significant others at the same time intervals in which other data were collected, as described earlier:

(1) How much has the patient progressed on a 0 to 4+ scale?
(2) How well is the patient following through with treatment on a 0 to 4+ scale?

Table 10.6 *Correlation Coefficients Between Change Scores in Self-Reports of Averaged, Combined Deviant Behaviors and in Averaged Termination Penile Plethysmograph Determinations*

Diagnostic Group	Correlation Coefficient (X^2)
Heterosexual pedophilia (N = 2,865)	0.63
Homosexual pedophilia (N = 855)	0.53
Exhibitionism (N = 770)	0.68
Rape (N = 145)	0.32
Public masturbation (N = 75)	0.64
Voyeurism (N = 70)	0.59
Frotteurism (N = 60)	0.62
Transvestism (N = 60)	0.65

NOTE: Data are from three test stimuli across the eight major diagnostic categories (N = 4,900). Self-reports include both overt and covert sexual behaviors combined.

The first question is a check on progress in other people's eyes while the second is an observation of treatment compliance.

Responses to these questions were obtained from a significant other for 2,393 offenders at the termination of treatment. For the remaining patients, no significant other was available (1,822 cases) or the significant other's contact with the patient was terminated during treatment (785 cases). The data are presented, divided into diagnostic categories, in Table 10.7. Again, it can be seen that relatively high ratings (an average of 3.1) were obtained in all categories except for men who rape. There was no significant difference among groups outside of this sole exception.

Another means of viewing compliance is to analyze records of attendance. However, there was no significant difference by diagnostic category in attendance. Upon reviewing attendance records further, the major finding appeared to be that "involuntary" patients, such as those who had to obtain therapy as a requirement of probation or parole, had slightly fewer missed appointments. These data have been reported elsewhere (Maletzky, 1980b).

Table 10.7 *Average Observers' Reports (0 to 4+) at the Termination of Treatment for the Eight Major Diagnostic Categories (N = 4,900)*

Diagnostic Group	Question #1: How much has the patient progressed?	Question #2: How well is the patient following through with treatment?
Heterosexual pedophilia (N = 2,865)	3.4	3.2
Homosexual pedophilia (N = 855)	2.9	2.7
Exhibitionism (N = 770)	3.1	3.0
Rape (N = 145)	2.1	2.2
Public masturbation (N = 75)	3.4	3.1
Voyeurism (N = 70)	3.0	2.9
Frotteurism (N = 60)	3.1	2.7
Transvestism (N = 60)	3.2	3.0

NOTE: All differences between rape and each of the three other categories are significant at the p greater than 0.1 level.

ESTIMATES OF HOMEWORK PERFORMANCE

Although individual therapists often made judgments about how well a patient followed through with homework, unfortunately, no objective data could be collected on this issue. Significant others were routinely asked about this information, but their observations seemed too uncertain to be quantified. Often, a therapist would ask the patient to demonstrate how he listened to a tape, smelled a foul odor, chewed a bitter pill, and so on to check on understanding and compliance. Occasionally, the therapist would ask a patient to come to the clinic two or three times a week and use an empty office to follow through on homework assignments. Because evaluation of these areas was not systematically obtained, no data are offered here. Hopefully, future clinician-researchers may devise objective measurements of homework performance and efficacy.

LEGAL RECORDS

The Sexual Abuse Clinic is indebted to local police for their coordination in sharing seized materials and providing access to data in police files. Because such data are routinely stored in large computers, it is possible to scan printouts from time to time (typically monthly) to see if patients already treated, or those in the midst of treatment, have recently been charged with, arrested for, or convicted of sexual abuse. Such cases were counted as treatment failures, even if a charge or arrest did not lead to conviction. Such conservatism was believed to be important to prevent staff from overestimating the positive effects of their own treatments. This method of data collection is not entirely without fault, however.

- A 32-year-old heterosexual pedophile reported no deviant urges or behaviors during a six-month course of treatment. Other measures improved only slowly, however. A legal record check revealed no apparent criminal charges. It was only after an arrest was made during an act of oral-genital contact with a 7-year-old girl that it became clear that this patient had changed his name five to ten times a year and had lived in five states during the year prior to treatment.

Although some patients may use aliases, this can be cross-referenced within the computer system. Offenses reported in a different area of the country may not be entered; however, many local states share this information through computer terminal connections.

Table 10.8 displays the legal records of each diagnostic category for 110 men who were charged with sexual crimes during active treatment or follow-up. These may not have been the only men who offended during these time periods but only those detected by the computer check. The table presents these data as a percentage of men who were charged, given the entire number of all men treated in that diagnostic category. It is immediately apparent that this percentage was reasonably low for all groups except for men who rape, although the percentage for that group was not as high as would have been expected based upon the other outcome findings already reported.

To further analyze these data, the table presents a comparison by diagnostic category of plethysmograph data for the repeat offenders. Again, the plethysmograph data represent a mean percentage of full tumescence in response to three test stimuli, presented at the termi-

Table 10.8 *Diagnostic and Plethysmographic Outcome Data on Offenders*
Apprehended by Legal Authorities During Treatment or Follow-Up
(N = 110)

Primary Diagnostic Category	Number Apprehended	Percentage of Total Within Category	Termination Plethysmograph Measurement[a]
Heterosexual pedophilia	38	1.3	9.5
Homosexual pedophilia	35	4.1	17.3
Exhibitionism	15	1.9	14.3
Rape	20	13.8	27.6
Voyeurism	2	2.3	15.5
Public masturbation	0	0	N/A
Frotteurism	0	0	N/A
Transvestism	0	0	N/A
Fetishism	0	0	N/A
Obscene telephone callers	0	0	N/A
Sadomasochism	0	0	N/A

a. Expressed as a percentage of mean full tumescence in response to three test stimuli never associated with aversive stimuli.

nation session for these particular offenders but never associated with aversive stimuli. The table demonstrates a close correlation between plethysmograph data and reoffending, but with some surprising differences: In men who molested boys, there was a slight disparity between plethysmograph readings and charges, arrests, and convictions. Within this group, there were relatively higher deviant arousals on the plethysmograph compared with the legal records, in contrast to all other groups. Although homosexual pedophiles possessed treatment outcomes almost as favorable as other groups based upon legal records, their improvements occurred less rapidly than those for other categories, although they eventually reached similar, though not exactly equivalent, levels. Therapists often expressed the belief that this group was more difficult to treat. This may have appeared to be so only because of the slower decline in deviant sexual arousal rather than because there were any significant differences in eventual outcome.

As can be seen in Figures 10.7 and 10.8, and in Tables 10.6 to 10.8, and as expected from the results already discussed, men who raped had a poorer outcome in these comparisons, whether measured by speed or eventual level of response or by computer search of legal records. This group did not appear to enjoy the magnitude of successful outcome seen in all other diagnostic categories.

The Persistence of Change

OVERALL FOLLOW-UP RESULTS

In attempting to evaluate whether these initial and early follow-up results were overly optimistic, offenders were followed from the end of all booster sessions at yearly intervals. Although attempts were made to contact all discharged offenders, a number of individuals were lost to follow-up. Some had simply moved without leaving a forwarding address, while others were located yet refused to attend follow-up plethysmograph testing sessions. How are these latter offenders to be regarded? They could be viewed by the cautious observer as still harboring deviant sexual arousal and afraid this would become clear on follow-up plethysmograph evaluation. The optimist, however, might view their reticence as simply a wish not to be reminded of an unpleasant period in their lives.

The following compromised guidelines, and their rationales, were established to identify a "treatment success" or a "treatment failure."

A treatment success was an individual who

(1) completed all treatment sessions,
(2) demonstrated no sexual arousal (under 20% of full tumescence) to three test stimuli,
(3) demonstrated no deviant sexual arousal on plethysmograph testing at any annual follow-up testing session,
(4) reported no deviant sexual arousal in terms of deviant covert or overt sexual behavior at any time since treatment ended, and
(5) had no legal record of any charges of, or arrests or convictions for, deviant sexual activity, even if unsubstantiated.

A treatment failure was an individual who was not a treatment success. This last statement is not as gratuitous as it appears. Any offender who did not complete treatment for any reason was counted as failure.

- A 27-year-old logger, suspected of molesting his stepdaughter but not mandated for treatment, refused to return for a second visit, insisting he could prevent future offenses through his newly discovered religious convictions.
- A 67-year-old homosexual pedophile showed adequate reductions in deviant sexual arousal in the first 11 treatment sessions but was lost to follow-up after a serious motor vehicle accident.
- A 19-year-old developmentally disabled youth with an IQ of 82 spent three and a half years in treatment for aggressive sexual fantasies with palpable, yet minor, reductions in misbehavior.
- An elderly homosexual pedophile was charged with remolesting a neighbor's 8-year-old son, but the boy then claimed he had lied.
- A 14-year-old boy, treated one year earlier for exhibitionism, was returned to the juvenile detention hall on suspicion of exposing in a school yard; he was released the next day in an apparent case of mistaken identity.

These cases may not appear to be failures, but, in actuality, they were and have been tallied as such. Treatment personnel must be able to modify their therapy situations and their own behaviors to maximally increase the probability that each patient will continue in treatment. Although there may be circumstances beyond anyone's control, it is best to place this responsibility on the presumably broader shoulders of the therapist than on the patient.

It is also in the best interests of objectivity that previously treated offenders who are suspected of remolesting, reexposing, and so on be considered guilty therapeutically and statistically, even if innocent judicially. Using such stringent outcome criteria may help to avoid therapeutic complacency: Even one repeated sexual offense had a victim and should not be tolerated.

It must be acknowledged that, by and large, follow-up data are presented on only those offenders choosing to make themselves available for testing, an obvious biasing factor. To partially help restore balance, it also must be remembered that any repeat offense or even suspicion of one automatically made a patient "available" for follow-up and rendered him a treatment failure, as did any refusal to complete treatment. This leaves, however, a group of offenders who successfully completed treatment and were never suspected of a repeat offense but either could not be contacted for follow-up plethysmograph testing or were contacted but refused it.

With these disclaimers in mind, data are presented in Table 10.9 on the follow-up of 3,795 sexual offenders (approximately 75.9% of the original 5,000 patients). These patients represented those offenders ending treatment who were able to be followed thereafter. Follow-ups were as short as one year (never briefer), in 19% of offenders, or as long as 17 years (none longer, thus far), in just 2% of offenders. Although the remainder ranged in between, the majority, over 65%, have been followed for over three years.

The factors enumerated in the table cannot yet be thought of as definitely *indicative* of failure or *predictive* of dangerousness. Prospective studies now underway may help in this regard. Each variable has been examined for the 9% of patients who subsequently failed during or after completion of treatment and contrasted with the 91% of patients who have not (yet) failed or reoffended. It can be seen that certain factors strongly associated with treatment failure seem predictable and in the direction of common sense. Thus the two most important factors in this review found to be associated with failure were situational familiarity and number of victims: If the offender did not live with the victim, the chance he would fail was eight times as high as if he did, a finding significant at the .001 level of probability. Equally significant, if the patient had offended against several victims, the chance of failing in treatment was also eight times as high as if he had but a single victim. These findings underscored the distinction (though at times blurred) of the situational as opposed to the preferential (predatory or even obligatory) offender, a topic further evaluated in Chapter 11.

Moreover, if an offender was a relative stranger to his victim(s), the likelihood he would fail was almost five times as high than if he was well known to them. A recent review reported that, in 65% of cases of sexual abuse, the offender was known to the victim (Groth, 1979a), while another study observed that 44% of abusers were relatives; in that study, 93% of offenders were known to either the victim and/or his or her family (Laws & Osborn, 1983), a result almost exactly matched by a similar report from a different treatment center (Earls & Marshall, 1983). A current retrospective review again underscores the seriousness and risk of escalation toward more aggressive sexual crimes in men who offend against strangers (Stermac & Hall, 1989).

The manner in which the patient regarded his offender behavior also bore some relevance to the issue of failing treatment. For example, an offender who wholly denied allegations of sexual abuse was

Table 10.9 *Factors Associated with Failure During Treatment and Follow-Up for All Sexual Offenders Treated and Able to Be Followed (N = 3,995)*

| Factor | Percentage Having Factor | | |
	Treatment Successes (N = 6,635)	Treatment Failures (N = 360)	p
Victim characteristics:			
not living with victim(s)	8.1	65.7	< .001
more than one victim	7.6	60.5	< .001
offender not well-known to victim(s)	11.7	54.0	< .001
Offender characteristics:			
total denial of crime	15.4	48.2	< .001
denial of need for treatment	9.3	22.7	< .01
low intelligence	2.8	4.5	< .10
lack of remorse	16.1	23.5	<.10
offender a victim as a child	21.3	18.7	NS[a]
Assessment characteristics:			
high pretreatment deviant arousal (greater than 80%)	18.9	57.8	< .01
low pretreatment nondeviant arousal (less than 15%)	33.9	47.9	< .05
Offending behavior characteristics:			
use of force	20.1	53.8	< .01
presence of multiple paraphilias	4.1	22.7	< .01
presence of homosexual pedophilia	16.8	23.4	< .10
use of threats	23.7	37.2	< .10
duration of offending behavior(s) greater than 5 years	47.0	50.3	NS
frequency of offending behavior(s) greater than 10 times per year	36.8	40.1	NS
Socioeconomic characteristics:			
unstable employment history[b]	17.9	71.4	< .001
unstable history of social relationships[b]	12.5	47.3	< .001

a. NS = difference not significant.
b. Please see definitions in text.

three times as likely to fail than the offender who even partially admitted his complicity. Similarly, an offender who was totally opposed to treatment had a two and a half times greater likelihood of failing than the offender who at least minimally accepted (even if begrudgingly) the necessity of treatment.

In addition, if an offender demonstrated high pretreatment plethysmographic arousal to deviant stimuli, his chance of failing in treatment was approximately three times greater than if the normal arousal pattern was seen. Conversely, the offender beginning treatment with low nondeviant arousal had a one and a half times greater likelihood of failure. Often, such offenders also had multiple paraphilias.

Aspects of the offending behavior itself offered some additional clues to the probability of failing treatment. Thus a man who used physical force to inflict abuse upon his victim(s) was over two and a half times as likely to fail than a man who eschewed the use of force entirely. Similarly, men who coerced victims into compliance using threats of harm were one and a half times more likely to fail than those who practiced no such coercion.

As hinted at in the presentation of outcome data earlier in this chapter, men who molest boys were at slightly greater risk of failing treatment; it must be stressed, however, that the vast majority of homosexual pedophiles (over 86%) completed treatment successfully and were evaluated as continuing successes during follow-up. However, if offenders with multiple paraphilias, regardless of type, are examined separately, they carried a higher risk of failure than those with a single diagnosis, regardless of type. Prominent examples included offenders molesting both young girls and young boys or exposing and raping.

While these results seem generally to fall into an expected direction, a number of factors strongly associated with failures seem peculiarly unrelated to the commission of sexual crimes. Thus, if a man had worked at three or more jobs during the three years prior to his offense and/or was unemployed at the time of the offense, his likelihood of failing was fully four times as high as if he had worked at only one or two jobs during that same period of time and if he remained steadily employed. If an offender had divorced or separated during that time period and/or was living alone at the time of the offense, the chance of failure was also four times as high compared with a man who had a more stable family configuration, a result in agreement with another recent outcome study (Tracy, Donnelly, Morganbesser, & MacDonald, 1983). However, a confounding factor here could be homosexuality, as homosexual men generally incurred a greater likelihood of transient relationships.

Even stranger, there was no relationship between the duration of the offense, the frequency of offending behaviors, and the propensity to fail in treatment. In addition, whether the offender was himself a victim of sexual abuse as a child did not influence his chance of failure. Although some of these data are not dissimilar to those reported in other psychiatric conditions, in that job and family stability are correlated with exacerbations of some mental illnesses (Slaughter, 1976), they are nonetheless not in entirely expected directions.

Which, if any, diagnoses, are most closely associated with success in this form of treatment? Table 10.10 lists overall success rates using the criteria listed earlier, by diagnostic category, for all 5,000 offenders entering treatment. (In contrast, Table 10.9 reported data on the 3,995 offenders actually completing treatment who were available for follow-up.) Although these success rates are comfortable, deficiencies are apparent. Men who rape had the lowest success rate among all offenders with single diagnoses. Basic differences in the conceptualization and operation of rape may underlie these findings. Although almost three-quarters of rapists entering treatment reached the criteria for successful completion of therapy, a clinic cannot be satisfied that more than 25% of rapists currently undergoing treatment may rape again in the future. Obviously, further clinical work is essential to improve therapeutic techniques in this particular population of offenders.

Of equal concern are comparatively low success figures for men who molested both girls and boys (75.7%) or who had other multiple paraphilias (71.7%). Although these men could be considered to have had a higher libido, and hence, intuitively, a more entrenched problem, this explanation may be overly simplistic. Although, in treatment, each paraphilia was addressed separately, it may also be that techniques tripped over one another, so to speak, creating a confusion of effects.

In evaluating these figures, it must again be noted that all these data have been presented only on those offenders willing to present themselves for (free) follow-up evaluation sessions. However, the data are clearly biased against artificially high success rates by the very stringent criteria for success enumerated earlier, including the need to complete all sessions, to manifest continuing abstinence by

Table 10.10 *Percentage of Offenders Satisfying Criteria for Successful Treatment Outcome[a] (N = 5,000)*

Diagnostic Category[b]	Percentage Successful at Time of Last Follow-up
Heterosexual pedophilia (N = 2,865)	94.7
Homosexual pedophilia (N = 855)	86.4
Heterosexual and homosexual pedophilia combined (N = 112)	75.7
Other multiple paraphilias (N = 54)	71.7
Exhibitionism (N = 770)	93.1
Rape (N = 145)	73.5
Public masturbation (N = 75)	91.1
Voyeurism (N = 70)	88.1
Frotteurism (N = 60)	80.6
Transvestism (N = 60)	91.7
Fetishism (N = 30)	88.8
Obscene telephone callers (N = 25)	100.0
Sadomasochism (N = 25)	80.0
Zoophilia (N = 20)	100.0

a. See text for definition of criteria.
b. Total number of offenders exceeds 5,000 due to the addition of two categories that might contain patients from the primary diagnostic groupings. Thus among all homosexual pedophiles, a number would also be placed in the heterosexual and homosexual pedophilia combined category.

plethysmographic evaluation of no deviant sexual arousal, and to maintain scrupulously "clean" legal records.

There is also obviously a difference between failure, using these criteria, and remolestation. The majority of failures did not molest after entering therapy. It is most critical, parsimonious, and objective, however, to err on the side of conservatism in regarding any of these "failures" (such as those who dropped out of treatment) as potential reoffenders.

If the data presented here are representative of results in other large clinics, they represent a good start in calling for recommendations about the kinds of therapy that will be effective in the treatment and prevention of sexual abuse. They also help in the determination of the *location* of treatment; clearly, some offenders are not suitable for outpatient therapy and will require hospitalization or institutionalization in order to undergo treatment under the safest of conditions.

- A 39-year-old movie projectionist had been exposing to young girls for over 20 years. For the past 6 years, however, he had also begun fondling girls' vaginal and breast areas and approaching victims in parks and school yards. He had worked at five different jobs during the past 3 years and had been divorced twice. During evaluation, he denied ever touching any youngsters, although he admitted to exposing to them. He agreed that he needed treatment. Factors indicating dangerousness to be at large in this case included
  — multiple victims
  — multiple paraphilias
  — offender a relative stranger to victims
  — minimization and denial
  — unstable employment history
  — unstable history of personal relationships
  Factors indicating safety included
  — absence of force used in the crime
  — amenability to treatment
  Recommendations included treatment in an institutional setting.
- When a 23-year-old truck driver was accused of molesting his 4-year-old son, he admitted to an ongoing attraction to young boys since his early teenage years but denied any other sexual problems. His wife of five years professed support for him. A plethysmograph evaluation revealed no other paraphilias. The clinic recommended to the court that he have no contact with boys under the age of 18, live apart from his son until treatment had been effective, and engage in a mandated behavioral treatment program as a part of his probation. He was believed to be safe to remain at large based upon the following factors
  — single victim
  — single paraphilia
  — offender living with victim
  — offender well known to victim
  — absence of force used in the crime
  — admission of the problem
  — amenability to treatment
  — stable employment history
  — stable history of personal relationships
  Just one negative factor emerged:
  — The presence of homosexual pedophilia
- A 33-year-old construction worker had committed two rapes during a period of three years, all at knife point. However, on several other occasions when his would-be victim fought back, he became frightened and ran away. He had worked steadily and had been married for

ten years. He freely admitted his complicity in these acts, including several attempts that had not been previously reported, and urgently requested treatment. Factors indicating dangerousness included
— multiple victims
— offender a stranger to victims
— use of force in the crime
Factors indicating safety included
— single paraphilia
— admission of the problem
— amenability to treatment
— stable employment history
— stable history of personal relationships
Believing the negative factors outweighed the positive, the clinic recommended treatment in an institutional setting.

Obviously, such recommendations cannot, as yet, be based upon a quantitative weighing of the various risk factors and hence will contain some subjective judgments. Work is now ongoing to place some quantitative value on each of these factors and hence to be able to report to official agencies the statistical likelihood of reoffense. As in the last case example, recommendations for inpatient treatment are usually made in cases of rape, especially in those cases involving a weapon, although some might propose outpatient treatment with depo-Provera in certain cases. In a review of clinic recommendations, it appears that staff have tended to be conservative, believing the value of community safety outweighed that of personal liberty. Decision-making agencies, of course, such as children's services division, corrections divisions, and the courts may weigh such recommendations in the balance with other factors in which treatment personnel may not be expert. It has also become clear that multiple sources of input must be considered in formulating recommendations. Data from police reports, victim and other official reports, significant others, past treatment records, the presentence investigation, the patient's own history, and the penile plethysmograph record will all determine the most sensible recommendations in each case.

In a similar vein, clinic personnel must also make recommendations regarding disposition once outpatient therapy is advised and initiated.

- Following the revelation that a 45-year-old physician had molested his 12-year-old stepdaughter, he was entered into outpatient therapy with the following recommendations:
    — no contact with girls under the age of 18, supervised or unsupervised
    — no frequenting locations where children might congregate, such as video game stores, fast-food restaurants, parks, playgrounds, and school yards
    — court-mandated behavioral treatment

  He was subsequently placed on probation and required to move out of his house and undertake treatment in the clinic. Following demonstration of improvement over the first four months of treatment, clinic personnel advised the following steps to his probation officer:
    — limited contact with the victim through family therapy sessions for several months
    — should this proceed without complication, supervised visits at home for several more months
    — overnight and weekend visits thereafter for several more months
    — should all these work well, a move back home with the concurrence of all family members, the probation officer, the family therapist, and the behavioral therapist
    — once home, no unsupervised contact with the victim
    — plethysmograph and polygraph evaluations prior to succeeding to each next step
- A 67-year-old man had molested several granddaughters and grandsons, at times under the influence of alcohol. He typically did so around swimming pools the family owned. Clinic recommendations included the following:
    — no contact with children under the age of 18, supervised or unsupervised
    — avoidance of places where children might congregate, such as pools, parks, and playgrounds
    — a court-mandated behavioral treatment program
    — an inpatient alcohol treatment program followed by
    — a monitored Antabuse program and attendance at Alcoholics Anonymous
    — plethysmograph and polygraph evaluations at six-month intervals

  As treatment progressed, slow improvement was demonstrated. At six months, recommendations to his probation officer included the following:
    — supervised contact with his grandchildren
    — no contact with them, however, even supervised, around swimming pools, lakes, or at the ocean

Recommendations were made to his children and to him that, even after treatment, he should not be in the company of his grandchildren without another adult being present.

- A 28-year-old divorced factory worker molested his 6-year-old daughter during visitations with her. Following a year of treatment, the following recommendations were made in conjunction with his ex-wife, the victim's mother.
  — visitations with the victim only in the grandparents' home for several months
  — if these proceeded well, visits alone with the victim in public places such as restaurants, movie theaters, circuses, and fairs for several more months
  — if these proceeded well, and if plethysmograph and polygraph evaluations were negative, unsupervised visitations

Such recommendations have usually been offered as treatment is progressing and improvement can be documented. At first, clinic personnel usually have advised no contact with minors, even supervised, with the (as yet unproven) fear that even supervised contact could lead to the strengthening of deviant fantasy formation, especially in the early phases of treatment. Again, this represents a bias toward safety, even at the risk of separating families for periods of time. It has proven helpful to have some empiric basis for these recommendations in dealing with agencies; a review of the offending history with an emphasis on the safety factors elucidated above can assist in providing reasonable advice not only on safety to be at large but also on the rate and circumstances of a return to contact with the victim and, ultimately and hopefully, healing of wounded families.

Some confidence can be ascribed to these recommendations partly due to the large data base from which they emanate and partly due to the successful outcomes in the vast majority of offenders. However, more than 9% of offenders were failures and, ostensibly, at risk to harm victims in the future. Some of these men represented poor risks for visiting victims or returning home. Demographic comparisons *alone* are evidently not helpful in predicting danger to the community and potential failure in treatment. Thus there are no statistically significant differences between successful and unsuccessful offenders when compared in terms of age, educational or occupational level, presence of other psychiatric diagnoses, or presence of prior sexual or nonsexual charges. With some exceptions, the characteristics of an offender appear less crucial than the *parameters of the offending behavior itself* in predicting ultimate treatment success and, by extension, danger to be at large. To recapitulate, men who *might* fail in treatment and/or reoffend are those who

(1) are not living with their victim(s)
(2) have multiple victims
(3) have multiple paraphilias
(4) offend against relative strangers
(5) use force in their offense(s)
(6) totally deny their participation in the offense(s)
(7) totally deny the need for treatment
(8) demonstrate high pretreatment deviant arousal
(9) demonstrate low pretreatment nondeviant arousal
(10) manifest employment instability
(11) manifest instability of personal relationships

Discussion

The data presented here indicate that sexual offenders can be successfully treated with techniques of behavior modification, although this statement cannot yet be extended as confidently to men who rape. This conclusion must be tempered with the recognition of drawbacks in the way the data were generated and presented. These patients were not treated identically; rather, a variety of techniques were employed as befit each individual's needs. Some of these patients were entered into double-blind controlled research (Maletzky, 1973a, 1973b, 1974b, 1977, 1980a, 1980b; Maletzky & Price, 1984); others were treated as routine clinic patients. Therefore, data collection methods were partially subjective and largely retrospective. In addition, averaged data were usually presented, thus increasing the risk of blurring subtle distinctions.

However, some strengths within these data should also be recognized: A large number of patients have been studied; treatment assessment techniques were varied yet standardized; and treatment conditions were typically clinical. Thus observations made for this many patients in a nonresearch environment can be considered representative of treatment conditions across a multitude of settings.

Although these data and the conclusions they intimate are not to be substituted for more precise controls and measurements, they can serve in two ways: They can point the way for future, smaller, better controlled studies and they can indicate for the clinician not only what is likely to be helpful but what is feasible as well.

But what is to be made of the relatively poor results among men who rape? As indicated above, this group may differ either because of an overall difference when compared with other groups of sexual offenders or because of the group's possible heterogeneous nature. For example, the rapist usually does not repeat his crime at the frequency of the pedophile; neither does he always have excessive deviant arousal to aggressive sexual fantasies.

A comparison between self-reported covert and overt acts between all other groups and rapists revealed a combined frequency of 7.2 per week for all other groups as opposed to 3.6 for rapists, a difference significant at the .001 level. Averaged plethysmograph values for arousal to deviant stimuli were low in rapists as a group. A number of men had no deviant arousal whatsoever. The percentage of heterosexual pedophiles with no deviant arousal at the beginning of treatment was 34.7%. This percentage among men who had raped was 53.7%, a difference significant at the .01 level.

It is possible that men who rape do so partly because of denied or frustrated sexual feelings at the time rather than as an expression of deviant arousal. There is no current evidence, however, that links other offender groups to a thwarted sexual drive. While other sexual offenders can be divided into situational (circumstantial or opportunistic) and predatory (preferential or obligatory) groups (see Chapter 11), rapists are often considered entirely predatory. However, distinctions can be drawn between one group of men who rape, yet prefer consenting sexual relations, and men who show arousal chiefly to the aggressive elements of sexual activity (Abel, Blanchard, Becker, & Djenderedjian, 1978; Malamuth & Clark, 1983). Also, in contrast to other sexual offenders (with the exception of exhibitionists), rapists show significantly higher rates of sexual crimes in the summer months, if inhabiting temperate zones (Michael & Zumpe, 1983). It appears that some men who rape have relatively nonaggressive fantasies during mutually consenting, as opposed to forcible, sexual scenes (Murphy, Krisak, Stalgaittis, & Anderson, 1984). Nonetheless, a sizeable and distinctive minority seem to derive pleasure from aggressive elements in the sexual act (Abel, Becker, & Cuningham-Rathner, 1984; Groth, 1979a).

Work now ongoing in the clinic may be helpful in distinguishing these groups. A set of six standard story lines are read to rapists beginning with purely sexual scenes followed by mixed sexual and aggressive scenes and then, finally, scenes of a nonsexual but aggressive nature (Abel & Blanchard, 1974). The order of presentation is varied randomly. Patients' responses on the plethysmograph are monitored continuously. This work has already demonstrated a dichotomy of responses, as depicted in Figure 10.9. One group of men without histories of particularly aggressive rapes ($N = 55$) showed clearly elevated sexual responses to frankly sexual scenes and reduced responses to purely aggressive scenes (see Groth, 1979a). Another group with histories of extreme aggression ($N = 25$) demonstrated the opposite pattern: They became aroused only as the aggressive elements were intensified; 9 of these men demonstrated erections to scenes of aggression alone without any sexual content. These findings underscore the belief, previously voiced, that rapists may not be a homogeneous population.

If these data on all sexual offenders are confirmed in future trials, they lend themselves to explorations of the genesis of maladaptive sexual approach disorders. Do unifying mechanisms exist that produce these disorders? Is the acquisition of these disorders the result of spurious sexual associations made at times of critical sensitivity in the development of the central nervous system? Is there a biological or genetic component predisposing individuals to the development of deviant sexual arousal?

An informal retrospective survey of all 5,000 patients' charts indicated a history of the patients having been molested as children in an uncommonly high number: Fully 29% of sexual offenders had such a history, with molestation usually having taken place between the ages of 5 and 12. The event was often remembered in graphic detail.

Genetic histories were obtained from all 5,000 sexual offenders:

— 22% had first-degree relatives with an affective disorder
— 27% had first-degree relatives with a history of sexual offenses themselves
— 44% had first-degree relatives with a history of alcoholism

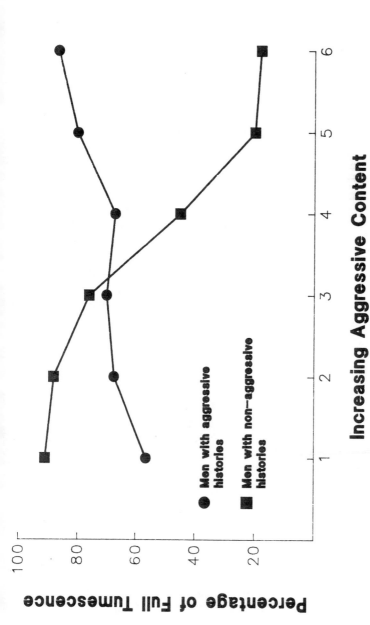

Figure 10.9 Average Plethysmograph Responses to Increasingly Aggressive Sexual Scenes in Two Sets of Rapists: Those With ($N = 15$) and Those Without ($N = 18$) Aggressive Histories ($N = 33$)

The unexpectedly high number of relatives who themselves had offended may actually be an underestimate; this figure included only those relatives *known to the patient* who had offended. Other offenders in the family may have existed, yet knowledge of them might well have been camouflaged.

In reviewing these data, a number of additional questions emerge: Can a streamlined treatment package be economically organized? What should its main components be? Can assessment techniques become more sophisticated? For which offenders will group therapy be helpful? For which should medications (chiefly depo-Provera) be reserved? The results defined in this chapter can only indicate the way for future, better controlled research.

With the increasing awareness of sexual abuse, a plethora of treatment techniques have evolved, often administered by diverse populations of therapists who adhere to a variety of schools of therapy. Some therapies do not lend themselves well to scientific scrutiny, however, and some therapists are reluctant to subject themselves to such rigorous inquiry. It is unlikely that replications of prior research demonstrating the efficacy of behavioral techniques will be of value in setting standards for treatment. It is possible, however, that an ounce of public exposure in the form of popular articles, television discussions, and educational seminars may accomplish more than a pound of rigorous objective research.

Conclusions

The experiences of a single sexual abuse clinic in a metropolitan area over a period of 17 years have been reviewed. Data have been presented regarding characteristics of the study population, methods of assessment, and treatment results. While the population of sexual offenders thus described is large, methodological flaws prevent the data from being conclusive. Nonetheless, the cross-correlation among a variety of assessment techniques, and the large number of offenders treated, engenders some confidence in the application of the various treatment methods described.

Assessment techniques employed included patients' own reports, observers' reports, the penile plethysmograph, and scrutiny of computerized police files. Patients were treated in a clinical, rather than an academic, environment, although several well-controlled studies occurred during the generation of these data.

A number of tentative conclusions can be summarized:

(1) The majority of sexual offenders can be effectively treated with behavioral techniques.

(2) Treatment of the sexual offender is not necessarily prolonged or expensive.

(3) A separate subgroup of sexual offenders, men who rape, have poorer outcomes when compared with all other categories of offenders, for reasons not immediately apparent.

(4) Success in treatment can be reliably measured using a variety of assessment techniques.

(5) It is safe to treat many, *but not all*, sexual offenders on an outpatient basis.

(6) Although small, well-controlled studies are needed to verify these conclusions, there are sufficient data to recommend the use of behavioral methods in the treatment of the sexual offender.

Notes

1. The Exodus Trust, 1623 Franklin Street, San Francisco, California 95109, maintains an enormous library of pornographic material in a variety of media; those interested should write the Trust directly.

2. Contact the Association for the Behavioral Treatment of Sexual Abusers, P.O. Box 66028, Portland, Oregon 97266.

(3) Personal communication from H. N. Wagner and J. J. Frost, Johns Hopkins University Medical School, Baltimore, Maryland.

11

Summary and Future Directions

The principles of behavior modification were formulated decades ago, but their practical application in treating behavioral disorders has come about only recently and to a lesser extent than had been hoped. Behavior therapy has still not achieved clinical success in conditions in which, from a theoretic perspective, it should have been helpful. This is true in the addictive disorders such as alcoholism or narcotic dependencies and also in what are now called "personality disorders" (Marks, 1981a, pp. 249-287). This is also true in psychiatric disorders such as schizophrenia and manic-depressive illness. Limited changes in behavior can be produced in these populations by exerting total environmental control and by manipulating vital contingencies such as has been accomplished with inpatient token economies (Kazdin, 1985). But such programs have not yielded improvement in the central core of these disorders.

Thus behavioral techniques can increase the probability that the regressed patient with schizophrenia will improve his personal hygiene and display good table manners, yet that patient may still be bedeviled with hallucinations and have trouble attending to any task due to overwhelming distractibility. This is not to belittle the gains made in increasing independence and reducing symptoms in these populations; however, the theory and practice of such operant conditioning has been applied in these conditions as an adjunctive, rather than primary, treatment technique. Indeed, many clinicians and researchers hold that schizophrenia and the major affective disorders are genetic and biochemical illnesses. If so, operant conditioning techniques can be helpful in the same fashion that they have been applied to the management of many chronic medical disorders. Thus modeling and praise can teach a young diabetic how to administer his own medication; principles of stimulus control can help a patient with high blood pressure to lose weight.

Such techniques of operant conditioning in the treatment of the sexual offender have been detailed in Chapter 6, where they were presented as aids to treatment rather than as sufficient treatments in themselves. Instead, respondent techniques such as covert sensitization or aversive behavior rehearsal have been presented as the major modalities in the treatment of sexual abuse. This accurately represents the current scope of clinical practice but should not be taken to mean that further change is unthinkable. The treatment of the sexual offender is a major area of research interest, partly because of the explosion of public awareness of this phenomenon and partly because of the emergence of effective treatment techniques. Moreover, in the treatment of the sexual offender, the principles of behavior modification actually work in the expected direction: The pairing of deviant sexual arousal with aversive stimuli reduces or eliminates the deviant response. It might be argued that the *exact* mechanism for this change is uncertain, but this is only true in a neurophysiological sense: The neural pathways involved are speculative; even this area is now under investigation (Maple, 1977).

Lest this appraisal sound self-congratulatory, it must be quickly added that respondent and operant techniques have not eliminated deviant sexual arousal in all sexual offenders. Most clinics report a high success rate, but few data are available to examine the reasons that 10% to 15% of sexual offenders apparently derive little or no benefit from such techniques. This chapter will address this and other unanswered problems certain to be causes of concern in the future treatment of the sexual offender.

Efficacy of Treatment

Approximately 9% of typical sexual abuse clinic patients either show no benefit from treatment or show minor and/or temporary improvement. This rate generally holds across all subcategories with one major exception: men who rape. Chapter 10 raises the question of whether this group is truly comparable to other sexual offenders. Even eliminating this group, however, does little to change the approximate 9% failure rate, due to the much larger numbers of pedophiles and exhibitionists in the patient population. This failure rate, however, might be inflated to some extent because it included *all patients who entered treatment but failed to complete it,* even if they discontinued treatment after one session. These were regarded as failures because whatever treatment techniques were used in early treatment sessions failed to help these patients continue their treatment.

A retrospective review of one large sexual abuse clinic practice was presented in Chapter 10. Table 10.9 of that chapter divides all treated sexual offenders into successes or failures based upon multiple assessment techniques. For this purpose, *success* was defined as the completion of all treatment sessions, under 20% of full tumescence to deviant test stimuli at the end of treatment and no increase in arousal at annual follow-up, no reports of covert or overt deviant sexual activity, and an absence of any new charges of sexual abuse during treatment and follow-up. The table demonstrates that neither duration nor frequency of offending behaviors could help in distinguishing successful patients from treatment failures. The table also shows a tendency for poorer outcome in men who were either unmarried or living alone and for men who could not sustain gainful employment. Why should living with a companion promote treatment success? Why should maintaining a steady job help as well? Currently, there are only unsatisfying and vague guesses: Those in a stable relationship and those with job consistency may have possessed traits that enabled them to work harder in treatment. Perhaps those with a good prognosis were more settled and experienced and thus might have learned sufficient coping skills to utilize techniques in a more productive fashion. Clearly, these tentative answers are unsuitable and show that even the questions in this area of research cannot be posed with sufficient precision to facilitate the generation of satisfactory answers.

In the treatment of a patient not showing adequate progress, it is important to evaluate all the assessment techniques available and to be flexible in altering treatment programs, when necessary.

- A 26-year-old married metal worker who had digitally penetrated the vagina of his 4-year-old biological daughter, and molested several nieces as well, made apparently rapid progress in treatment, showing eradication of plethysmograph responses to sexual stimuli involving young girls over a period of three months. He maintained improvement at one-year follow-up but was rearrested and convicted six months thereafter for digital penetration of his 6-year-old niece. Six months later, he still demonstrated no sexual arousal on plethysmograph testing. However, a detailed log, kept by his wife, revealed occasions on which he called out two names of his victims in his sleep. He had also related heterosexual pedophiliac dream content to her, and she had observed that he continued to keep photographs of a number of young girls beneath other materials in his desk drawer.

- After reoffending, a 40-year-old construction worker was referred back to the clinic, where, five years earlier, he had been labeled a treatment failure. Similar techniques were employed in his treatment the second time, but it was noted that he had a special aversion to foul taste. His subsequent treatment program combined foul odor, electric shock, and foul taste in a random design, with foul taste being used twice as frequently as the other two aversive stimuli. Frequency records and the plethysmograph revealed good progress, and a three-year follow-up indicated that gains had been sustained.

In the first example, data were collected from the sexual offender and his significant other, law enforcement officials, and the plethysmograph as well as from his own reports. Only an evaluation of all these assessment devices yielded clues that treatment was not as successful as the patient and the therapist wished. The second example demonstrates the value of individualizing treatment: Idiosyncratic responses must be explored. Therapists should be cautious in developing a "treatment package" to fit all offenders. A treatment program for one offender cannot be assumed to be appropriate for another.

With the current level of understanding, some guiding principles can be offered about treatment failures, always bearing in mind that rigorous scientific scrutiny has yet to be applied to this important area:

(1) If treatment is failing, the particular set of sexual stimuli being used and the aversive stimuli used to reduce deviant sexual arousal should be examined.

(2) As much information as possible should be collected from significant others.

(3) The aid of the patient must be enlisted in determining any reasons for inordinately slow progress.

(4) Concurrent, nonsexual problems should be explored--these may be blocking progress.

(5) Multiple treatment techniques should be used.

(6) Multiple assessment measures should be used.

These suggestions will not cure every treatment failure, but they may assist some patients for whom treatment may otherwise not succeed.

Follow-Up

Generalization from treatment conditions to real-life situations is of pivotal concern in all behavior therapy. It assumes additional significance in treating the sexual offender because his behavior is thought to be responsive to the situation in which he finds himself, and these cannot be directly controlled by the therapist or, if so, only to a limited extent. In addition, the sexual offender often poses a danger to the community, thus increasing the importance of transfer from in vitro to in vivo situations. Generalization is enhanced by the real-life techniques described, particularly in Chapter 9. The practice of aversive conditioning and reconditioning techniques "in the field" has been particularly helpful. Assessments reported at follow-up were, in reality, testing the success of such generalization.

How long should treatment last? Most workers believe that treatment and follow-up should continue as long as practically possible. Data reviewed in Chapter 10 have been presented for a large group of sexual offenders treated and followed over a period of 17 years. However, only a minority of these patients have had adequate follow-up assessments exceeding 10 years. Of those who have, many were given different treatments and assessed with a wide variety of measurement techniques. Still, these data represent some of the longest follow-ups currently in the literature.

In addition to the "booster" phases of treatment already described, generalization and persistence of therapeutic effects can be enhanced through an active program of relapse prevention such as recently advocated by Pithers, Marquis, Gibat, and Marlatt (1983). Such a program consists of a number of steps, carefully explored with each offender, well before the end of active therapy:

(1) Avoiding overconfidence. The offender is encouraged to regard the need for treatment as perpetual and the need for caution extreme.

(2) Self-monitoring. The offender is coached in recognizing the earliest steps leading to recurrent deviant sexual arousal, especially those that initially appear harmless.

(3) Problem solving. Rational problem-solving skills, such as brainstorming and then evaluating options, are taught to the offender to use in provocative situations.

(4) Environmental control. The offender is encouraged to review lifestyle changes he can produce to lower the risk of entering dangerous situations.

(5) Cognitive restructuring. Thought-changing and substituting techniques are detailed with the offender in an effort to relabel thinking errors and impose greater self-control.

(6) Coping skills. The offender is taught relaxation training, anger management skills, and impulse control training; he is encouraged to use physical exercise as a release and is coached in relapse rehearsals to prepare him for a sexual arousal "emergency." He is taught to practice such skills until they are overlearned and become automatic. A card is often provided with instructions and reminders of techniques to practice and telephone numbers to call if an urgent situation arises. A potential benefit lies in the practice of encouraging, or even, via a probation situation, enforcing, participation in community activities to prevent sexual abuse. Thus the former offender may

be assigned to lead several therapy groups for current offenders, give talks to school or church groups on how to recognize and prevent sexual abuse, and assist probation and parole officers in obtaining information for ongoing cases of abuse.

These procedures must be implemented as a part of each offender's final hours of therapy. While it is likely that such relapse prevention for sexual offenders will be tested more widely in the near future, it should also be borne in mind that the altogether attainable goal of behavioral treatment is the *elimination* of deviant sexual arousal rather than only its *control*. Admittedly, a portion of offenders must settle for the enhanced self-control over deviant fantasies and behaviors implied as the treatment result in relapse prevention models; however, the majority of offenders can lose all arousal to their deviant stimuli with adequate behavior therapy. Yet, even for those who ostensibly do, as measured by the plethysmograph and follow-up of legal records, relapse prevention programs will still be necessary to ensure ongoing safety in the community.

In light of the importance of safety, it does not seem unreasonable to expect that all clinics, both in- and outpatient, engaged in this work, should keep accurate records of demographic information, treatment techniques employed, and outcome over time, documenting assessment techniques used. Hopefully, this last will include an attempt to use a variety of outcome measures. Sophisticated double-blind research is not the goal here; rather, clinically relevant and realistic data are needed to be certain of which techniques are providing the best therapeutic outcomes.

Of special importance in this regard is the ability to continue contact with as many sexual offenders as possible. This cause is greatly aided by establishing good rapport with the patient early in treatment and maintaining contact even after active treatment is completed. If at all possible, follow-up assessments for the collection of such data should not be billed to the patient. The economic consequences of this policy will, hopefully, be outweighed by the contribution such knowledge can make in advancing our understanding of the treatment of the sexual offender.

Efficiency of Treatment

Questions of cost have only recently arisen in the behavioral literature (Mason, Louks, & Backus, 1985), although such issues have been a part of medical practice for some time (Coclen, Hamilton, & Walter, 1980). Certainly, issues of efficiency will continue to be discussed when decisions on care of the sexual offender must be made, particularly in the face of the rising numbers of sexual offenders referred for treatment and the increasing cost of providing psychological and medical care. While consumers will be heard in this debate, those who are third-party payers, including the federal government, may become the most persistent. It may not suffice to demonstrate that a treatment works; it may instead be necessary to document that it does so at less cost than any other reasonable approach. This will be a new area to many researchers, but one in which clinicians have already been immersed.

- When a 61-year-old homosexual pedophile was first seen in a Sexual Abuse Clinic, he had been through a three-year course of treatment with psychoanalysis. He was referred after reoffending and, with 16 weeks of aversive therapy, plethysmograph arousal to young boys was essentially eliminated. However, he began to complain of increasing depression and of no one "understanding" him. He made a suicide gesture with an overdose; after being rereferred to a psychoanalyst, his mood quickly improved.

- A high school student was repeatedly arrested for exposing himself to young girls. Little progress was being made using standard behavior therapy techniques. Thus he was referred for group therapy in addition to his behavioral program. Within several weeks, self-reports and plethysmograph readings demonstrated improvement. He believed that the experience of learning about other sexual offenders, and their lack of criticism toward him, allowed behavior therapy to become increasingly effective.

Both examples document the need for flexibility in designing a treatment program for the sexual offender. It is not uncommon to incorporate, within the same treatment program, plans for different methodologies, even some that may seem mutually antagonistic, such as psychoanalysis; reality therapy; self-help groups such as Parents United, Recovering Offenders, and Sexaholics Anonymous;

and behavior therapy. However, with the current state of knowledge, it is difficult to predict the most efficient or economical approach for *each* offender. There is no doubt that many patients receive "too much" treatment or "too many" approaches, reflecting therapeutic uncertainty and, perhaps, a desire to overtreat to ensure safety.

Unfortunately, the clinician may feel compelled to offer the treatment with which he or she is most familiar. Another approach has been to offer, at first, what appears to be the least costly alternative.

- Because of a new legislative ruling, one western state established a program in which sexual offenders could be sentenced to receive depo-Provera. Cost assessments seemed to document the efficacy of this approach. No time constraints were imposed, however. In addition, no provision was made for behavioral treatment. Early experience indicated incomplete success and the necessity for additional treatment programs, with concomitant escalating costs and delays.

Although it is tempting to decry a lack of controlled studies in addressing this question, there are now some data, even if preliminary, that can help delineate treatment directions:

(1) Comparative cost of different prospective treatments can be estimated.
(2) The comparative effectiveness of several treatment approaches is reasonably well known (Maletzky, 1980a).
(3) Progress during treatment can be closely monitored and changes in treatment techniques can be made using ongoing evaluation.

Hopefully, the scientific literature will begin to address this issue in a more complete fashion and, thereby, establish some standards for treatment. That this issue is delicate should not cause it to be ignored.

Prediction of Dangerousness

Psychologists and psychiatrists have been vigorously and repeatedly reproached for attempting to predict human behavior (Wettstein, 1984). By extension, such criticism casts doubt on the ability of the professional to correctly foretell (with a greater than chance probability) who is likely to offend and who is not, to whom a reoffense might be directed, and when it might occur. Although some data exist to help clarify this issue for the sexual offender, they must be regarded as tentative and preliminary. As previously mentioned, one problem is a lack of prospective controlled research. However, large and clear double-blind studies are not likely; it is difficult to ethically justify a control group in a natural environment given that members of such a group, whether receiving no treatment or receiving traditional therapy, are at high risk for reoffending. Therefore, retrospective data must be scrutinized. To partly compensate for this deficiency, large numbers of patients can be studied without creating a potentially dangerous situation.

Prognostic factors might be found in several areas of inquiry: demographic information, diagnosis, duration and/or frequency of inappropriate sexual behavior, presence or absence of violence, and early treatment response. Table 10.9 in Chapter 10 displays data culled from the records of a total sample of 3,995 sexual offenders divided into those who failed in treatment and those who did not. It should be noted that not all of these treatment failures reoffended. Evidence from self-admissions and police reports indicates that fewer than one-third of offenders not meeting the treatment success criteria enumerated in Chapter 10 actually reoffended. Conversely, a sexual offender might have yielded an improving plethysmograph or other signs of success but still have reoffended during or after treatment. Alternatively, a patient might have shown no sign of improvement on multiple measures yet might never have reoffended, at least up to the maximum duration of follow-up in the current population, a total of 17 years.

An additional review of these data reveals only a few factors of significance. However, these are not ones that would automatically have been apparent. Some very strong predictors of future offending relate to demographic characteristics rather than to variables of the sexual behavior itself. Thus a stable pair-bond and a steady employment history proved of significance in predicting safety as opposed to the duration or frequency of the inappropriate sexual behavior.

This result was true of the sample as a whole. However, if data from pedophiles, both heterosexual and homosexual, are isolated, two additional factors assume importance: the number of victims and the places in which the offense has occurred. Thus if an offender had more than one victim at one time, his chance of reoffending was eight times as great as the offender who had but a single victim.

Similarly, the offender who committed sexual crimes both inside and outside his home had an eightfold greater likelihood of reoffending when compared with offenders who committed sexual crimes solely within their homes. These data underscore a distinction now coming into sharper focus, particularly for pedophiles, as more offenders are evaluated and treated, that is, the differences between two types of pedophiles--the situational offender and the predatory one.

- A 54-year-old blind homosexual pedophile had purchased several new video games and let this be known in his new apartment complex. When several boys asked to see his games, he allowed them in, gave them marijuana and beer, and then showed them an X-rated pornographic videotape. He made sexual advances toward them as they became aroused to the movie. This pattern was repeated a number of times. When outcry arose against him in the apartment building, he would plead innocence on the basis of his visual handicap and would from time to time move to another complex.

- When a 41-year-old millworker married his current wife, he joined her and her two daughters, 5 and 7 years of age. He fell into habits of wrestling with the older girl and would become aroused during those times. He also began to create situations in which he could undress and be naked around her as he also enjoyed her looking at him in that state. He began to "wander" into the girls' unlocked bathroom to discover if his victim was there, taking a bath. If so, he would fondle her vagina at those times and began to insist she draw his erect penis on paper. Twice he masturbated while fondling her, then ejaculated into a spoon and demanded she ingest the ejaculate. On several occasions, he took Polaroid photographs of the sexual activity with her. No sexual activity occurred with his younger stepdaughter.

- A 23-year-old roofer often volunteered to teach Sunday school and began to lead camping trips for youngsters in his church. He would direct the sleeping arrangements to his advantage and fondle the young girls' genital areas in the middle of the night; were they to awaken, he would reassure them he was just checking on them to make certain they were safe. On several occasions he had parked his car near school yards and masturbated while watching young girls at play. He had also begun, just prior to treatment to drive his car around neighborhoods near schools and offer to give young girls rides home.

The first and third examples noted above were of the predatory type. While these men have also been termed *preferential offenders*, there are insufficient data to indicate that they would *always* choose sexual activity with a child rather than an adult. It has been theorized that these offenders are different in some central fashion from cases typified by the second example above in which an offender molests a child, apparently because the situation presents itself (Abel & Becker, 1984; Carmen, Reiker, & Mills, 1984; Kroop, 1984; Maletzky, in press; Mayer, 1983). This area is too new and tender to pluck out new theories with any confidence: Would most men be sexually aroused when living with a 12- to 14-year-old girl not their biological kin whom they did not raise from infancy? Would most of these men, if aroused, be able to control their actions, leaving the situational pedophile guilty of a sexual impulse control problem rather than a deviant arousal one? What factors would be powerful enough to overcome the natural taboo most individuals possess that prohibits sexual arousal for youngsters they have raised since infancy (see Finklehor, 1984)? Different answers to these questions compel different treatment strategies. Similarly, should a predatory offender demonstrate a higher plethysmograph response to deviant than to nondeviant stimuli? Logically, this may be so, but, in actual practice, often the reverse is true. There is no shortage of potential research material within these dilemmas.

It would seem that the situational offender should have a more favorable prognosis than his predatory counterpart. Table 11.1 reports outcome data from a retrospective review of most pedophiles in this sample, categorized into situational or predatory patterns. To cast potential patterns into clearer perspective, an attempt was made to eliminate uncertain cases. Thus some cases were not entered into the table. For example, a man who molested two stepdaughters and their next-door friend was not included; neither was an offender who molested his own son and the boy's cousin, whom he had just met when his family stayed at his house during a two-week vacation. It is immediately apparent from the table that the data fall into anticipated patterns. Thus just knowing that an offender fits a situational profile--as defined by a victim or victims residing with the offender and the absence of multiple paraphilias--allows one to account for over 85% of the variance in an analysis performed on these data. The risk of reoffending and/or failing in this clinic was almost two and a half times as great for the predatory as for the situational pedophile. (The data in this table cannot be compared directly with those in Table 10.9, in which all offenders, not just pedophiles, were evaluated, regardless of pattern of offense. In that table, the data are

Table 11.1 *Treatment Outcomes of Situational and Predatory Pedophiles*
             (N = 3,315)

Type of Pedophile[a]	Treatment Successes[b] (N = 3,083) (percentage)	Treatment Failures[b] (N = 232) (percentage)	p[c]
Situational (N = 2,450)	92.7	7.3	< .001
heterosexual (N = 2,072)	93.4	6.6	< .001
homosexual (N=378)	88.9	11.1	< .001
Predatory (N = 865)	82.5	17.5	
heterosexual (N = 600)	83.1	16.9	< .001
homosexual (N = 265)	79.2	20.8	< .001
Situational—predatory Difference—all pedophiles[d]	< .05	< .05	< .01
heterosexual difference	< .05	< .05	
homosexual difference	< .05	< .05	

NOTE: Table terminology is defined as follows. *Situational* pedophiles have the following factors: (1) living with the victim(s), (2) offender well-known to victim(s), and (3) single paraphilia. *Predatory* pedophiles have the following factors: (1) not living with the victim(s) or living with one victim but having at least one other victim in the community, (b) offender not well known to at least one victim, and (c) single or multiple paraphilias. Cases that did not fit clearly into these definitions were omitted from data presentation. See text for details.
a. Offenders with multiple paraphilias are listed according to their major paraphilia.
b. See definitions in text.
c. Horizontal column differences.
d. Vertical column differences.

expressed as a percentage of successful or unsuccessful outcomes *for each characteristic*. In Table 11.1, pedophiles alone are evaluated with arbitrary definitions for situational and predatory offenders, and successes and failures are given as percentages *for each type of offender*.) It appears that the clinical notion of two kinds of offending behaviors--a less dangerous situational pattern and a more dangerous predatory one--is borne out by these preliminary data.

As more clinicians accumulate knowledge and understanding about sexual abuse, there is no doubt its treatment will become increasingly sophisticated. Recent work has begun not only to document the effectiveness of treatment programs but to raise additional questions about who may or may not be qualified to treat sexual offenders and the impact sexual abuse programs may have on the communities they serve (O'Connell, Leberg, & Donaldson, 1990). Economic considerations may continue to have an impact on treatment conditions. If so, outpatient treatment will continue to be a necessary component of a total sexual offender treatment program.

Such programs will need to depend upon valid and reliable predictors of safety to be at large and likelihood of successful treatment. Thus far, profiles have emerged that appear productive. The patient who offends at home against a single victim, who knows him or her well, who avoids physical force, who is relatively honest about his crimes, who agrees that treatment is necessary, and who has enjoyed a stable employment history and stable social relationships has an excellent chance of eliminating the possibility of molesting again, with appropriate treatment. The patient who preys upon multiple victims in the community, some of whom might not know him well, who may have several paraphilias, who uses physical force, who minimizes or denies his offenses, who actively resists treatment, and who has erratic histories of employment and social relationships possesses a greater uncertainty of treatment success and a higher risk for reoffending, particularly within the first several months of therapy when behavioral approaches have not yet significantly affected him. Even though, for most such offenders, behavioral treatment will markedly reduce or eliminate deviant sexual arousal, it is still to those for whom treatment does not reduce or eliminate arousal that we must extend our most earnest and urgent efforts.

Summary and Future Directions

A multitude of questions remain: What variety of causes give rise to the maladaptive sexual approach disorders? If deconditioning can eliminate deviant sexual arousal, are conditioning factors at crucial developmental stages involved? Are these conditions possible in anyone, given the same upbringing, or is some genetic or behavioral susceptibility necessary? What are the most effective treatment components within a sexual offender program? Which are the most efficient? What are the best ways to evaluate treatment? Can sexual offenders truly be "cured" or will there always be some potential to reoffend?

In calling for more research on these issues, some consideration must be given to data already at hand. It is unlikely that large, retrospective reports of the efficacy of behavior therapy will add anything to the current literature. Similarly, anecdotal single-case reports will also not be helpful. However, meaningful studies will be

possible for the clinician as well as the researcher across several
dimensions:

(1) Single-case A-B-A-B and A-B-A-C designs can help to tease out crucial
    variables within a total treatment package.
(2) Single- or small-case designs can also address theoretic questions of
    the etiology and nature of the maladaptive sexual approach disorders.
(3) Intermediate, multiple-case studies can further document the role
    individual variation plays in determining treatment outcome.
(4) Intermediate, multiple-case studies can also clarify the pivotal factors
    in treatment success and hence approach the issue of
    cost-effectiveness.
(5) Long-term, larger studies can address the problem of treatment
    failures and the issue of reoffending.

There is no shortage of material to interest future researchers in the
pursuit of understanding and treating maladaptive sexual approach
behaviors, sometimes termed the *disorders of desire*. It is hoped that
this work will assist in some small measure toward attaining those
goals.

APPENDIX A:

The Sone Sexual History Background Form

Name: _____   Date: _____

1. Where did you get most of your sexual information as a child?

    _____

2. With what degree of comfort was sex discussed in your home?

    _____

3. How old were you when nocturnal emissions (wet dreams) began? _____

4. Were there any special feelings (pride, embarrassment, etc.) you
    associated with nocturnal emissions? Please comment.

    _____

5. When did you get the "whole picture" together (menstruation for the
    female, erection for the male, intercoruse, conception, delivery, etc.)?
    How did you feel about this?

    _____

    _____

6. Do you recall playing sex games as a child? What age? What kinds of
    games? With whom? _____

    _____

7. As a child or adolescent, were you punished for sexual activities?
    ( ) Often ( ) Once ( ) Never Caught ( ) Caught, but not punished
    ( ) Had none   Please comment. _____

    _____

    _____

8. Were you sexually molested as a child? By whom and in what way? How
    old were you? _____
    _____
    _____

9. At what age do you recall first having any pelvic (genital) feelings that
    were pleasurable? Were they in connection with any particular thoughts,
    activities, or situations? _____
    _____
    _____

10. At what age did you first begin to masturbate? _____

11. Did you often use fantasy while masturbating during adolescence? Any
    special "theme?" Describe as many kinds of fantasies as you remember.
    _____
    _____
    _____

12. At what age did you have your first heterosexual (boy-girl) date? _____

13. At what age did you have your first sexual experience (genital touching,
    kissing, mutual masturbation, etc.) with a member of:
    _____ Same Sex   _____ Opposite Sex

14. What kind of sexual experience was this - describe.
    _____
    _____

15. As a child, did you ever watch animals or humans, accidently or
    otherwise, involved in sexual activities? Please comment.
    _____
    _____

16. As a teenager, how did you view girls who went "all the way?"

_____

17. As a teenager, how did you view boys who went "all the way?"

_____

18. How would you describe your sexual activities during adolescence? Check as many as apply, indicating frequency by writing Never, Seldom, Often, Sometimes, as it applies. Comment as needed.

_____None   _____Oral-Genital Stimulation.

_____Some kissing & making out   _____Simulating intercourse with

_____Petting - Not to Orgasm.   clothes on - no penetration.

_____Petting - Leading to Orgasm _____Sexual Intercourse.

_____Mutual Masturbation (Touching

        each others' genitals).

    Comments: _____

19. With whom were you involved sexually as an adolescent?

Always with girls _____   Equally with both _____

Always with boys _____   No sexual experiences _____

Usually girls, sometimes boys _____ Adult males _____

Usually boys, sometimes girls _____ Adult females _____

20. How would you describe the usual feelings you had following sexual activities? (Use as many adjectives as needed, such as guilty, loved, etc.) _____

_____

_____

21. At what age and with whom (steady girlfriend, prostitute, etc.) did you first experience intercourse? _____

_____

22.   Was this a good or bad experience for you at the time? Did you
       experience any difficulty with your erection or ejaculation? _____
       _____

23.   Approximately how often and with how many different partners did you
       experience intercourse?
       A.   Before the age of 10   _____
       B.   Ages 10 - 15   _____
       C.   Ages 15 - 18   _____
       D.   Ages 18 - 21   _____
       E.   Age 21 to present time   _____
       Indicate, for each age, your most frequent partner. (Prostitute, casual
       acquaintance, person with whom you were having a close relationship,
       spouse, or any other)
       A.   _____   B.   _____   C.   _____
       D.   _____   E.   _____

24.   As an adolescent, did you have any problems with either getting or
       maintaining an erection or with ejaculating. If yes, please comment on
       the type of problem and how often it occurred.
       _____
       _____
       _____

25.   How do you rate yourself as a sexual partner?
       As an adolescent   _____
       As an adult   _____
       Please comment.   _____
       _____
       _____

26.   In what kinds of sex play have you participated?

Frequency   Rating (0-10)

_____ _____   A. Manipulating of partner's genital area.
                              Male or female?

_____ _____   B. Partner's manipulation of your genital area.

_____ _____   C. Performing cunnilingus (oral sex) on
                              female partner.

_____ _____   D. Performing fellatio (oral sex) on male
                              partner.

_____ _____   E. Partner performing fellatio on you. Male
                              or female?

_____ _____   F. Performing anal sex on partner. Male or
                              female?

_____ _____   G. Male partner performing anal intercourse
                              on you.

_____ _____   H. Intercourse (vaginal).

Using scale of 0 to 10, rate A through H as to degree of pleasure you
derived (usually) from each of these activities: 0 = no pleasure at all,
10 = the most pleasure you've experienced. Rate frequency with Never,
Seldom, Sometimes, or Often.

27.   As an adult, and up until the time you began Sex Offender Program, how
      frequently did you masturbate? _____ Were there
      specific situations connected with your masturbation? (comment if
      necessary) _____

      _____

      _____

What kinds of fantasies did you use to masturbate to? Be specific about fantasized person and situation. _____

_____

_____

28.   As an adult, what are the kinds of sexual dreams you've had most frequently? _____

_____

_____

29.   As an adult, have you had difficulty with any of the following? Comment when necessary.

A.   Techniques of petting and foreplay _____ ( )

B.   Positions in intercourse _____ ( )

C.   Partner's inactivity _____ ( )

D.   Partner not achieving orgasm _____ ( )

E.   Difficulty in achieving erection _____ ( )

F.   Difficulty in maintaining erection _____ ( )

If answer to E or F is yes, how often does difficulty occur (100% of time - 50% of time, etc.) _____

At what point do you usually lose erection _____

Are there certain situations where difficulty in achieving or maintaining an erection is likely to occur? _____

_____

What are your thoughts about this when it occurs? _____

_____

G.   Difficulty in ejaculation _____ ( )

During what sexual activity do you usually ejaculate? _____

_____

BENEFITS

The principal benefit of taking MPA is that you will not be thinking about sex as often as you did in the past, and you will not feel compelled to act on the sexual thoughts you have. Freedom from these sexual thoughts will allow you to work on other issues in your life, like communicating with others, developing another outlet for your sexual urges, or finding ways to relate to others in nonsexual ways. There will be less risk that you will act out on your sexual impulses in ways that can get you into difficulty with the law.

EVALUATION FOR THE PROGRAM

If no medical problems are present, you will be seen by a doctor to determine if you can benefit from this program. The doctor may ask you detailed questions about your sex life, about the incident that got you into trouble with the law, what kinds of things you find exciting sexually, and what medical problems, if any, you have had in the past.

The evaluation may also involve a test with an instrument called the penile plethysmograph. You will be asked to slip a plastic ring, filled with mercury (the same substance that is in a thermometer) around the base of your penis. This instrument *will not* shock you or give you any physical pain of any kind. You will be shown slides of sexual situations of many kinds, or be asked to listen to tapes of sexual situations, and be asked to fantasize about what you hear and see. As you begin to have an erection, more blood flows into your penis, which enlarges; the instrument continuously measures this enlargement.

You will probably find this to be an embarrassing situation. The evaluator will not be observing you directly, and every effort will be made to make you as comfortable as possible. This test is important and may be used later to aid in treatment.

HOW OFTEN AND HOW MUCH OF THE DRUG IS GIVEN

MPA is given by injection on a weekly or twice-monthly basis. The amount of MPA may be monitored by a blood test from time to time to determine the amount of testosterone (male hormone) in your bloodstream.

OTHER TREATMENT YOU WILL RECEIVE

MPA is *not* a cure for sexual problems, and, *in addition* to taking the drug, you will be expected to participate in other treatment programs. This may include counseling sessions, either in a group or individually, counseling with your living partner, and helping you become sexually aroused to persons and situations that will not get you into trouble with the law. You will be invited to become involved in the development of your own treatment plan.

LENGTH OF TREATMENT

Each person is unique, thus the duration of MPA treatment varies. The average length of treatment, however, is four months. By this time, other therapies should be starting to become effective, and the medication can be safely discontinued.

DISCONTINUING THE MEDICATION

If the court, the parole board, or your probation or parole officer has not ordered treatment: You can decide at any time that you want to stop the medication. If you develop any medical problem and are unable to continue taking MPA, you will be taken off the program.

If any of the above things happen, you will be asked to come to a meeting where your case will be discussed. Every effort will be made to find some alternative that meets your needs.

If the court or your probation or parole officer has ordered treatment: You can decide at any time that you want to stop the medicine. If you develop any medical problem and are unable to continue taking MPA, you will be taken off the program. If you decide to stop the medicine, a report to that effect must be sent to the court or to your probation or parole officer.

If any of the above things happen, you will be asked to come to a meeting where your case will be discussed. Every effort will be made to find some alternative that meets your needs. A report will be written and presented to the court or to your probation or parole officer, who will make the final decision.

REPORTS TO THE COURT OR TO YOUR PROBATION OR PAROLE OFFICER

If the court or your probation or parole officer has ordered your evaluation, or ordered you to be in the program, you will be asked to sign a release of information form that will allow staff of the Sexual Abuse Clinic to talk with that officer. All staff in the clinic have a responsibility to protect the information you give them and to report only the information that is necessary to evaluate your participation in the program. At the same time, staff have a responsibility to protect the community from sexual crimes. If you report other crimes that you have not been arrested for or convicted of, or if you report committing new crimes, this information *may* be given to the court, to your probation or parole officer, or to the district attorney's office.

* * *

Application for the Use of depo-Provera (MPA)

I have read all the information in the preceding pages explaining depo-Provera (MPA). A doctor from the Sexual Abuse Clinic has answered any questions I have asked, to my satisfaction, about the medication. I understand that I will be expected to have regular injections of MPA and will also participate in other counseling programs. I understand that if I disclose new or unreported crimes to anyone in the clinic, this information may be reported to the court or to my probation or parole officer, or to the district attorney's office. I understand that I may stop the program at any time, and if the court or my probation or parole officer has ordered me into the program, this decision will be reported to them. I understand that my application for this program means I will receive an evaluation to see if I can benefit from it.

I, _____, DO or DO NOT (circle the choice you have made) want to be evaluated in order to receive depo-Provera. If this evaluation shows I can benefit from the medication, I want to receive it, and I understand both the potential risks and the benefits of the program.

_____   _____
Applicant's Signature   Date

_____   _____
Doctor's Signature   Date

APPENDIX D:

Equipment and Associated
Procedures
Used in a Sexual Abuse Clinic

Information is offered here on the actual setup and use of equipment needed in a sexual abuse clinic. This information is presented in sufficient detail to enable clinicians to employ this equipment and these techniques but also with the understanding that individual variations may be necessary in any single setting. Hopefully, sufficient standardization of equipment and techniques can occur in the future so as to make interclinic comparisons feasible.

In basic science, it is often a breakthrough in technology, such as equipment design or novel materials, that propels a cascade of new findings and even new theories. There is no such parallel in behavioral science, in which equipment already existing is more often modified for clinical use. The penile plethysmograph, for example, was created as a tool to assess impotence; electric shock devices were employed for many years in a panopoly of conditions before their use in treatment of the sexual offender.

Currently, however, there is sufficient evidence that the behavioral techniques described here are sufficiently successful to warrant the purchase of equipment necessary to employ all the methods described in this book. This equipment need not intrude into, or hamper, the therapist-patient alliance, yet many of those trained in the behavioral sciences may hold some contempt and even fear of this equipment. Its presence, however, can be carefully explained to the patient, and its use easily mastered by the therapist.

316

Moreover, its results can contribute to the therapeutic goals of eliminating deviant sexual arousal, reunifying families, enhancing self-esteem, and improving social skills.

The two basic purposes of devices to help in the treatment of the sexual offender are to present stimuli and to measure patient response. A variety of stimuli must be presented--sexual, aversive, arousal, and attention stimuli. In addition, they must be presented in a variety of modes--visual, auditory, olfactory, gustatory, and proprioceptive. The measurement of patient response would seem simpler: the assessment of a single dimension, that of sexual arousal. However, even this assessment can be measured in several ways--through erection responses, self-report, and reports of significant others.

The work on equipment in behavioral treatment often refers to "laboratories," perhaps somewhat of a presumption, because detailed, highly controlled research is rarely conducted there. Nonetheless, if a clinic is outfitted as described, research *can* occur--perhaps almost as valid a reason to encourage the purchase of such equipment as for the treatment of the sexual offender itself.

The well-equipped clinic, in presenting stimuli and measuring sexual response, represents an attempt to replicate some of the "natural" conditions of the sexual world confronting the offender. That it possesses obvious shortcomings by artificially doing so is not a reason to forgo such an attempt. The research and accumulated experience of those working with thousands of offenders prompts the use of analog settings. Indeed, in matters sexual, it is often the analog--the picture, the image, the fantasy--that precedes, promotes, and often even surpasses the real thing.

Equipment to Present Stimuli

Visual stimuli. The chief means of presenting visual stimuli were and still are 35 mm slides. A slide projector is necessary, preferably one that can accommodate trays with large numbers of slides. While standard trays hold 80 slides, 140-slide trays are far better in presenting a large number of stimuli without the need to switch trays.

A screen is usually not necessary if a white or off-white painted wall is available. The Association for the Treatment of Sexual Abusers (ATSA) recommends a 48-inch × 30-inch image. The client should be relaxed in a lounge chair approximately six to ten feet from the image.

Movies offer a different type of visual stimulus as they act over a longer time and can develop sexual themes such as aggression and domination. A 16 mm projector is preferable to an 8 mm one for quality, but, in reality, many more 8 mm than 16 mm pornographic moves are currently available.

Videotapes are only now being explored as alternatives for both slides and movies. Sexual stimuli presented on videotape require a camera to record material already encoded only on slides and movies. A four-head "freeze-frame" videorecorder and a television monitor are recommended, preferably of 23-inch size. Some experimenters believe (with some research evidence) that greater levels of arousal are achieved with the presence of frank sexual stimuli on the ubiquitous television screen. Another advantage of the video format is the simplicity and convenience of presenting all visual stimuli in one mode. A disadvantage is the need to fast-forward or reverse quickly to present scenes in the proper order for each client, as each offender may be using a different order, and, often, there are differences for the same offender from one session to the next. By noting the sequential counter number corresponding to "freeze-frame," stimuli that once were slides can be presented on the TV screen as well. Thus far, it has appeared that the shifting about on each tape has proven as feasible as rapidly switching from one slide to a distantly removed one in the same carousel tray.

The Sexual Abuse Clinic has weighed the pros and cons of slides and videotape and decided to transfer all visual stimuli to videotape and standardize the mode of presentation. It is as conceivable, however, that slides and movies will remain as, or at times more, useful and popular in the future.

Auditory stimuli. Standardized tape recordings are available to assess sexual offenders and can be used with routine evaluations (Abel & Becker, 1984). In addition, and more valuable in treatment, however, are individualized audiotapes, recorded by the therapist, of scenes provided by offenders, victims, police reports, and presentence investigations. Excellent quality tape recordings must be employed. The infernal hiss of inexpensive machines is enough of a distraction, as are extraneous noises, to interfere with the concentration of the patient trying to imagine difficult scenes. An external microphone, not the built-in one usually specified, is helpful as well. So too are earphones, both in the office and at home. These have been particularly valuable because so many offices seem to conduct rather than shield outside noise. It is a nice touch, though hardly practical in many clinics, to provide some offenders with earphones to take home for practice. The patient should be encouraged to purchase his own; even an inexpensive pair is preferable to none at all.

Aversive Stimuli

Olfactory stimuli. While ammonia, valeric and butyric acids, and hydrogen sulfide have been advocated in the past, the most powerful stimulus to elicit nausea, and hence directly decondition sexual response, is rotting biological tissue. Any hospital or clinical laboratory should be able to obtain postsurgi-

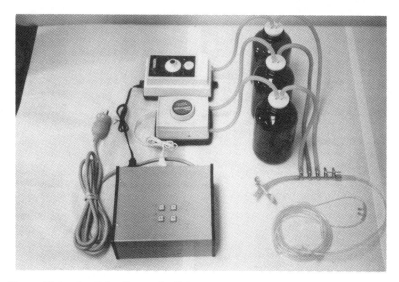

Figure D.1   An Odor Pump for Behavioral Conditioning

cal tissue, usually placenta. The tissue is cut into 2 cc blocks, placed in colored *glass* bottles, and inoculated with bacterial cultures of E. coli, Proteus, or Pseudomonas, already available as test cultures in most laboratories. They are then allowed to incubate at temperatures slightly above ambient ones for 48 hours. While the cultures are then ready for use, they often can be made even more foul-smelling by introducing organic matter such as urine, dog or cat feces, cheese, meat, or fish. Such cultures, exposed to the air occasionally, will retain a nauseating odor for six to twelve months. For those who wish to use chemical odors, ammonia and valeric or butyric acids can be obtained through a clinical laboratory or chemical supply house such as Abbott Laboratories.[1]

In the earliest work using such aversive odors, therapists would merely open a bottle of odor under a patient's nose at appropriate intervals during the visual or auditory stimulus presentation. Often, however, a patient would attempt to hold his breath or turn away. Moreover, the resulting stench would last longer than the stimulus, hence unwanted overlap or backward conditioning could occur. Moreover, the unhappy clinician would emerge from such repeated sessions with more aversion for himself than he expected.

Fortuitously, several generations of odor pumps have since been manufactured. Currently, an attractive model, pictured in Figure D.1, combines four odor reservoirs with a pump mechanism and tubing-and-cannula apparatus

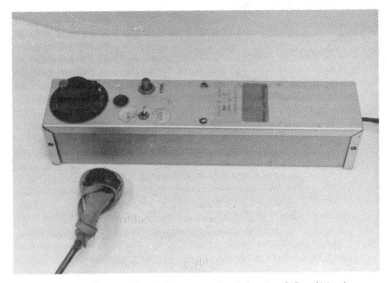

Figure D.2   An Electric Shock Generator for Behavioral Conditioning

to deliver pulses of varying odors directly to the patient's nasal passages.[2] While the patient is thus additionally encumbered, adaptation to the apparatus occurs rapidly. The reservoirs can contain foul odors such as the rotting tissue described above or valeric acid. They can also contain amyl nitrate, obtainable by prescription (it comes in crushable ampules), to enhance sexual arousal when appropriate (see Chapter 5). In addition, they can contain pleasant odors such as cedar or perfume or simply fresh air to wash away a foul odor and hence provide reinforcement for leaving a deviant scene or approaching an appropriate one. This flexibility allows greater accuracy in pinpointing which olfactory stimuli to use with which slides, videotapes, or passages of scenes.

   Electric stimuli. The most venerable aversive stimulus employed in all behavior therapy is electric shock, and it still occupies a niche in the treatment of the sexual offender, although probably not as the primary aversive stimulus used. Standard electric shock generators, such as pictured in Figure D.2,[3] use low voltage and amperage with appropriate safeguards via downgrading transformers and grounding devices. In a typical device, the strength of the stimulus can be infinitely varied from 0 to 10 milliamperes with a maximum open circuit of 1,000 millivolts. Stimuli are delivered through two electrodes so that the stimulus can flow through tissue. Typically, index and middle fingers are used, although the forearm can be used as well. Both of these areas are sensitive and accessible.

There is no theoretic or heuristic reason to stimulate the inner thigh, penis, or scrotum, as is feared by some offenders. Shock in those areas would only create undue fear and embarrassment. In all cases, electric shock should be self-administered by the therapist each time he or she is to use it on an offender to demonstrate its safety.

Most electric shock generators produce a variable output. It is best to let the offender set the dial at the lowest setting and gradually increase it on his own to the point at which he believes the shocks are sufficiently aversive. It is then suggested, though certainly left to the discretion of the offender, to increase the stimulus one more setting, explaining that this will ensure the efficacy of treatment, quicken the treatment course, and prevent the almost certain accommodation to milder stimuli.

Gustatory stimuli. The use of propantheline, a bitter pill, has been described in Chapter 3. A physician's prescription is necessary. This drug has been of most help in *in vivo* situations, where it can be unobtrusively employed in the presence of a deviant stimulus. Typically, one or two pills are provided each session; even one-quarter of a tablet is sufficient. The patient should be instructed to chew the pill thoroughly and then spit it out if possible. Even swallowing an entire tablet would not be dangerous; however, patients should not be given large quantities.

Tactile stimuli. Life-size dolls and anatomically correct dolls can be used for aversive behavior rehearsal.[4] While these have been helpful for aversive behavior rehearsal, they can also be used for interviewing victims if no agency has already done so. In aversive behavior rehearsal, the patient can demonstrate, with the dolls, what he actually did. The therapist can survey the plethysmograph at the same time to see if any arousal occurs and provide aversion, if appropriate. Chapter 3 provides the details of these techniques.

Biofeedback. The penile plethysmograph, described below, provides the assessment of erectile response, roughly equated with arousal. However, the instrument can be used for biofeedback and can provide information to the offender about his level of arousal, thus providing him an opportunity to alter it on his own, a form of sexual control. He is usually instructed to increase arousal to nondeviant stimuli and decrease it to deviant stimuli. To assist in this process, visual data are provided to the offender in the form of a bank of 20 lights that are connected to the plethysmograph's output and are positioned to the side of a video monitor screen.[5] Each 5% of plethysmographic arousal triggers a light above the next to flash on; signs by the lights tell the offender the level of arousal, spaced every four lights apart (20%, 40%, 60%, 80%, 100%). The offender can see his arousal increasing or decreasing and, combined with instructions from the therapist, can engage in attempts at self-control.

Attention stimuli. One light from the biofeedback array can serve the function of a visual attention control. The patient is asked to press a button (connected to a light under the therapist's monitor), or to raise a finger if a button hookup is cumbersome, whenever that light flashes on. The therapist can randomly light this stimulus to make certain the patient is paying attention to the visual stimuli (and not closing his eyes).

Sexual stimuli. All stimuli presented to the offender must try to approximate what would most arouse him in the natural world. Thus each stimulus represents a compromise: The clinician must combine the patient's reports of fantasies and sexual activities with police and victim reports, when available, to present the most arousing scenes possible.

Visual stimuli. Sets of slides exist and can be mail ordered from several firms: Farrell Instruments, Inc. or the Exodus Trust.[6] More effective still are slides or "freeze-frame" videos of photographs from real life or pornographic magazines that strive to match the fantasies of the offender. While local pornography stores should be perused, access to a large library of materials can be gained through combinations of mail-order and prepared slides with locally collected material. In addition, confiscated materials from offices of the district attorney, police, FBI, and the postal inspector provide important additions where available. It is vital to have a large library of truly hard-core materials, not easily and legally obtainable in this country, especially with pedophiliac subjects. The Sexual Abuse Clinic has been able to produce some of its own materials, but this is, of course, limited to consenting adults. The cooperation of law enforcement agencies and the sharing of materials between clinics within large geographic areas has been most helpful. Issues of confidentiality, informed consent, and even the legality of possession for distribution of such materials among clinics have yet to be tested in court.

Because of the practical problems in obtaining a wide variety of child pornographic slides, the legal questions surrounding their possession and use, and the ethical dilemmas in attempting to produce or procure such materials, clinics are commissioning drawings, to the patient's specifications or in accord with police and victim reports. An increasing deployment of such materials in the near future will help in evaluating the comparative efficacy of such made-to-order stimuli.

Movies and videotapes develop sexual themes of greater variety and longer duration than slides or still frames. Again, it is difficult to predict the perfect fit for each offender, but plethysmograph recordings can be helpful in learning which frames may be particularly arousing: These can then be identified and tagged for future use with that particular offender.

Auditory stimuli. As with visual stimuli, prepared tapes describing pedophiliac and aggressive sexuality exist (Abel & Becker, 1984). However, therapists must also produce tapes with idiosyncratic scenes graphically describ-

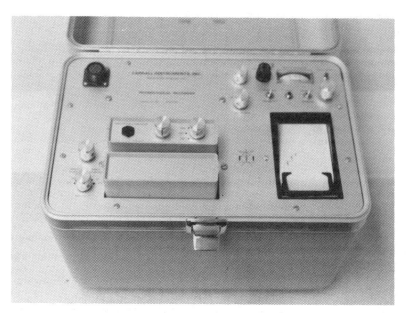

Figure D.3   The Penile Plethysmograph

ing the deviant and nondeviant activity with verve and emphasis in voice, though not with melodrama. Occasionally, female voices have been shown to elicit greater arousal. While the commercially prepared tapes are helpful for assessment, they cannot be expected to excite the highest arousal possible for each offender. Idiosyncrasy is vital in the production of useful sexual scenes.

In summary, sexual stimuli must be sufficiently personalized and idiosyncratic to be arousing; hence the ingenuity of the therapist is called into play to devise the most appropriate stimuli for each offender.

Equipment to Measure Sexual Response

The penile plethysmograph. The penile plethysmograph, pictured in Figure D.3, has become the standard device to measure male sexual arousal. It consists of a circumference gauge, as shown in Figure D.4,[7] usually mercury in rubber, to measure changes in penile tumescence, which are then transmitted electrically to the instrument that registers those changes with pen tracings on heat-sensitive moving chart paper. These responses can be read as electrical outputs, as, for example, voltage changes, or as a percentage of a previously obtained full erection.

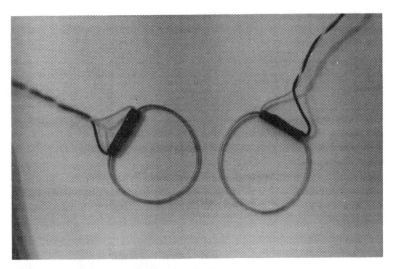

Figure D.4   Mercury-in-Rubber Strain Gauges

In practice, the offender places the gauge between the base and the mid-shaft of his penis. Then, while relaxing in a lounge chair, he views, listens to, or recites sexually related material while his arousal responses are recorded. Very subtle changes in blood flow, and hence penile circumference, can be recorded, as the rate of response. It is also helpful to elicit a full erection, if possible, with appropriate material and then measure the rate of decline, if any, with inappropriate stimuli.

Researchers and clinicians have wondered about a potential drawback of the plethysmograph. The strain gauge measures circumference with great sensitivity, but an erection may first produce an elongation of the penis; if so, instrument readings would remain constant or actually drop during this phase. A project in the planning stage will attempt to address that issue. If the offender is asked to place two strain gauges on his penis, one at the base and one near the head, an elongation *and* a circumference change can be evaluated. It remains, however, to assess whether such encumbering gadgetry will allow an adequate penile response.

The idea of publicly measuring such a private event as sexual arousal strikes many as inherently so artificial as to guarantee gross error. However, some studies have partially validated the instrument's use with offenders. Ongoing studies must now demonstrate the overall validity of the technique in a large normal population. Such studies are in progress across a variety of centers. Currently, the penile plethysmograph remains the only semiobjective device available to measure sexual response.

It is essential to familiarize the patient with the plethysmograph thoroughly and, except in single-trial assessments, to obtain repeated measures to enhance reliability. Measures to ensure the patient's privacy are essential. Hence the clinician usually is behind a partition or in an adjoining room during the examination, although the patient is aware that he or she is viewing the procedure through a one-way glass mirror. Extraneous noises and distractions must be minimized.

If good rapport is established and privacy maximized, reliable readings can be obtained with this instrument despite what would appear to be a highly intrusive and artificial procedure. The instrument, while first thought to be of most benefit in the assessment of the sexual offender, may actually be of optimal use in the repeated measurement of whether therapy is effective and in the provision of biofeedback to the offender in teaching control over sexual impulses. Given the current state of knowledge, it should never be used to prove or disprove whether an individual committed a sexual crime or as the only criterion in the decision of whether an offender is safe to be at large. Table D.1 lists the recently promulgated standards for the operation of the plethysmograph from the Association for the Behavioral Treatment of Sexual Abusers.[8] Detailed instructions on the actual operation of the machine will not be reviewed here but can be obtained from the manufacturer's manual accompanying the machine (see also Longo, 1983). Currently, the penile plethysmograph manufactured by Farrell Instruments, Inc., is the most widely used instrument.

Table D.1 *Association for the Behavioral Treatment of Sexual Abusers: Standards for Use of the Penile Plethysmograph*

I. Preliminary procedure guidelines

    A. The examiner should make attempts to gather supportive information, such as marital and family history, criminal history, present life situation, legal status, sexual history, and the reason for referral.

    B. Proper release of informational sources should be used by the examiner to secure supportive information, as mentioned above, or to allow the examiner to release the plethysmograph assessment to other sources.

    C. It is the responsibility of the examiner to document, in the evaluation, the source of supportive evidence used in the assessment.

    D. It is the responsibility of the examiner to screen the client for contamination factors, such as drug use, medication, last sexual activity (prior to use of plethysmograph), emotional state, physical impairment, and so on.

    E. Previous to the examination, the examiner should take precautionary steps to ensure that the examination will not be interrupted. The client should be given the opportunity to empty his bladder prior to the commencement of the assessment.

Table D.1 *Continued*

F. No client with an active sexually transmittable disease or parasite should be tested. Clinicians should understand the various sexually transmitted diseases and parasites and check client for these prior to testing. The client should sign a disclaimer as to any knowledge of a sexually transmitted disease.

II. Legal concerns/informed consent
   A. The consent form regarding the penile plethysmograph procedure should be read, signed, and dated by the client prior to the assessment.
   B. Release forms should be legally sound and dated for both incoming and outgoing informational sources.
   C. Raw data forms must provide information for retrieval of specific stimulus materials that were used in the assessment.

III. Laboratory equipment
   A. The plethysmograph machine must have a continuous chart paper readout, which runs at 1 mm per second.
   B. The manufacturer's instructions for setup and use must be followed.
   C. An armchair or lounge chair with a cleanable surface, such as vinyl or leather, must be provided. A reclining lounge chair is preferred.
   D. Disposable examination paper, on the chair seat and on the arms of the chair, is required for each patient.
   E. Mercury-in-rubber, Indium-gallium, or Barlow gauges must be used, and each gauge must be tested and periodically calibrated.
   F. A calibration device or cone is required in 0.5 cm increments, with a minimal range of 6 cm.
   G. Security devices must ensure the patient's privacy but must also include an emergency entrance with the safety of the patient in mind.
   H. A slide projector for visual material should be capable of projecting to an approximate image of 48 inches x 30 inches.
   I. A sound system for communication between the patient and the examiner should provide distortion-free material.
   J. The clinician must have a protocol for fitting gauges and for troubleshooting breakdowns and malfunctions.
   K. The instrument should be initially calibrated and repeatedly checked. Gauges should be checked prior to each assessment. (Note: Certain gauges may have a specific shelf life.)
   L. The clinician must ensure that the mercury gauge is stretched at least 10%, but not more than 20%, when placed on the penis prior to any tumescence.
   M. The clinician should be cautioned to ensure that sizing is within minimal and maximum strain.
   N. Placement of the gauge on the penis should be between base and mid-shaft.
   O. The patient should place the gauge on his own penis.
   P. The clinician should assure that wiring from the gauge is not hanging loose (placing a weight or pulling on the gauge), or clinical error may result. Clothing should not touch the penis or inhibit full erection.
   Q. Recording of full penile tumescence should be obtained whenever possible. Data are most readily interpreted when full erection is obtained.

Table D.1 *Continued*

    R. Gauges will be disinfected prior to use, utilizing a liquid immersible or other accepted laboratory disinfection procedure.

    S. The patient should place the gauge in a receptacle after use before leaving the room. The patient should also dispose of protective coverings before leaving.

    T. The patient should cleanse hands before leaving the room.

    U. The clinician should use an antibacterial soap after contact with the gauges. Any items or articles that have been in contact with the patient should also be disinfected.

IV. Stimulus materials

    A. The clinician will have available a range of explicit sexual stimulus materials, which will include a variety of both appropriate and deviant sexual themes.

    B. Visual materials

        1. Visual materials will include nude or clothed poses, provocative nude poses, and depictions of scenes involving explicit sexual acts.

        2. Age ranges recommended for visual material are 0–3, 4–9, 9–12, 13+, and adults. Categories should include both sexes and multiple races.

        3. A minimum number of slides to be used per assessment is 15, with a two-minute exposure to the client.

        4. The client must have diminished tumescence for a minimum of 30 seconds before new stimulus materials are presented.

    C. Audiotapes

        1. The audio material should include the following categories: consenting sex, children, rape, and aggressive sexual scenarios. Tapes will depict both genders and ages ranging from children to adults.

        2. A minimum of six audiotapes will be used during each assessment. Audiotapes are to be three to four minutes in duration.

V. Documenting assessment data

    A. The clinician should not make absolute statements regarding plethysmograph data.

    B. Written reports should include:

        1. a description of the method for collecting data

        2. the range of physiological responses exhibited by the client

        3. relevant data from the client's medical or psychological sexual history

        4. any indication of suppression or falsification by the client

        5. an indication of the validity of the data (validity controls used should be noted in the examination)

        6. the types of stimulus materials used

        7. a summary of highest arousal in each category

        8. the time involved in the assessment process

        9. a description of the client's anxiety level

      10. denials or minimizations by the client

      11. the level of client cooperation

328

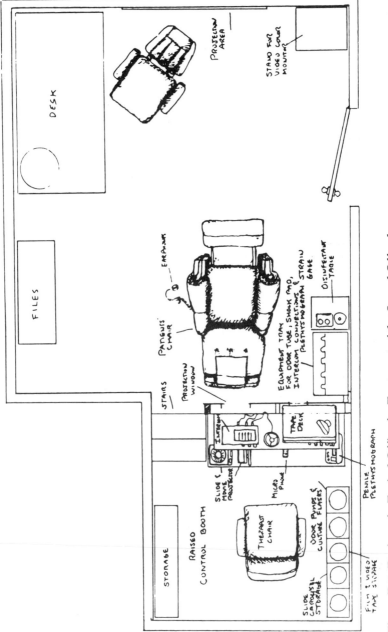

Figure D.5 Design of a Typical Office for Treatment of the Sexual Offender.

Table D.2 *Association for the Behavioral Treatment of Sexual Abusers: Standards for Use of the Penile Plethysmograph*

1. The patient space must be separated from the clinician's work area by an opaque partition to be a minimum of seven feet high, or preferably a stationary wall, to ensure the patient's privacy.
2. An intercom or speaker system must be used when the patient is in a stationary enclosure.
3. A means of maintaining constant room temperature must be provided. The temperature range should be between 72° and 78° Fahrenheit.
4. The patient space must have adequate ventilation.
5. Adjustable lighting should be available.
6. A carpet or rug, insulation, or other sound-deadening measures should be used to ensure that the patient's space is as sound-proof as possible. Isolation from extraneous noise is necessary.
7. Security measures must be provided for not only the laboratory but for the stimulus materials as well.
8. The patient space should be at least five feet by eight feet in dimension.
9. The clinician must establish a system determining stimulus-attention detection so that assurances can be made that the patient was, in fact, exposed to the sexual stimulus materials.

The best method of gaining skill with such equipment is to use it continuously. A transition from awkward experimentation to facile use will occur with accumulated experience.

The ambience of a clinical office for the treatment of the sexual offender differs from a usual office, not only due to the presence of necessary electronic equipment but because of the partition (or separate anteroom) needed as well. Figure D.5 illustrates only one of many possibilities that have proven useful. Table D.2 lists suggestions from ATSA in designing a "clinical space." For reference, Table D.3 lists the items of equipment necessary for the operation of a clinic for the treatment of the sexual offender.

Notes

1. Abbott Laboratories at Abbott Park, P.O. Box 68, Chicago, Illinois 60064.
2. MECTA Corporation, 7015 McEwan Road, Lake Oswego, Oregon 97035.
3. Farrell Instruments, Inc., P.O. Box 1037, Grand Island, Nebraska 68802.
4. Migima Designs, Inc., 1243 1-2 Oak Street, Eugene Oregon 97401.
5. MECTA Corporation (see note 2, above).
6. Farrell Instruments, Inc. (see note 3, above); the Exodus Trust, 1523 Franklin Street, San Francisco, California 94109.
7. Parks Medical Electronics, Inc., 19460 S.W. Shaw Street, Aloha, Oregon 97006.
8. Association for the Treatment of Sexual Abusers, P.O. Box 66028, Portland, Oregon 97266.

Table D.3 *Equipment Necessary to Operate a Sexual Abuse Clinic*

I. Equipment to present sexual stimuli
   A. slide projector
   B. movies
   C. movie screen or light-colored blank wall
   D. audiotape cassette recorder with earphones
   E. videotape camera (optional)
   F. videotape cassette recorder (VCR)
   G. video monitor (television screen)
   H. array of biofeedback and attention lights
II. Equipment to present aversive stimuli
   A. odor reservoir/pump with nasal cannulas
   B. electric shock generator
   C. dolls
      1. life-sized: boys and girls
      2. anatomically correct dolls (generally smaller than life-size): girl, boy, woman, man
III. Sexual stimuli
   A. slides
   B. movies
   C. videotapes
   D. audiotapes
IV. Aversive stimuli
   A. a variety of foul odors
      1. bacterial cultures
      2. valeric acid
   B. propantheline tablets
V. Positive stimuli
   A. pleasant odors
   B. amyl nitrate
VI. Recording equipment
   A. penile plethysmograph
   B. supply of penile gauges
   C. calibration gauges for standardization of plethysmograph
VII. Miscellaneous equipment
   A. leather/vinyl recliner
   B. dubbing machine
   C. disinfectant solution to clean gauges and cannulas
   D. partition/screen with one-way mirror and ports for projection equipment
   E. ceiling mirror to check eye contact to screen and to check status of plethysmograph
   F. disposable examination paper

References

Abel, G. G. (1976). Assessment of sexual deviation in the male. In A. S. Bellack & M. Hersen (Eds.), *Behavioral assessment: A practical handbook.* New York: Pergamon.

Abel, G. G. (1984, November). *Reflections on the treatment of the sexual offender.* Presented to the Oregon Corrections Division Conference on the Sexual Offender, Portland.

Abel, G. G., Barlow, D. H., Blanchard, E. B., & Guild, D. (1973). The components of rapists' sexual arousal. *Archives of General Psychiatry, 34,* 895-908.

Abel, G. G., & Becker, J. V. (1984). *The treatment of child molesters* (NIMH Grant MH 36347-01202, and BRSA Grant #903, E5040). New York: New York State Research Foundation for Mental Hygiene, Columbia University.

Abel, G. G., Becker, J. V., & Cuningham-Rathner, J. (1984). Complications, consent, and cognitions in sex between children and adults. *International Journal of Law and Psychiatry, 7,* 89-103.

Abel, G. G., & Blanchard, E. B. (1974). The role of fantasy in the treatment of sexual deviation. *Archives of General Psychiatry, 30,* 467-475.

Abel, G. G., Blanchard, E. B., & Barlow, D. H. (1980). Measurement of sexual arousal in several paraphilias: The effects of stimulus modality, instructional set and stimulus content on the objective. *Behaviour Research and Therapy, 19,* 25-33.

Abel, G. G., Blanchard, E. B., Barlow, D. H., & Maviscakalian, M. (1975). Identifying specific erotic cues in sexual deviations by audiotaped description. *Journal of Applied Behavior Analysis, 8,* 247-280.

Abel, G. G., Blanchard, E. B., Becker, J. V., & Djenderedjian, A. (1978). Differentiating sexual aggressives with penile measures. *Criminal Justice and Behavior, 51,* 315-332.

Abel, G. G., Blanchard, E. B., Murphy, W. D., Becker, J. V., & Djenderedjian, A. (1981). Two methods of measuring penile response. *Behavior Therapy, 12,* 320-329.

331

Abel, G. G., Gore, D. K., Holland, C. L., Camp, N., Becker, J. V., & Rathner, J. (1989). The measurement of the cognitive distortions of child molesters. *Annals of Sex Research*, 2, 135-153.

Abel, G. G., Lewis, D. J., & Clancy, J. (1970). Aversion therapy applied to taped sequences of deviant behavior in exhibitionism and other sexual deviations: A preliminary report. *Journal of Behavior Therapy and Experimental Psychiatry*, 1, 59-66.

Adams, H. E., & Sturgis, E. T. (1978). Status of behavioral reorientation in the modification of homosexuality: A review. *Psychological Bulletin*, 84, 1171-1188.

Adams, H. E., Tollison, C. D., & Carson, T. P. (1981). Behavior therapy with sexual deviations. In S. M. Turner, K. S. Calhoun, & H. E. Adams (Eds.), *Handbook of clinical behavior therapy* (pp. 318-346). New York: John Wiley.

Adams, H. E., Webster, J. S., & Carson, T. P. (1980). Comments: Appropriate behavioral assessment and modification of sexual deviation: A comment on "biosyntonic" therapy. *Journal of Consulting and Clinical Psychology*, 48, 106-108.

Adams-Tucker, C. (1982). Proximate effects of sexual abuse in childhood: A report on 28 children. *American Journal of Psychiatry*, 139, 1252-1256.

Alberti, R., & Emmons, M. (1975). *Stand up, speak out, talk back.* New York: Simon & Schuster.

Alcoholics Anonymous. (1978). New York: Alcoholics Anonymous World Services, Inc.

Allen, D. W. (1974). *The fear of looking or scopophilia-exhibitionist conflicts.* Charlottesville: University of Virginia Press.

Allen, D. W. (1980). A psychoanalytic view. In D. J. Cox & R. J. Daitzman (Eds.), *Exhibitionism: Description, assessment, and treatment* (pp. 59-82). New York: Garland.

American Psychiatric Association. (1987). *Diagnostic and statistical manual* (3rd ed.). Washington, DC: American Psychiatric Association Press.

Bancroft, J. A. (1970). A comparison study of aversion and densenitization in the treatment of homosexuality. In E. L. Burns & J. L. Worsley (Eds.), *Behavior therapy in the 1970's.* Bristol, England: Wright.

Barlow, D. H. (1977). Assessment of sexual behavior. In A. R. Cemenero, H. E. Adams, & K. S. Calhoun (Eds.), *Handbook of behavioral assessment.* New York: John Wiley.

Barlow, D. H., & Abel, G. G. (1981). Recent developments in assessment and treatment of paraphilias and gender identity disorders. In W. E. Craighead, A. E. Razdin, & M. H. Maharey (Eds.), *Behavior modification: Principles, issues, and applications* (2nd ed.). Boston: Houghton Mifflin.

Barlow, D. H., Abel, G. G., Blanchard, E. B., Bristow, A. R., & Young, D. C. (1977). A heterosocial skills checklist for males. *Behavior Therapy*, 8, 229-239.

Barlow, D. H., & Agras, S. (1973). Fading to increase heterosexual responsiveness in homosexuals. *Archives of General Psychiatry*, 28, 509-576.

Barlow, D. H., Reynolds, E. H., & Agras, W. S. (1973). Gender identity change in a transsexual. *Archives of General Psychiatry*, 28, 569-576.

Bártová, D., Náhurek, K., Svetzka, J., & Hajnová, J. (1979). Comparative study of prophylactic lithium and diethylstilbestrol in sexual deviants. *Acta Nervosa Scandinavica Supplement (Praha)*, 21, 103-104.

Beck, A. T., & Rush, A. J. (1976, December). *Research on suicide, depression, and anxiety.* Paper presented to the American Association of Behavior Therapy, New York.

Becker, J. V., & Abel, G. G. (1981). Behavioral treatment of victims of sexual assault. In H. E. Adams, C. D. Tollison, & T. P. Carson (Eds.), *Handbook of clinical behavior therapy* (pp. 347-379). New York: John Wiley.

Becker, J. V., Skinner, L. J., & Abel, G. G. (1983). Sequelae of sexual assault: The survivor's perspective. in J. G. Greer & I. R. Stuart (Eds.), *The sexual aggressor: Current perspectives on treatment* (pp. 240-266). New York: Van Nostrand Reinhold.

Bem, D. J. (1972). Self-perception theory. In L. Berkowitz (Ed.), *Advances in experimental social psychology.* New York: Academic Press.

Berlin, F. S. (1981). Ethical use of antiandrogenic medications [Letter to the editor]. *American Journal of Psychiatry, 138,* 1515-1516.

Berlin, F. S. (1983). Sex offenders: A biomedical perspective and a status report on biomedical treatment. In J. G. Greer & I. R. Stuart (Eds.), *The sexual aggressor: Current perspectives on treatment* (pp. 83-123). New York: Van Nostrand Reinhold.

Berlin, F. S., & Coyle, G. S. (1981). Sexual deviation syndromes. *The Johns Hopkins Medical Journal, 149,* 119-125.

Berlin, F. S., & Meinecke, C. F. (1981). Treatment of sex offenders with antiandrogenic medication: Conceptualization, review of treatment modalities, and preliminary findings. *American Journal of Psychiatry, 138,* 601-607.

Berliner, L., & Wheeler, J. R. (1987). Treating the effects of sexual abuse on children. *Journal of Interpersonal Violence, 2,* 415-434.

Blair, C. D., & Lanyhon, R. I. (1981). Exhibitionism: Etiology and treatment. *Psychological Bulletin, 89,* 439-463.

Blanchard, E. B. (1979). Biofeedback and the modification of cardiovascular dysfunctions. In H. J. Gatchel & K. P. Price (Eds.), *Clinical applications of biofeedback: Appraisal and status.* New York: Pergamon.

Bohmer, C. (1983). Legal and ethical issues in mandatory treatment: The patient's rights versus society's rights. In J. G. Greer & I. R. Stuart (Eds.), *The sexual aggressor: Current perspectives on treatment* (pp. 3-21). New York: Van Nostrand Reinhold.

Bonheur, H., & Rosner, R. (1980). Sex offenders: A descriptive analysis of cases studied at a forensic psychiatry clinic. *Journal of Forensic Science, 25,* 3-14.

Bradford, J. M. W. (1983). Research on sex offenders: Recent trends. *Psychiatric Clinics of North America, 6,* 715-731.

Braun, M. (1976). Instrumental learning. In M. P. Feldman & A. Broadhurst (Eds.), *Theoretical and experimental bases of the behavior therapist.* New York: John Wiley.

Brownell, K. D., & Barlow, D. H. (1976). Measurement and treatment of two sexual deviations in one person. *Journal of Behavior Therapy and Experimental Psychiatry, 7,* 349-354.

Brownell, K. D., & Barlow, D. H. (1977). The behavioral treatment of sexual deviation. In E. Foa & A. Goldstein (Eds.), *The handbook of behavioral interventions.* New York: John Wiley.

Brownell, K. D., Hayes, S. C., & Barlow, D. H. (1977). Patterns of appropriate and deviant sexual arousal: The behavioral treatment of multiple sexual deviations. *Journal of Consulting and Clinical Psychology, 45,* 1144-1155.

Burnstein, J. G. (1983). *Handbook of drug therapy in psychiatry.* Boston: John Wright, PSG Inc.

Caffaro-Rouget, A., Lang, R. A., & VanSanten, V. (1989). The impact of child sexual abuse on victims' adjustment. *Annals of Sex Research, 2,* 30-47.

Caird, W. R., & Wincze, J. P. (1977). *Sex therapy: A behavioral approach.* Hagerstown, MD: Harper & Row.

Carmen, E., Reiker, P. P., & Mills, T. (1984). Victims of violence and psychiatric illness. *American Journal of Psychiatry, 141,* 378-383.

Carnes, P. (1984). *The sexual addiction*. Minneapolis, MN: Comp Care.

Carson, T. P., & Adams, H. E. (1981). Affective disorders, behavioral perspectives. In S. M. Turner, R. S. Calhoun, & H. E. Adams (Eds.), *Handbook of clinical behavior therapy* (pp. 318-346). New York: John Wiley.

Carte, J. R., Rosen, C., Saperstein, L., & Shermack, R. (1985). An evaluation of a program to prevent the sexual victimization of young children. *Child Abuse and Neglect, 9*, 391-328.

Cautela, J. R. (1967). Covert sensitization. *Psychological Record, 20*, 459-468.

Coclen, C., Hamilton, D., & Walter, R. (1980). The national hospital rate-setting study. In *Health care financing grants and contract report*. Washington, DC: Office of Research, Demonstrations, and Statistics, HCFA.

Colson, C. E. (1972). Olfactory aversion therapy for homosexual behavior. *Journal of Behavior Therapy and Experimental Psychiatry, 3*, 185-187.

Comfort, A. (1972). *The joy of sex: A gourmet's guide to love making*. New York: Simon & Schuster.

Comings, D. E., & Comings, B. G. (1982). A case of familial exhibitionism in Tourette's Syndrome successfully treated with haloperidol. *American Journal of Psychiatry, 139*, 913-915.

Conger, J. C., & Farrell, A. D. (1981). Behavioral components of heterosocial skills. *Behavior Therapy, 12*, 41-55.

Conrad, S. R., & Wincze, J. P. (1976). Orgasmic reconditioning: A controlled study of its effects upon sexual arousal and behavior of adult male homosexuals. *Behavior Therapy, 7*, 155-166.

Cooper, A. A. (1963). A case of fetishism and impotence treated by behaviour therapy. *British Journal of Psychiatry, 109*, 649-652.

Cooper, A. J. (1981). A placebo-controlled trial of the antiandrogen cyproterone acetate in deviant hypersexuality. *Comprehensive Psychiatry, 22*, 458-465.

Cox, D. H., & Maletzky, B. M. (1980). Victims of exhibitionism. In D. J. Cox & R. J. Daitzman (Eds.), *Exhibitionism: Description, assessment, and treatment* (pp. 289-293). New York: Garland.

Cunningham, J., Pearce, T., & Pearce, P. (1988). Childhood sexual abuse and medical complaints in adult women. *Journal of Interpersonal Violence, 3*, 131-144.

Curran, J. P. (1977). Skills training as an approach to the treatment of heterosexual-social anxiety: A review. *Psychology Bulletin, 84*, 140-157.

Diamet, C., & Wilson, G. T. (1975). An experimental investigation of the effects of covert sensitization in an analogue eating situation. *Behavior Therapy, 4*, 499-504.

Dimock, P. T. (1988). Adult males sexually abused as children. *Journal of Interpersonal Violence, 3*, 203-221.

Earls, C. M., & Marshall, W. L. (1981). *The relationship between penile length and diameter*. Paper presented to the Canadian Psychological Association, Toronto, Canada.

Earls, C. M., & Marshall, W. L. (1983). The current state of technology in the laboratory assessment of sexual arousal patterns. In J. G. Greer & I. R. Stuart (Eds.), *The sexual aggressor: Current perspectives on treatment*. New York: Van Nostrand Reinhold.

Eber, M. (1977). Exhibitionism or narcissism? [Letter to the editor]. *American Journal of Psychiatry, 134*, 153.

Emrick, C. D. (1975). A review of psychologically oriented treatment of alcoholism 2: The relative effectiveness of treatment versus no treatment. *Quarterly Journal of Studies on Alcohol, 36*, 88-108.

Evans, D. R. (1968). Masturbatory fantasy and sexual deviation. *Behaviour Research and Therapy, 6,* 17-19.

Evans, D. R. (1980). Electrical aversion therapy. In D. J. Cox & R. J. Daitzman (Eds.), *Exhibitionism: Description, assessment, and treatment* (pp. 85-122). New York: Garland.

Faller, K. C. (1984). Is the child victim of sexual abuse telling the truth? *Child Abuse and Neglect, 8,* 473-481.

Farkas, G. M., Evans, S. M., Sine, L. F., Eiffert, G., Wittlieb, E., Vogelman, & Sine, S. (1979). Reliability and validity of the mercury-in-rubber strain gauge measure of penile circumference. *Behavior Therapy, 10,* 555-561.

Fay, J. (1979). *He told me not to tell.* Seattle, WA: King County Rape Relief Society.

Ferster, C. B., & Skinner, B. F. (1957). *Schedules of reinforcement.* New York: Appleton.

Finklehor, D. (1984). *Child sexual abuse: New theory and research.* New York: Free Press.

Finklehor, D. (1988). *Nursery crimes.* Newbury Park, CA: Sage.

Fookes, B. H. (1969). Some experiences in the use of aversion therapy in male homosexuality, exhibitionism, and fetishism-transvestism. *British Journal of Psychiatry, 115,* 339-341.

Foregt, J. P., & Kennedy, W. (1971). Treatment of overweight by aversion therapy. *Behaviour Research and Therapy, 9,* 29-34.

Freeman-Longo, R., & Bays, L. (1989). *Who am I and why am I in treatment?* Orwell, CT: Safer Society Press.

Freund, K. (1975). The present state of the phallometric test of erotic preference. *European Journal of Behavioral Analysis and Modification, 1,* 27-28.

Freund, K. (1980). Therapeutic sex drive reduction. *Acta Psychiatrica Scandinavica, 62,* (Suppl. 287), 5-38.

Freund, K., Char, S., & Coulthard, R. (1979). Phallometric diagnosis with "non-admitters." *Behaviour Research and Therapy, 17,* 451-457.

Freund, K., Scher, H., & Hucker, S. (1983). The courtship disorders. *Archives of Sexual Behavior, 12,* 369-379.

Gagné, P. (1981). Treatment of sex offenders with medroxyprogesterone acetate. *American Journal of Psychiatry, 138,* 644-646.

Geary, J. M., & Goldman, M. S. (1978). Behavioral treatment of heterosexual social anxiety: A factorial investigation. *Behavior Therapy, 9,* 971-972.

Gebhard, P. H., Gagnon, J. H., Pomeroy, W. R., & Christiansen, C. Y. (1965). *Sexual offenders.* New York: Harper & Row.

Gilmour, D. R., McConaich, I. A., & DeRuiter, C. A. (1981). Group assertion training for adult male offenders: Internal validity. *Behavior Therapy, 12,* 274-279.

Gold, S., & Neufeld, I. L. A. (1965). A learning theory approach to the treatment of homosexuality. *Behaviour Research and Therapy, 2,* 201-204.

Goldfried, M. R., & Tsier, C. S. (1974). Effectiveness of relaxation as an active coping skill. *Journal of Abnormal Psychology, 83,* 348-355.

Goodman, G. (1984). The child witness. *Journal of Social Issues, 40,* 113-119.

Gray, J. J. (1970). Case conference: Behavior therapy in a patient with homosexual fantasies and heterosexual anxieties. *Journal of Behavior Therapy and Experimental Psychiatry, 1,* 225-232.

Greene, R. L. (1980). *The MMPI: An interpretive manual.* Orlando, FL: Grune & Stratton.

Greer, J. G., & Stuart, I. R. (1983). *The sexual aggressor: Current perspectives on treatment.* New York: Van Nostrand Reinhold.

Groth, A. N. (1979a). *Men who rape: The psychology of the offender.* New York: Plenum.

Groth, A. N. (1979b). Sexual trauma in the life histories of rapists and child molesters. *Victimology: An International Journal, 4,* 10-16.

Hackett, T. P. (1971). The psychotherapy of exhibitionists in a court clinic setting. *Seminars in Psychiatry, 3,* 297-306.

Haley, J. (1963). *Strategies of psychotherapy.* New York: Grune & Stratton.

Hall, R. (1988). Self-efficacy ratings. In R. Laws (Ed.), *Relapse prevention with sex offenders.* New York: Guilford.

Halleck, S. L. (1981). The ethics of antiandrogenic therapy [Editorial]. *American Journal of Psychiatry, 138,* 642-643.

Hampton, R. L., & Newberger, E. H. (1985). Child abuse incidence reporting by hospitals: Significance of severity, class, and race. *American Journal of Public Health, 75,* 56-60.

Harbison, J. J., Quenn, J. T., & McAllister, H. (1970). An attempt to shape human penile response. *Behaviour Research and Therapy, 9,* 286-290.

Hayes, S. C., Brownell, K. D., & Barlow, D. H. (1978). The use of self-administered covert sensitization in the treatment of exhibitionism and sadism. *Behavior Therapy, 9,* 283-289.

Heimberg, R. G., & Becker, R. E. (1981). Cognitive and behavioral models of assertive behavior: Review, analysis, and integration. *Clinical Psychology Review, 1,* 353-373.

Heimberg, R. G., Madsen, C. H., Montgomery, D., & McNabb, C. E. (1980). Behavioral treatments for heterosocial problems. *Behavior Modification, 4,* 147-172.

Hein, N. (1981). Sexual behavior of castrated sex offenders. *Archives of Sexual Behavior, 10,* 11-19.

Henson, D. E., & Robin H. B. (1971). Voluntary control of eroticism. *Journal of Applied Behavior Analysis, 4,* 37-44.

Herman, J. (1976). Issues in the use of psychotherapy to assess female sexual dysfunction. *Journal of Sex and Marital Therapy, 2,* 197-204.

Hindman, J. (1987, April). *Evaluating the female sexual offender: A physiological approach.* Paper presented at the conference "The Sexual Assault of Children and Adolescents," Alexandria Associates, Ontario, Oregon.

Hollander, M. H., Brown, C. W., & Roback, H. B. (1977). Genital exhibitionism in women. *American Journal of Psychiatry, 134,* 436-438.

James, S. (1978). Treatment of homosexuality 2: Superiority of desensitization/arousal as compared with anticipatory avoidance conditioning: Results of a controlled trial. *Behavior Therapy, 9,* 28-36.

James, S., Orwin, A., & Turner, R. K. (1972). Treatment of homosexuality 1: Analysis of failure following a trial of anticipatory avoidance conditioning and the development of an alternative treatment system. *Behavior Therapy, 8,* 840-848.

Jason, J., Williams, S. L., Burton, A., & Rochat, R. (1982). Epidemiologic differences between sexual and physical child abuse. *Journal of the American Medical Association, 247,* 3344-3348.

Jehu, D. (1939). Mood disturbances among women sexually abused in childhood: Prevalence, etiology, treatment. *Journal of Interpersonal Violence, 4,* 164-184.

Jones, I. H., & Frei, D. (1977). Provoked anxiety as a treatment of exhibitionism. *British Journal of Psychiatry, 131,* 295-300.

Jones, J. G. (1982). Sexual abuse of children. *American Journal of Diseases of Children, 136,* 142-14〔

Josiason, R. C., Fantuzzo, J., & Rosen, R. C. (1980). Treatment of pedophilia using multistage aversion therapy and social skills training. *Journal of Behavior Therapy and Experimental Psychiatry, 11*, 55-61.

Kazdin, A. E. (1978). *History of behavior modification*. Baltimore: University Park Press.

Kazdin, A. E. (1985). Token economy. In A. S. Bellack & M. Hersen (Eds.), *Dictionary of behavior therapy techniques* (pp. 224-227). New York: Pergamon.

Kelly, R. J. (1982). Behavioral reorientation of pedophiliacs: Can it be done? *Clinical Psychology Review, 2*, 387-393.

Kennedy, W. A., & Foregt, J. (1968). Control of eating behaviors in an obese patient by avoidance and conditioning. *Psychological Reports, 23*, 571-573.

Knight, R. A. (1989). An assessment of the concurrent validity of a child molester typology. *Journal of Interpersonal Violence, 4*, 131-150.

Knight, R. A., Carter, D. L., & Prentky, R. A. (1989). A system for the classification of child molesters. *Journal of Interpersonal Violence, 4*, 3-23.

Kolvin, I. (1967). "Aversive imagery" treatment in adolescents. *Behaviour Research and Therapy, 5*, 245-248.

Kremsdorf, R. B., Holman, M. L., & Laws, D. R. (1980). Orgasmic reconditioning without deviant imagery: A case report with a pedophile. *Behaviour Research and Therapy, 18*, 203-207.

Kroop, F. H. (1984). *Retraining adult sex offenders: methods and models*. Syracuse, NY: Safer Society Press.

Lande, S. D. (1980). A combination of orgasmic reconditioning and covert sensitization in the treatment of a fire fetish. *Journal of Behavior Therapy and Experimental Psychiatry, 11*, 291-296.

Lang, R. A., Langevin, R., Bain, J., Frenzel, R. R., & Wright, P. (1989). An examination of sex hormones in genital exhibitionists. *Annals of Sex Research, 2*, 67-75.

Langevin, R. (1983). *Sexual strands: Understanding and treating these anomalies in men*. Hillsdale, NJ: Lawrence Erlbaum.

Langevin, R., Paitrich, D., Hucker, S., Newman, S., Ramsey, G., Pope, S., Geller, G., & Anderson, C. (1979). The effectiveness of assertiveness training, Provera, and sex of therapist in the treatment of genital exhibitionism. *Journal of Behavior Therapy and Experimental Psychiatry, 10*, 225-282.

Langevin, R., Wortzmang, G., Wright, P., & Handy, L. (1989). Studies of brain damage and dysfunction in sex offenders. *Annals of Sex Research, 2*, 163-179.

Laws, D. R. (Ed.). (1988). *Relapse prevention with sex offenders*. New York: Guilford.

Laws, D. R., & Osborn, C. A. (1983). How to build and operate a behavioral laboratory to evaluate and treat sexual deviance. In J. G. Greer & I. R. Stuart (Eds.), *The sexual aggressor: Current perspectives on treatment* (pp. 293-335). New York: Van Nostrand Reinhold.

Ledwidge, B. (1979). Cognitive behavior modification or new ways to change minds: Reply to Mahoney and Rasdin. *Psychological Bulletin, 86*, 1050-1053.

Lee-Evans, M., Graham, P. J., Harbison, J. J. M., McAllister, H., & Quinn, J. T. (1975). Penile plethysmographic assessment of sexual orientation. *European Journal of Behavioral Analysis and Modification, 1*, 20-26.

Leichtenstein, E., & Kretzer, C. S. (1969). Investigation of diverse techniques to modify smoking: A follow-up report. *Behaviour Research and Therapy, 7*, 139-140.

Levin, S. M., Barry, S. M., Gambero, S., Wolfinsohn, L., & Smith, A. (1977). Variations of covert sensitization in the treatment of pedophilic behavior: A case study. *Journal of Consulting and Clinical Psychology, 10,* 896-907.

Lewinsohn, P. M., Bigland, A., & Zeiss, A. M. (1976). Behavioral treatment of depression. In P. O. Davidson (Ed.), *The behavioral management of anxiety, depression, and pain.* New York: Brunner/Mazel.

Lipton, D. N., & Nelson, R. O. (1980). The contribution of initiation behaviors to dating frequency. *Behavior Therapy, 11,* 59-67.

Little, L. M., & Curran, J. P. (1978). Covert sensitization: A clinical procedure in need of some explanations. *Psychological Bulletin, 85,* 513-531.

Lombardo, R. W., & Turner, S. M. (1979). Use of thought-stopping to control obsessive ruminations in a chronic schizophrenic patient. *Behavior Modification, 3,* 207-232.

Longo, R. E. (1983). Administering a comprehensive sexual aggressive treatment program in a maximum security setting. In J. G. Greer & I. R. Stuart (Eds.), *The sexual aggressor: Current perspectives on treatment* (pp. 177-197). New York: Van Nostrand Reinhold.

LoPiccolo, J. (1985, March). *Diagnosis and treatment of male sexual dysfunction.* Paper presented at the Seventeenth Banff International Conference on Behavioral Sciences.

LoPiccolo, J., & Steger, J. (1978). The sexual interaction inventory: A new instrument for assessment of sexual dysfunction. In J. LoPiccolo & L. LoPiccolo (Eds.), *Handbook of sex therapy.* New York: Plenum.

Lovibond, S. H. (1963). The mechanism of conditioning of enuresis. *Behaviour Research and Therapy, 1,* 17-81.

MacCulloch, M. J., & Feldman, M. P. (1967). Aversion therapy in the management of 43 homosexuals. *British Medical Journal, 2,* 544-597.

MacCulloch, M. J., Snowden, P. R., Wood, P. J., & Millis, H. E. (1983). Sadistic fantasy, sadistic behaviour and offending. *British Journal of Psychiatry, 143,* 20-29.

MacCulloch, M. J., Waddington, J. L., & Sanbrook, J. E. (1978). Avoidance latencies reliably reflect sexual attitude during aversion therapy for homosexuality. *Behavior Therapy, 9,* 562-577.

MacLean, P. D. (1965). New findings relevant to the evolution of psychosexual functions in the brain. In J. Morey (Ed.), *Sex research: New developments.* New York: Holt, Rinehart & Winston.

MacMurray, B. K. (1988). The nonprosecution of sexual abuse and informal justice. *Journal of Interpersonal Violence, 3,* 197-202.

MacMurray, B. K. (1989). Criminal determination for child sexual abuse: Prosecutor case-screening judgments. *Journal of Interpersonal Violence, 4,* 233-244.

Malamuth, N. M., & Clark, J. V. P. (1983). Sexual arousal to rape depictions: Individual differences. *Journal of Abnormal Psychology, 92,* 55-67.

Malamuth, N. M., & Donnerstein, E. (1982). The effects of aggressive-pornographic mass media stimuli. In L. Berkowitz (Ed.), *Advances in experimental social psychology.* New York: Academic Press.

Malcolm, P. U., Davidson, P. R., & Marshall, W. L. (1981). Control of penile tumescence: The effects of arousal level and stimulus content. *Behaviour Research and Therapy, 23,* 320-328.

Maletzky, B. M. (1973a). "Assisted" convert sensitization: A preliminary report. *Behavior Therapy, 4,* 117-119.

Maletzky, B. M. (1973b). The treatment of homosexuality by "assisted" covert sensitization. *Behaviour Research and Therapy, 11*, 655-657.

Maletzky, B. M. (1974a). Assisted covert sensitization for drug abuse. *International Journal of the Addictions, 9*, 411-429.

Maletzky, B. M. (1974b). "Assisted" covert sensitization in the treatment of exhibitionism. *Journal of Consulting and Clinical Psychology, 42*, 34-40.

Maletzky, B. M. (1977). "Booster" sessions in aversion therapy: The permanency of treatment. *Behavior Therapy, 8*, 460-463.

Maletzky, B. M. (1980a). Assisted covert sensitization. In D. J. Cox & R. J. Daitzman (Eds.), *Exhibitionism: Description, assessment, and treatment* (pp. 187-285). New York: Garland.

Maletzky, B. M. (1980b). Self-referred versus court-referred sexually deviant patients: Success with assisted covert sensitization. *Behavior Therapy, 11*, 306-314.

Maletzky, B. M. (1981). Clinical relevance and clinical research. *Behavioral Assessment, 3*, 283-288.

Maletzky, B. M. (1984a, March). *The initiation and continuing management of sex offender programs.* Presented to the Correctional Services of Canada Symposium on Sexual Aggressives, Vancouver, British Columbia.

Maletzky, B. M. (1984b, March). *The management of sexual offender programs.* Presented to the Treatment and Research Symposium on Sexual Aggression, Simon Fraser University, Vancouver, British Columbia.

Maletzky, B. M. (in press). *Predicting the dangerousness of the sexual offender.*

Maletzky, B. M., & Price, R. C. (1984). Public masturbation in men: Precursor to exhibitionism? *Journal of Sex Education and Therapy, 10*, 131-136.

Maple, T. (1977). Unusual sexual behavior of nonhuman primates. In J. Moreg & H. Musaph (Eds.), *Handbook of sexology* (pp. 319-345). New York: Excerpta Medica.

Marks, I. M. (1981a). *Cure and care of neuroses.* New York: John Wiley.

Marks, I. M. (1981b). Review of behavior psychotherapy 1: Sexual disorders. *American Journal of Psychiatry, 138*, 750-753.

Marks, I. M. (1981c). Review of behavior psychotherapy 2: Sexual disorders. *American Journal of Psychiatry, 138*, 754-756.

Marquis, J. (1970). Orgasmic reconditioning: Changing sexual object choice through controlling masturbation fantasies. *Journal of Behavior Therapy and Experimental Psychiatry, 1*, 263-271.

Marquis, J. K., Day, D. M., Nelson, C., & Miner, M. H. (1989, July). *The sex offender treatment and evaluation project* (Third report to the California legislature in response to PC 1365 by the California Department of Mental Health), Sacramento, CA.

Marshall, W. L. (1973). The modification of sexual fantasies: A combined treatment approach to the reduction of deviant sexual behavior. *Behaviour Research and Therapy, 11*, 557-564.

Marshall, W. L. (1979). Satiation therapy: A procedure for reducing deviant sexual arousal. *Journal of Applied Behavior Analysis, 12*, 377-389.

Marshall, W. L., & Lippers, R. (1977). The clinical value of boredom: A procedure for reducing inappropriate sexual interests. *Journal of Nervous and Mental Disease*, 283-287.

Martin, G., & Pea, J. (1988). *Behavior modification: What it is and how to do it.* West Nyack, NY: Prentice-Hall.

Mason, J. C., Louks, J., & Backus, R. (1985). Patient-predicted length of stay and diagnosis-related-group reimbursement. *American Journal of Psychiatry, 142,* 369-371.

Masters, W., & Johnson, V. (1970). *Human sexual inadequacy.* Boston: Little, Brown.

Mathis, J. L. (1980). Group therapy. In D. J. Cox & R. J. Daitzman (Eds.), *Exhibitionism: Description, assessment, and treatment* (pp. 41-58). New York: Garland.

Mathis, J. L., & Collins, M. (1970a). Mandatory group therapy for exhibitionists. *American Journal of Psychiatry, 126,* 1162-1167.

Mathis, J. L., & Collins, M. (1970b). Progressive phases in the group therapy of exhibitionists. *International Journal of Group Psychotherapy, 20,* 167-169.

Mayer, A. (1983). *A treatment manual for therapy with victims, spouses, and offenders.* Homes Beach, FL: Learning Publications, Inc.

McFall, R. M. (1982). A review and reformulation of the concept of social skills. *Behavioral Assessment, 4,* 1-33.

McGonaghy, N. (1971). Aversive therapy of homosexuality: Measures of efficacy. *American Journal of Psychiatry, 127,* 1221-1224.

McGonaghy, N. (1972). Aversion therapy. *Seminars in Psychiatry, 4,* 139-144.

McGovern, K., & Jensen, S. (1985). Behavioral group treatment methods for sexual disorders and dysfunctions. In D. Uppen & S. Ross (Eds.), *Handbook of behavioral group therapy* (pp. 421-442). New York: Plenum.

McGovern, K., & Peters, J. (1988). Guidelines for assessing sexual abusers. In L. Walker (Ed.), *Handbook of sexual abuse of children.* New York: Springer.

McGuire, R. J., Carlisle, J. M., & Young, B. G. (1965). Sexual deviations as conditioned behavior. *Behaviour Research and Therapy, 2,* 185-190.

Meichenbaum, D. H. (1974). *Cognitive behavior modification.* Morristown, NJ: General Learning Press.

Meichenbaum, D. H., & Turk, D. (1976). The cognitive-behavioral management of anxiety, anger, and pain. In P. O. Davidson (Ed.), *The behavioral management of anxiety, depression, and pain.* New York: Brunner/Mazel.

Michael, R. P., & Zumpe, D. (1983). Sexual violence in the United States and the role of season. *American Journal of Psychiatry, 140,* 883-886.

Miller, H. L., & Haney, J. R. (1976). Behavior and traditional therapy applied to pedophilica exhibitionism: A case study. *Psychological Reports, 39,* 1119-1124.

Miller, J. A. (1980). A song for the female finch. *Science News, 117,* 58-59.

Miller, W. R. (1983). Controlled drinking: A history and critical review. *Journal of Studies on Alcohol, 44,* 68-83.

Millon, T. (1977). *Millon clinical multiaxial inventory: Manual.* Minneapolis: NCS Interpretive Scoring Systems.

Morganstern, F. S., Pearce, J. F., & Linford-Ness, W. (1965). Predicting the outcome of behavior therapy by psychologic tests. *Behavior Research and Therapy, 3,* 191-200.

Murphy, W. D., Krisak, J., Stalgaittis, S., & Anderson, K. (1984). The use of penile tumescence measures with incarcerated rapists: Further validity issues. *Archives of Sexual Behavior, 13,* 545-554.

Nadelson, C. C., Nothan, M. T., Zackson, H., & Gornick, J. (1982). A follow-up study of rape victims. *American Journal of Psychiatry, 139,* 1252-1256.

Newmark, C. (1985). *Major psychological assessment instruments.* Boston: Allyn & Bacon.

Nichols, H. R., & Molinder, I. (1984). *Molinder multiphasic sex inventory.* (Available from Nichols & Molinder, 437 Bowes Drive, Tacoma, Washington, 98466).

Nolan, J. D., & Sandman, C. (1978). "Biosyntonic" therapy: Modification of an operant conditioning approach to pedophilia. *Journal of Consulting and Clinical Psychology, 46,* 1133-1140.

Nyman, N. W. (1989). Prevention education: A developmental view. *Journal of Interpersonal Violence, 4,* 254-256.

O'Connell, M. A., Leberg, E., & Donaldson, C. R. (1990). *Working with sex offenders: Practical guidelines for therapist selection.* Newbury Park, CA: Sage.

Paveza, J. (1988). Risk factors in father-daughter child sexual abuse: A case-control study. *Journal of Interpersonal Violence, 3,* 290-306.

Paykel, E. S. (1979, June). *Sexual offender research.* Paper presented to the Society for Psychotherapy Research, Oxford.

Petrovich, M., & Templer, D. I. (1984). Heterosexual molestation of children who later became rapists. *Psychological Reports, 54,* 810.

Prithers, W. D., & Laws, R. (in press). The penile plethysmograph: Uses and abuses in assessment and treatment of sexual aggressors. In B. Schwartz (Ed.), *Sex offenders: Issues in treatment.* Washington, DC: National Institute of Corrections.

Prithers, W. D., Marquis, J. K., Gibat, C. C., & Marlatt, G. A. (1983). Relapse prevention with sexual aggressives: A self-control model of treatment and maintenance of change. In J. G. Greer & I. R. Stuart (Eds.), *The sexual aggressor: Current perspectives on treatment* (pp. 214-239). New York: Van Nostrand Reinhold.

Prithers, W. D., Martin, R., & Cummings, B. (1988). Vermont treatment program for sexual aggressors. In R. Laws (Ed.), *Relapse prevention with sex offenders.* New York: Guilford.

Quinsey, V. L., & Chaplin, T. C. (1988). Penile responses of child molesters and normals to descriptions of encounters with children involving sex and violence. *Journal of Interpersonal Violence, 3,* 259-274.

Quinsey, V. L., Chaplin, T. C., & Carrigan, W. F. (1980). Biofeedback and signaled punishment in the modification of inappropriate sexual age preventions. *Behavior Therapy, 11,* 567-576.

Quinsey, V. L., Chaplin, T. C., Maguire, A. M., & Upfold, D. (1988). The behavioral treatment of rapists and child molesters. In E. R. Morris & C. J. Brackman (Eds.), *Behavioral approaches to criminal delinquency: Applications, research, and theory.* New York: Plenum.

Quinsey, V. L., Chaplin, T. C., & Varney, G. A. (1986). A comparison of rapists' and non-sex offenders' sexual preferences for mutually consenting sex, rape, and physical abuse of women. *Behavioral Assessment, 3,* 127-135.

Quinsey, V. L., & Marshall, W. L. (1983). Procedures for reducing inappropriate sexual arousal: An evaluation review. In J. G. Greer & I. R. Stuart (Eds.), *The sexual aggressor: Current perspectives on treatment* (pp. 262-289). New York: Van Nostrand Reinhold.

Rachman, A. J., & Teasdale, J. (1969a). Aversion therapy: An appraisal. In C. M. Franks (Ed.), *Behavior therapy: Appraisal and status.* New York: McGraw-Hill.

Rachman, A. J., & Teasdale, J. (1969b). *Aversion therapy and behavior disorders: An analysis.* London: Routledge & Kegan.

Rader, C. M. (1977). MMPI profile types of exposers, rapists, and assaulters in a court service population. *Journal of Consulting and Clinical Psychology, 45,* 61-69.

Rallman, W. M., & Gilmore, J. D. (1980). Vascular disorders. In S. M. Turner, R. S. Calhoun, & H. E. Adams (Eds.), *Handbook of clinical therapy* (pp. 380-405). New York: John Wiley.

Reckers, G. A., & Vasni, J. W. (1977). Self-monitoring and self-reinforcement process in a pre-transsexual boy. *Behaviour Research and Therapy, 10,* 211-216.

Reid, G. J., Tombaugh, T. N., & Heunel, R. V. (1981). Application of contingent physical restraint to suppress stereotyped body-rocking of profoundly mentally retarded persons. *American Journal of Mental Deficiencies, 86,* 78-85.

Remburg, O. (1975). *Borderline conditions and pathological narcissism.* New York: Jason Aronson.

Reston, C., & Yamashita, A. (1983). Orgasmic reconditioning: A behavior based treatment for redirecting sexual arousals of sex offenders. *Dissertation Abstracts International, 44,* 1251-B.

Richmond, G., & Bell, J. C. (1983). Analysis of a treatment package to reduce a hand-mouthing stereotype. *Behavior Therapy, 14,* 567-581.

Rieber, I., & Sigusch, V. (1979). Psychosurgery on sexual offenders and sexual "deviants" in West Germany. *Archives of Sexual Behavior, 8,* 523-527.

Riggs, D. S., Murphy, D. M., & O'Leary, R. D. (1989). Intentional falsification in reports of inter-partner aggression. *Journal of Interpersonal Violence, 4,* 220-232.

Rimm, D. C., & Lefebvre, R. C. (1981). Phobic disorders. In S. M. Turner, R. S. Calhoun, & H. E. Adams (Eds.), *Handbook of clinical behavior therapy* (pp. 12-40). New York: John Wiley.

Rooth, F. G., & Marks, I. M. (1974). Persistent exhibitionism: Short-term response to aversion, self-regulation, and relaxation treatments. *Archives of Sexual Behavior, 3,* 227-248.

Rosen, R. C., & Kopen, S. A. (1978). Role of penile tumescence measurement in the behavioral treatment of sexual deviation: Issues of validity. *Journal of Consulting and Clinical Psychology, 46,* 1519-1521.

Rosenthal, T. L., Rosenthal, R. H., & Chang, A. F. (1977). Vicarious, direct, and imaginal aversion in habit control: Outcomes, heart rate, and subjective perceptions. *Cognitive Therapy and Research, 1,* 143-159.

Sajwaj, T., Libet, J., & Agras, S. (1974). Lemon-juice therapy: The control of life-threatening rumination in a six-month old infant. *Journal of Applied Behavior Analysis, 7,* 557-563.

Sanbrook, J. E., MacCulloch, M. J., & Waddington, J. L. (1978). Incubation of sexual attitude change between sessions of instrumental aversion therapy: Two case studies. *Behavior Therapy, 9,* 477-485.

Schatzberg, A. F., Orsulak, P. J., Rothschild, A. J., Salaman, M. S., Lerbinger, J., Rizuka, P. P., Cole, J. O., & Schildkraut, J. J. (1983). Platelet MAO activity and the Dexamethasone Suppression Test in depressed patients. *American Journal of Psychiatry, 140,* 1231-1233.

Schmidt, G., & Schorsch, E. (1981). Psychosurgery of sexually deviant patients: Review and analysis of new empirical findings. *Archives of Sexual Behavior, 10,* 301-323.

Server, M. (1970). Shame aversion therapy. *Journal of Behavior Therapy and Experimental Psychiatry, 1,* 213-215.

Slaughter, C. (1976). *Relations.* New York: Pocket Books.

Smith, S. R. (1980). Legal stand toward exhibitionism. In D. J. Cox & R. J. Daitzman (Eds.), *Exhibitionism: Description, assessment, and treatment* (pp. 11-38). New York: Garland.

Smith, S. R., & Meyer, R. G. (1980). Workings between the legal system and the therapist. In D. J. Cox & R. J. Daitzman (Eds.), *Exhibitionism: Description, assessment, and treatment* (pp. 311-338). New York: Garland.

Smith, W. S. (1981). *When I say no I feel guilty.* New York: Bantam.

Snaith, R. P., & Collins, S. A. (1981). Five exhibitionists and a method of treatment. *British Journal of Psychiatry, 138,* 126-130.

Sone, L. (1984). *The Sone sexual history background form* (Unpublished document available from Alternatives to Sexual Abuse, P.O. Box 25537, Portland, Oregon 97225).

Spohn, H. E., Cogne, L., LaCoursiere, R., Mazur, D., & Hayes, K. (1985). Relation of neuroleptic dose and tardive dyskinesia to attention, information-processing, and psychophysiology in medicated schizophrenics. *Archives of General Psychiatry, 42,* 849-859.

Stampfl, T. G., & Levis, D. J. (1968). Implosive therapy: A behavioral therapy? *Behaviour Research and Therapy, 6,* 31-36.

Stang, D. J. (1974). Methodological factors in more exposure research. *Psychological Bulletin, 81,D, 1014-1025.*

Stermac, L., & Hall, K. (1989). Escalation in sexual offending: Fact or fiction? *Annals of Sex Research, 2,* 153-162.

Sturgis, E. T., & Meyer, V. (1981). Obsessive-compulsive disorder. In S. M. Turner, R. S. Calhoun, & H. E. Adams (Eds.), *Handbook of clinical behavior therapy* (pp. 68-102). New York: John Wiley.

Sugar, M. (1983). Sexual abuse of children and adolescents. *Adolescent Psychiatry, 11,* 199-211.

Suim, R. M., & Richardson, F. (1971). Anxiety management training: A nonspecific behavior therapy program for anxiety control. *Behavior Therapy, 2,* 498-510.

Thorndike, E. L. (1935). *The psychology of wants, interests, and attitudes.* New York: Appleton-Century.

Thorpe, G. L. (1972). Learning paradigms in the anticipatory avoidance technique: A comment on the controversy between MacDarough and Feldman. *Behavior Therapy, 3,* 614-618.

Tollison, C. D., & Adams, H. E. (1979). *Sexual disorders: Treatment, theory, and research.* New York: Gardner.

Tollison, C. D., Adams, H. E., & Tollison, J. W. (1979). Physiological measurement of sexual arousal in homosexual, bisexual, and heterosexual males. *Journal of Behavioral Assessment, 2,* 53-59.

Tracy, F., Donnelly, H., Morganbesser, L., & MacDonald, D. (1983). Program evaluation: Recidivism research involving sex offenders. In J. G. Greer & I. R. Stuart (Eds.), *The sexual aggressor: Current perspectives on treatment* (pp. 293-335). New York: Van Nostrand Reinhold.

Twentyman, C., Boland, T., & McFall, R. M. (1981). Heterosocial avoidance in college males: Four studies. *Behavior Modification, 9,* 748-765.

Vanceventer, A. D., & Laws, D. R. (1978). Orgasmic reconditioning to re-direct sexual arousal in pedophiles. *Behavior Therapy, 9,* 748-765.

VanDijk, W. K., & VanDijk-Kauffman, A. (1973). A follow-up study of 211 treated male alcoholics. *British Journal of Addictions, 68,* 3-24.

Walker, P. A., & Meyer, W. J. (1981). Medroxyprogesterone acetate treatment for paraphiliac sex offenders. In J. R. Hays, T. K. Roberts, & K. S. Solway (Eds.), *Violence and the violent individual* (pp. 353-373). New York: S. P. Medical and Scientific Books.

Wells, K. (1985). Behavioral family therapy. In A. S. Bellack & M. Hersen (Eds.), *Dictionary of behavior therapy techniques* (pp. 25-30). New York: Pergamon.

Wettstein, R. M. (1984). The prediction of violent behavior and the duty to protect third parties. *Behavioral Sciences & the Law, 2*, 291-317.

Wheeler, L. (Ed.). (1987). *Handbook on sexual abuse of children: Assessment and treatment issues.* New York: Springer.

Whitman, W. P., & Quinsey, V. L. (1981). Heterosocial skill training for institutionalized rapists and child molesters. *Canadian Journal of Behavioral Science, 13*, 105-114.

Wickramaserka, I. (1972). A technique for controlling a certain type of sexual exhibitionism. *Psychotherapy: Theory, Research and Practice, 9*, 207-210.

Wickramaserka, I. (1976). Aversive behavior rehearsal for sexual exhibitionism. *Behavior Therapy, 7*, 167-176.

Wickramaserka, I. (1980). Aversive behavior rehearsal: A cognitive-behavioral procedure. In D. J. Cox & R. J. Daitzman (Eds.), *Exhibitionism: Description, assessment, and treatment* (pp. 123-149). New York: Garland.

Wille, R., & Beier, K. M. (1989). Castration in Germany. *Annals of Sex Research, 2*, 103-133.

Witzig, J. S. (1968). The group therapy of male exhibitionists. *American Journal of Psychiatry, 125*, 179-185.

Wolfe, R. (1984, March). *Community-based programs for the sexual offender.* Paper presented to the Correctional Services of Canada Symposium on Sexual Aggressives, Vancouver, British Columbia.

Wolpe, J. (1969). *The practice of behavior therapy.* New York: Pergamon.

Wolpe, J., & Lazarus, A. A. (1966). *Behavior therapy techniques: A guide to the treatment of neurosis.* Oxford: Pergamon.

Yates, A. J. (1958). The application of learning theory to the treatment of tics. *Journal of Abnormal Social Psychology, 58*, 175-182.

Zbytovsky, M., & Zapletálek, M. (1979). Cyproterone acetate in the therapy of sexual deviations. *Acta Nervosa Scandinavica Supplement (Praha), 21*, 162.

Zilbergeld, B. (1978). *Male sexuality: A guide to sexual fulfillment.* New York: Little, Brown.

Name Index

Subject Index

Active listening skills, 145-146
Activities log, 174
Adolescent offenders, 222
    empathy training and, 166
    paradoxical intention and, 167-168
    treatment considerations, 16
Adolescent sexual activities, 51
Adverse consequences, covert sensitization and, 72-75
Affective disorders, 264
Affective states, opposite, 124
Aggression. *See* Sexual aggression
Alcohol, medications and, 180
Alcohol abuse, 174-175, 264, 268
Alcoholics Anonymous, 175
Alternatives to Sexual Abuse, 35
Ammonia, 82
Amyl nitrate, 131-132
Anatomically correct dolls, behavior rehearsal and, 89-90
Anger management skills, 273
Antabuse, 175
Anticipatory avoidance, 78, 130, 141
Antidepressant drugs, 178
Antihypertensive drugs, 178
Anti-Parkinsonian drugs, 180
Anxiety reduction, 149-151, 205
Apomorphine, 68
Arousal. *See* Sexual arousal
Artane, 180
Arteriosclerosis, 178
Assertiveness, 61, 93, 151, 208
Assessment, 29-34, 35-66, 228-231, 234
    aberrant sexual arousal and, 40-41
    case example, 56-61
    clinical interview and, 36-39

    clinical perspectives, 62-64
    objective, 29
    ongoing, 65
    physiological, 41
    psychological, 46-51
    significant other interview and, 56
    subjective, 29
    supplemental reports and, 39-40
    treatment implications, 64-65
    victim interview and, 54-56
Assessment team, 46
Association for the Behavioral Treatment of Sexual Abusers, 42, 215
Associative conditioning, 78
Audiotapes, 215
    arousal patterns and, 43
    masturbation fantasies and, 103-104, 203-204
    relaxation training and, 119-120, 150
Autohypnotic suggestion, 162
Aversive behavior rehearsal, 33-34
    homework assignments and, 200-201
    patient acceptance of, 113
Aversive conditioning, 25, 26, 67-95
    associative, 83
    behavior rehearsal, 86-89
    booster sessions, 242
    covert techniques, 72-77
    desensitization and, 120
    fading and, 98
    effectiveness of, 90-94
    electric stimulation, 77-80
    homework assignments and, 196-201
    masturbation satiation and, 105
    negative practice, 89-90
    odor aversion, 80-84

About the Authors

Barry M. Maletzky is currently Professor of Clinical Psychiatry at the Oregon Health Sciences University and is also in the private practice of psychiatry in Portland. He is Director of the Sexual Abuse Clinic, an organization devoted to the treatment of the sexual offender and the victims and families affected by sexual abuse. With offices in a number of Pacific Northwest locations, the Sexual Abuse Clinic is a multispecialty clinic with experience in treating over 5,000 sexual offenders to date. Although specializing in the treatment of the sexual offender, he has written over 50 papers and three books, and has delivered numerous presentations in the United States and abroad, on a variety of topics. Other areas of specialization and publication include the treatment of the refractory affective disorders and the forensic and management aspects of crimes of violence.

    Kevin B. McGovern is Associate Clinical Professor of Psychiatry at the Oregon Health Sciences University and the founder of Alternatives to Sexual Abuse, an organization dedicated to providing education and training in the area of sexual abuse. He also holds positions on the graduate faculties of both the Oregon Professional School of Psychology, Pacific University, and the Department of Counseling

356

Psychology, Lewis and Clark College. Underscoring his concern about preventing sexual abuse, he has recently founded the "Sexual-Abuse-Free Environment," an institute that promotes sexual safety and publishes a variety of materials in this field, including *Preventing Sexual Abuse*, a quarterly of scholarly research reports, interviews, and opinions. He has written more than 15 publications on topics ranging from assessment and treating of the sexual offender to the acquisition of communication and social skills training. His teaching duties have centered on abnormal psychology and the assessment of a variety of sexual problems, including deviant sexual arousal. He has chaired more than 35 "Alternatives to Sexual Abuse" seminars presented throughout the United States and has delivered more than 60 presentations to professional and lay groups. He pursues an active private practice of psychology in Portland, including the supervision of a number of professionals involved in the assessment and treatment of the sexual offender.